Reconstructions in Early Modern History

Series Editors: John Morrill and Pauline Croft

Nobilities in Transition
1550–1700

Courtiers and Rebels in Britain and Europe

RONALD G. ASCH

Professor of Early Modern History,
Albert-Ludwigs-Universität Freiburg

A member of the Hodder Headline Group
LONDON
Distributed in the United States of America by
Oxford University Press Inc., New York

First published in Great Britain in 2003 by
Hodder Arnold, a member of the Hodder Headline Group,
338 Euston Road, London NW1 3BH

http://www.arnoldpublishers.com

Distributed in the United States of America by
Oxford University Press Inc.,
198 Madison Avenue, New York 10016

The advice and information in this book are believed to be true and
accurate at the date of going to press, but neither the author nor the publisher
can accept any legal responsibility or liability for any errors or omissions.

British Library Cataloguing in Publication Data
A catalogue entry for this book is available from the British Library

Library of Congress Cataloging-in-Publication Data
A catalog record for this book is available from the Library of Congress

ISBN 0 340 62528 7

1 2 3 4 5 6 7 8 9 10

Typeset in 10/12pt Sabon by Phoenix Photosetting, Chatham, Kent
Printed and bound in Malta

What do you think about this book? Or any other Arnold title?
Please send your comments to feedback.arnold@hodder.co.uk

Amicis
et
inimicis academicis

Contents

Preface

Despite differences in culture, power and status noblemen in early modern Europe were able to recognise each other if not as equals then at least as members of a particular social group. However vaguely defined, this group was united by ideals of conduct and values which, in their different regional and national variations, still bore a certain resemblance to each other, like members of a family descended from the same ancestors. Nevertheless, to write a comparative history of the European nobilities is by no means an easy task. The difference between a Florentine patrician and a Yorkshire squire, or between a Pommerian *Junker* and a Spanish *hidalgo*, seem just too great. Moreover, an individual historian is hardly able to digest the research of recent decades with equal thoroughness and completeness for all European countries. In fact, this book does not presume to give a comprehensive survey of the European nobilities and their history in our period. Rather, it addresses a limited number of key problems which affected most noble elites in different ways. Short case studies of national developments which have a paradigmatic significance for the history of other countries, for example, the changing relationships between Crown and nobility in France, are supplemented by a broad outline of structures and changes at European level. Some readers are bound to feel that some countries have been unduly neglected, for example, Scandinavia or Eastern Europe. In fact, as I freely admit, I had to concentrate on those areas of research most easily accessible to me. This means that next to France, whose nobility inevitably plays an important role in this book, Britain and central Europe figure prominently, whereas the history of the nobility in Italy, for example, and a number of other countries cannot be examined in any detail. Despite these limitations I hope that this book provides a clear and comprehensible outline of wider historical developments, while at the same time paying due attention to the specific particularities of national history in most of the major countries of western and central Europe.

For having completed this work I owe a great debt to my colleague and friend John Morrill. Not only did he first ask me to write a book (initially on a slightly different topic) for the *Reconstructions in Early Modern History* Series which he and Pauline Croft are editing, but his advice, criticism and encouragement were invaluable while discussing earlier drafts of this book. I am also grateful to Christian Windler (Freiburg i. Br.) and Guy Rowlands (Cambridge) for their advice on problems of Spanish and French history respectively, and to the latter for allowing me to consult his work on the French army under Louis XIV before publication. Jean Boutier invited me to the École des Hautes Études en Sciences Sociales in Marseille in March 2002 where I could revise the draft of this book while enjoying the amenities of southern France. I would like to thank him for his generous hospitality as well as for a number of fruitful historical discussions. Heartfelt thanks must also go to Angela Davies (London) for having checked and revised the text, correcting and perfecting my English. Finally I have to thank the Master and Fellows of Selwyn College Cambrige for having granted me a Bye Fellowship in Easter Term 2000. This enabled me to collect the material for writing this work, a task which which would have been much more difficult at home.

   Academic life in the age of 'prodspeak' (as a British colleague has called the new rhetoric of bureaucrats who believe that they can measure intellectual 'productivity' in the same way in which one can measure the output of a factory) and of an ever more widespread general contempt for the humanities is not always a great joy, in fact it is sometimes thoroughly depressing. One would be unable to endure it without the support of friends and the sometimes annoying but also invigorating challenge which the debate and struggle with those who pursue different objectives in academic politics than oneself presents. I therefore dedicate this book to my colleagues, friends and foes alike.

R.G.A.
Marseille/Osnabrück, March/August 2002

Abbreviations

EHR	*English Historical Review*
ESC	*Économies, sociétés, civilisations*
GH	*German History*
HJ	*Historical Journal*
HSS	*Histoire, sciences sociales*
HZ	*Historische Zeitschrift*
JMH	*Journal of Modern History*
MIÖG	*Mitteilungen des Instituts für Österreichische Geschichtsforschung*
PP	*Past and Present*
RHMC	*Revue d'histoire moderne et contemporaine*
TRHS	*Transactions of the Royal Historical Society*
ZHF	*Zeitschrift für Historische Forschung*

Introduction

I am a man just like anybody else
Only that God has granted me honour

Emperor Maximilian I,
early sixteenth century[1]

In 1605 a French nobleman, the Marquis de Beauvais-Nangis, suddenly left Paris with a friend and crossed the border into the Spanish Netherlands. Beauvais-Nangis and his friend, one Monsieur de Terrail, the real leader of this enterprise, wanted to join the Spanish army and take part in the siege of Bergen op Zoom. France and Spain were not at war at this time, but relations were tense and King Henry IV of France could hardly take pleasure in the fact that some of his noblemen chose to serve under his greatest rival and traditional enemy. However, when the French envoy in Brussels reproached de Terrail for his irresponsible behaviour, he argued that he and his friend had wanted to seek honour and acquire military experience so that they could serve their own monarch all the better – or so de Terrail claimed.[2] Even at the time this journey abroad, without royal permission, must have seemed risky and de Terrail told his companion that he would go to Hungary – to fight against the Turks – if the King tried to punish him for his adventure. Nevertheless it demonstrates that personal honour and military glory, no matter whether achieved at home or in foreign service, were of paramount importance to many noblemen, so much so that dynastic and national loyalties – even in a country such as France where national consciousness among noblemen was probably stronger than in most other parts of Europe at the time – could easily take second place if they came into conflict with their personal pride and ambition. A hundred years later many armies still had a fair share of foreign noblemen among their officers, but few nobles would have decided to leave their country on the spur of the moment for the sake of glory and adventure abroad. And if they had done so, they would have risked being punished by their own rulers without further ado.

This incident can serve to illustrate some of the key issues addressed in this book and the changes which affected the European nobilities in our period, changes in which cultural, religious and political developments interacted closely. In most parts of Europe the military, political and administrative resources of the dynastic state, despite military defeats, civil wars and bankruptcies, were visibly growing. By the later seventeenth century, the dynastic state had achieved a monopoly of military power which ended the capacity of individual noblemen, including the great magnates, to wage war or even to conduct local feuds. However, this process of state-building would not have been successful if monarchs had not found support among the noble elites themselves for their objectives. In fact, in many cases nobles took a leading part in this process and were its driving force, as military entrepreneurs, for example, or as royal officeholders or even as the Crown's creditors and financiers.

The new symbiosis between the monarchical state and nobilities which, often after a period of great tensions and open conflict, was achieved after the mid-seventeenth century in many countries, such as France or the (Austrian) Habsburg monarchy, but also in Brandenburg-Prussia and other German principalities, was as much the expression of cultural as of political changes. The new codes of conduct and social discipline which the confessional churches tried to impose, but also the ideal of urbanity and civility propagated by humanists initially posed a challenge to traditional noble culture. Confronted with these challenges noblemen and -women were almost forced to re-invent themselves. Their traditional virtues and claims to privilege were in danger of becoming obsolete. They therefore had to adapt to a new cultural climate while at the same time reasserting their cultural hegemony which was being challenged by new non-noble elites. The nobility was, however, largely able to assimilate cultural trends which were potentially hostile to its power in this period, and to subordinate them to its own value system. In fact, the new ideals guiding the personal behaviour of nobles were often based on a redefinition of honour and prestige by noble society itself and on a new self-discipline rather than on the simple acceptance of social norms imposed from above or from outside, for example, by princes at court or by clergymen in church.

This is not to deny that the change in noble attitudes and behaviour was profound. As late as the mid-sixteenth century, the typical nobleman had to demonstrate his social superiority by his ability to use physical and military force against his rivals and opponents.[3] The capacity to mobilise clients and tenants for warfare and feuding, or the possession of the necessary economic and political resources to maintain a large number of armed retainers, who often accompanied their lord on important public occasions, were still an essential precondition for gaining prestige and the respect of one's equals and social inferiors alike. What is more, noblemen were also expected to use physical force in person to intimidate or overcome opponents. It would be wrong to say that such habits had entirely disappeared 150 years later, but undoubtedly displays of physical force and martial prowess had become much subtler and more sophisticated. They had been diverted into closely confined channels which were deemed socially and politically acceptable. They could find expression, for example, in a professional military career. Admittedly the traditional culture of violence had not entirely disappeared, as the frequent duels among noblemen demonstrate. However, although frowned upon by judges, clergymen and non-noble officeholders, the duel was a highly ritualised and sophisticated form of interpersonal violence. It was to some extent an expression of the sophisticated court culture which had transformed noble codes of conduct in our period and had refined and sublimated traditional notions of honour but also, in some cases, given them a sharper edge.

The re-invention of noble values and models of conduct was visible not least in nobles' attitudes towards education and the arts. The ability to demonstrate good taste in fashion as much as in art or architecture, an air of casual elegance in appearance, gestures and words, and a good but practical rather than learned education were much more important than mere physical prowess at the end of the seventeenth century. Moreover, the capacity to pull strings at court or in the relevant administrative departments in the capital now often took precedence over mere local power which was based on the loyalty and deference of personal dependants and clients, although such local networks of influence certainly survived and continued to be an important basis of noble power.

In spite of these changes, the enduring cultural hegemony of the nobility is demonstrated by the fact that non-noble urban elites often tried to emulate and imitate the behaviour of nobles in the seventeenth century. Urban patricians as well as lawyers and financiers or tax farmers bought fiefs and tried to acquire seigniorial rights and titles. Their daughters attempted to marry the scions of great aristocratic houses and their sons sought to distinguish themselves as soldiers. Even in countries with a strong tradition of urban autonomy and independent civic elites, such as northern Italy, it became ever more important for those who wanted to succeed in politics and society to 'look and sound' like a nobleman or courtier in the seventeenth century.[4]

This 'refeudalisation', often emphasised by historians, was visible in many European countries in the seventeenth century, in particular its second half. Yet the earlier part of our period, especially the decades after *c.*1550, were marked by economic and social circumstances that were, at least initially, far from favourable for noble landlords. Many historians have, in fact, argued that these years were a time of profound crisis for the nobility. Economic trends, in particular the price inflation of the later sixteenth and early seventeenth centuries, posed a challenge to the noble capacity for survival, given that it was difficult to resist the social pressures for conspicuous consumption and overspending.[5] But then, economic problems affecting large sections of the nobility were nothing new, a fact sometimes forgotten by historians who do not specialise in medieval history. Many noble families, often in fact primarily the well-established ancient houses, with their many cadet branches, displayed a considerable ability to adapt to new economic and political circumstances. Moreover, growing debts were not necessarily a sign of economic mismanagement. They could also be the result of an attempt to invest more money than in the past in offices, government bonds and military power – in the form of units recruited or bought by their noble commanders – while mortgaging the landed estates and rights of jurisdiction which were the more traditional foundations of noble power.

The temptation therefore has to be resisted to see economic problems as sufficient proof of a general decline of noble power, as many historians were inclined to do in the past. Believing wholeheartedly in modernisation and its blessings no matter what form this process might take, these historians often took a dim view of noble power and its survival on principle. It was seen as an obstacle to the growth of the modern sovereign state just as much as to the rise of the middle classes or the eventual development of a liberal, enlightened and potentially egalitarian society.[6] From this point of view those periods in the history of the nobility when noble society seemed to be in crisis and decline, as in the late sixteenth and early seventeenth centuries, were of the greatest interest.

However, at the beginning of the twenty-first century – not least because of the virtual disappearance of Marxism as a theory claiming to provide a master narrative for the length and breadth of European history – historians are less certain that the urban middle classes or bourgeois elites were in some form or other the harbingers of a modern society governed by the principles of rational self-interest rather than by seemingly irrational notions of honour and social prestige. This allows us to take a new look at noble society, less dominated than in the past by a search for the alleged decline of noble power and political influence, but equally free of the superficial romantic nostalgia which sometimes leads historians to look for an ideal world full of glamour, chivalry and the virtues of a bygone age when dealing with our topic.

It is certainly true that recent research conveys the impression of a nobility triumphant rather than defeated in the seventeenth century.[7] Works on French history, for example, have corrected the traditional image of the early modern nobility as hidebound, backward-looking and condemned to economic failure. On the contrary it has been shown that noblemen and -women could adapt to new cultural trends as successfully as members of other elites. In fact, in the seventeenth century they were in many ways pioneers of an individualism – often seen as a particularly modern attitude to society – much more pronounced than among members of other elites.[8]

The history of the French nobility has benefited from the fact that it has never really been neglected by historians working on early modern France, whatever the reigning fashion in historiography. The role nobles played during the Wars of Religion and the *Fronde* and the place they held at the centre of the social, political and cultural life of the *Grand Siècle* were so prominent that they were simply impossible to ignore.[9] Moreover, even those historians who were inclined to greet the French Revolution as a great liberation from the oppressive rule of a decadent aristocracy could hardly deny that this aristocracy had a crucial impact on the structure of the Ancien Régime. In other countries attention paid to the history of the nobility was often more narrowly focused. For example, in England, next to the debate on the crisis of the aristocracy, which has now died down and hardly figures any longer in recent standard accounts of English social history, the search for the causes of the Civil War has often dominated historical debate, including many local studies concentrating on the gentry community in the counties, an approach which has both stimulated research and limited its agenda.[10]

In Germany and Austria, on the other hand, work on the various regional nobilities of the Holy Roman Empire has made comparatively slow progress over the last decades. Noblemen who, in other countries, would be classified simply as magnates or titled aristocrats – the princes and counts of the Empire – were able to create their own states or semi-independent dominions, even if they were sometimes diminutive in size. Research on these strata of noble society has therefore often been dominated by constitutional and political history wedded to the venerable tradition of *Reichsgeschichte*, and has paid less attention to the history of the nobility as a social group.[11] Social and cultural historians, on the other hand, were more likely to look at other sections of society such as the peasants or the urban elites, which appealed more strongly to the historical imagination, either because they embodied the fate of the oppressed and excluded or, alternatively, because they could be seen as linked to the forces of modernisation. Only recently have individual noble magnates or regional elites attracted more attention and become the subject of important and innovative studies.[12]

Comparative surveys of our topic are not infrequently dominated by an agenda derived from French history, because, in many ways, research on the French nobility has been more wide-ranging than that on other noble elites in Europe and has attained a particularly high overall standard. However, despite the often paradigmatic character of historical developments in France during our period, one should be wary of assuming that noble elites elsewhere more or less automatically followed the French example in outlook and behaviour, as some recent accounts have implied.[13] It is indeed true that especially in the second half of the seventeenth century noblemen all over Europe looked to the French court for cultural inspiration, that they spoke French and imitated the manners of the French aristocracy. But the ensuing similarities of mentality and social conduct often remained rather superficial; a Bohemian magnate ruling over thousands of serfs or the proud canon of a Westphalian cathedral chapter which would have been reluctant to accept even the highest ranking French prince as one of its members defined their position in society in a different way from a courtier in Versailles, let alone a judge in the *Parlement* of Paris, and such examples could be multiplied. Here as in other areas we are constantly reminded of the fact that the landscape of noble society in Europe was multifaceted and extremely diverse.

The heterogeneity of noble society in early modern Europe is striking and it is one of the aims of this book to draw readers' attention to this fact, not to conceal it. Nevertheless, when looking at the history of the noble elites in Europe a number of key problems and issues, which affected most European nobilities in our period, do emerge. The cultural changes of these 150 years which led nobles to develop new codes of conduct – new virtues and new vices in a manner of speaking – have already been emphasised. Equally important was the impact of the Reformation and Counter-Reformation on noble culture and mentality. The religious divisions and conflicts which engulfed Europe in the later sixteenth century threatened to cut across traditional ties of loyalty, kinship and friendship. At the same time, they confronted nobles with religious ideals and values which were not always easily compatible with the more conventional notions of noble virtue and valour. In fact, in the late sixteenth century clergymen, both Catholic and perhaps even more so radical Protestants, were eager to attack the nobility for its lack of religious fervour and its greed with regard to the property of the Church. Nevertheless many noblemen and -women found not only personal spiritual fulfilment but also a new political and social role in the struggle for the true faith, however defined. In the end, in most countries, a compromise between traditional aristocratic society and the new notions of religious orthodoxy and righteousness was achieved in the seventeenth century. Clergymen toned down their religious and moral enthusiasm in as far as it implied an attack on the traditional social order and nobles, as has already been stressed, adapted to the ideals of conduct which, inspired by the demands of religious reformers, were designed to mitigate the cult of military heroism to which many noblemen still subscribed in the late sixteenth century.

Self-control and the ability to master the subtler arts of self-assertion were even more important at court than in church. The court has often been seen as a place where noblemen ceased to be warriors and masters lording it over tenants and vassals, and became content to act as idle servants to an all-powerful monarch. This interpretation relies far too heavily on the admittedly widespread contemporary criticism of the court, often by disappointed courtiers, and has been thoroughly revised by recent research. Nevertheless, there is no doubt that ideals of conduct and patterns of behaviour first developed for the court and at court, such as the idea that the true nobleman had to display a seemingly effortless, casual air of superiority to succeed in society and triumph over his rivals, increasingly influenced and transformed the behaviour of all noblemen, no matter whether they lived in the country, in town or at court itself.

However, while the court was a place where new cultural standards and ideals of noble conduct were developed, it was also a focus for bitter conflicts between aristocratic factions and their competing claims to dominate access to the ruler and to control royal or princely patronage. Noble rebellion – a conspicuously widespread phenomenon in a number of European countries in the late sixteenth century and at the beginning of the seventeenth century – was certainly motivated by more than the frustrations and resentments of former or potential courtiers who had failed to gain the monarch's favour, but nevertheless, such grievances often played a considerable part in the domestic unrest of this period. In fact, for a number of European countries the century *c*.1560–1660 was a time of prolonged and violent political confrontation between princes and noblemen. After 1560 the French monarchy was almost destroyed by more than 30 years of civil war in which significant sections of the nobility, although perhaps numerically only a minority, took an active and at certain stages decisive part. Moreover the series of civil wars and noble revolts continued in the early seventeenth century and did not end until the 1660s. Although at least in its heartlands it enjoyed a far greater degree of stability, the Spanish monarchy was at the same period confronted by a number of regional or national revolts in its remoter provinces which were often led, or at least supported and abetted by noblemen. England, Scotland and Ireland were shaken by civil wars in the 1640s in which initially aristocratic magnates also played a prominent part and the Austrian Habsburgs saw their authority challenged by the rebellion of the Bohemian Estates in 1618–20.

Not until the second half of the seventeenth century was stability and peace re-established. The new political power structure emerging from the conflicts of an earlier age have often been seen as an expression of royal or princely absolutism, which solved the problem posed by rebellious, overmighty subjects once and for all. However, recent research has questioned the very idea of 'absolutism' and has sometimes even rejected the term itself as largely meaningless.[14] Few monarchs were able to rule for more than a limited period without the co-operation of significant sections of the traditional noble elite. In fact, kingship would have been almost inconceivable in a society which lacked a powerful nobility. But as we shall see, it would be wrong to assume that the structure of politics and society at the end of the seventeenth century was still largely the same as it had been 150 years earlier. The greater authority of the state was visible not least in the very definition of noble status. More than in the past, at the end of the seventeenth century disputes over claims to noble status were decided by law courts and royal or princely officeholders, and not just by the collective judgement of the local community – noble and non-noble – and its acknowledged leaders. This is not even to mention the grant of new noble titles by letters patent, a process which in some countries led to a true inflation of honours. In fact, the tendency to replace less formal customary definitions of nobility by statutory criteria applied by legal experts was one of the crucial developments affecting most European elites during our period. Moreover the growth of the early modern state led to important changes affecting both military organisation, financial administration and the role of the law courts in resolving conflicts, as has already been emphasised. By the end of the seventeenth century a new political and social equilibrium had emerged, but in many countries it had only been achieved after serious conflicts and domestic turmoil. Looking at the balance of continuity and change between 1550 and 1700 it may be tempting to conclude that everything had to change so that everything could remain the same, as a Sicilian aristocrat was to put it much later, commenting on the even more profound upheavals of the nineteenth century.[15] In the following chapters we will examine how plausible such a statement is.

1

Status and the quest for exclusiveness

The foundations of noble identity

Introduction

At first glance it seems that in the early modern period noblemen all over Europe shared a common outlook and held similar ideals and values dominated by ideas such as honour, lineage and military valour.[1] Until the later seventeenth or early eighteenth century, when many sovereigns tried to prevent their subjects of whatever status from serving a foreign monarch, noblemen often sought a career at court or in war outside their own country of origin. In fact, the original Grand Tour or *Kavalierstour* often served the purpose of giving young noblemen military experience on foreign battlefields as much as the objective of improving their knowledge and education (see below pp. 57–60) In some sense, therefore, the nobility, and its upper echelons in particular, was a genuinely European elite, whose members recognised each other as equals, a recognition which found its expression not least in intermarriage.[2]

Further examination reveals however, that the social meaning of 'being noble' depended very much on a national or even regional context, and that one can speak of a European nobility only in a very limited sense. The standards and norms which determined noble status differed greatly from one country to the next. In some parts of Europe a certain amount of – preferably landed – wealth, the right marriage and a certain way of life were sufficient or almost sufficient to establish some claim to noble status, whereas other countries demanded documentary proof of noble descent going back several generations. German cathedral chapters, for example, were particularly strict in this respect (see below, pp. 20–21). They tended not to acknowledge noble titles acquired abroad at all. They distrusted the proofs provided by foreign corporations or authorities, because they were based on different notions of nobility. In the eighteenth century some German lawyers argued that only titles derived from imperial grants were valid in Germany. Just as the Emperor could not claim a seat in the English House of Lords even if he had '16,000 noble ancestors', no foreign nobleman could claim membership of a German noble corporation even if he could demonstrate the necessary 16 quarters of nobility in the generation of his great-great-grandparents.[3] This example shows that for contemporaries – even in the eighteenth century – there was not one European nobility. Rather there were different national and regional noble elites, each with their own definitions of status and rank, although these various elites were about to become more homogeneous by the end of the old régime.[4]

Furthermore even within the great composite monarchies of early modern Europe such as the Spanish Empire or within countries, definitions of nobility were by no means always clear cut. In the early seventeenth century a French writer, Guez de Balzac, argued that it was almost impossible to define nobility. To be noble, he suggested, was in some sense a quality more imagined than real. Nobility existed only in the opinions of men. One had to believe in it and to rely on what others said about it. 'Beauty could be seen, riches could be touched, but nobility had to be imagined or to be taken on faith.' ('Elle n'est guère que dans l'opinion des hommes: Il faut la croire, et s'en rapporter à la bonne foy d'autruy. La beauté se voit, et les richesses se touchent, mais la noblesse s'imagine, et se présuppose.')[5] This may have been a radical point of view, at least for somebody who himself belonged to the nobility, but Balzac's remarks point to one of the central problems faced by the nobility in our period: what criteria defined noble status and who applied them to validate or reject claims to such a status? Quite clearly to claim the privileges of a nobleman was worth little if almost everybody could do so, as was the case, for example, in some parts of Poland and Spain.[6] Only if there was a clear division between the – preferably small – minority of noble families and the mass of the population, could one really take pride in being noble and enjoy the fiscal, legal and political advantages this entailed.

It is hardly an exaggeration to say that the life of a nobleman – and, in different ways, of female members of noble families as well – had one principal purpose: to prove their claim to honour and superiority, to prove that they really belonged to the privileged elite. The display of military prowess in war or in tournaments or duels, the coats of arms which decorated tombs, gatehouses and carriages alike, the country houses and castles dominating the countryside all served this purpose, to which marriage arrangements and education were equally subjected. Nevertheless, pedigrees proving the ancient lineage of a family could be invented and in many countries manors and castles could be acquired by commoners as well as by noblemen – at least before the seventeenth century. The question thus remained: who was to sit in judgement over controversial claims to noble status? In the past, the collective judgement of those who were already by common consensus socially accepted as members of the nobility had often been the decisive criterion; this initially quite informal collective judgement had been more formally articulated since the fifteenth century, for example, in the rules governing admission to tournaments (from which non-noble contestants were normally excluded),[7] but also in the admission practice of spiritual and secular noble corporations such as cathedral or collegiate chapters, orders of knighthood or the noble estates forming part of the provincial or national representative assemblies.[8]

From customary to statutory definitions of nobility

In the last resort, however, only the state which increasingly sought to replace more informal methods of government by clearly defined administrative and legal procedures could really enforce strict status criteria. Nobilities which wanted to maintain their social exclusiveness either had to ensure that they controlled the state themselves as in republics such as Venice or in ecclesiastical principalities with their elective rulers (the German prince bishoprics offer an example of this model, as does the sovereign Order of St John of Jerusalem which ruled over the island of Malta), or they had to appeal to the monarch to act as a defender of noble exclusiveness and noble honour. Often monarchs were only too ready to respond to such appeals, for they increasingly saw the right to investigate claims to nobility combined with the right to create new nobles as a source of power and, not least, of additional revenues. In fact, in many countries, 'the authority to issue letters of nobility became like minting gold coins, a measure of sovereignty.'[9]

Thus, in many parts of Europe, the later sixteenth and the seventeenth centuries witnessed a process by which noble status was more clearly defined in legal terms than it had been in the past either by noble corporations or by royal or princely officeholders. To some extent this tendency to restrict the definition of nobility had become necessary because the increasing tax burden had made the status of nobleman dangerously attractive, all the more so as the feudal obligation to perform personal military service for the Crown at times of war had largely become obsolete in an age when battles were fought by armies of professional soldiers and no longer by the feudal host.

In fact, it has been argued for Germany that the first attempts to develop a comprehensive definition of the nobility as an estate comprising both magnates and rural squires were made in the fifteenth century when taxation and other burdens imposed by the rulers on their subjects had first become a real political problem.[10] Not to belong to the 'misera plebs contribuens', the miserable tax-paying plebs, became increasingly attractive and therefore barriers had to be erected against those whose claim to noble status had no real foundation. In countries where noblemen had to pay taxes like

everybody else, the need to define the nobility in legal terms was correspondingly smaller. This explains to some extent why in England, where
simple gentlemen as well as peers were liable to taxation, the gentry never
became an estate with clear legal boundaries.[11]

However, as we shall see, the difference between England and continental
countries such as France, with their more rigid definitions of status, was a
gradual and not an absolute one in the late sixteenth century. Ultimately
wealth, in particular landed estates, the possession of offices, a claim to
ancient lineage and a particular lifestyle, and not least the ability to arrange
the right sort of marriage for oneself and one's children, continued to be as
important in demonstrating noble status in France or Germany as it was in
England or in other countries which lacked clear legal criteria defining
nobility. Royal control over admissions to the noble estate, and even more
crucially, royal ability to exclude from the nobility those who could not
prove their status according to strict legal criteria was limited, at least until
the mid-seventeenth century, in spite of all attempts to regulate and restrain
social mobility. In fact, even in the later seventeenth century the prevailing
rhetoric of social exclusiveness often formed a marked contrast to social
practices which continued to leave considerable scope for social mobility,
upwards as well as downwards.[12]

Hard social and economic facts certainly played a part in constituting
noble status, for example, wealth or the ability to exercise rights of lordship
over villages or towns, but equally important was the social rhetoric which
gave meaning and significance to these facts. Thus it has been argued for
Germany that the nobility as an estate, comprising both the higher nobility
(princes, earls and barons) and simple knights, did not really exist before the
fifteenth century, when the idea of nobility was first invented as a concept,
not least to distinguish rural from urban elites.[13] If one accepts this argument, it could be said that the new concept of a nobility comprising all those
fully capable of holding feudal fiefs first created the nobility as a social reality in Germany.

Given the importance of the prevailing social grammar governing the way
in which people thought, spoke and wrote about problems of social order
and hierarchy, it was essential for those social groups which were seeking to
improve their own status to change or manipulate the language of status
and hierarchy. Lawyers and academics who argued that academic degrees
gave a man the same status as a grant of nobility certainly tried to do so in
the sixteenth century,[14] and while their success in countries such as
Germany may have remained limited, the French *noblesse de robe*, an elite
of proprietary officeholders, was significantly more successful in laying
claim to noble status from the late sixteenth century onwards (see below,
pp. 37–8). Many *robins* bought noble fiefs in order to demonstrate their
newly acquired status as members of the noble elite.

Such phenomena as the aspirations to noble status of proprietary officeholders, however, soon provoked counter-measures. In 1579 the King of

France, Henry III, had a new law, the *Ordonnance* of Blois, enacted. One of its clauses (art. 258) stated that men of non-noble origin who bought noble fiefs should remain members of the third estate in future; the silent elevation to the status of nobleman was thereby declared illegal. In the late Middle Ages and the earlier sixteenth century, it had been normal practice for wealthy urban citizens, lawyers, officeholders and even rich farmers to acquire fiefs, rights of jurisdiction, and castles, and to adopt a way of life suitable for a nobleman – for example, avoiding all visible mercantile activities or, even more important, manual work – thus gradually persuading local society that they actually were noblemen and had never been anything else. Such a process might take time, one or two generations and sometimes even longer, but for those powerful and influential enough to persuade local officeholders to strike their names off the tax rolls – noblemen were exempt from the most important direct tax, the *taille*, in the north of France – or the registers of those who had to pay a special fee, the tax of the *franc-fief*, because they owned noble fiefs without actually being noble, success was mostly a matter of time.[15] Outside the few provinces such as Normandy where the Crown already exercised some formal control over noble status, patents of nobility were rarely sought to confirm this silent social process (ennoblement by virtue of office was a different matter); in fact, for many noblemen the idea that the king could by a stroke of his pen automatically transform a commoner into a nobleman seemed almost monstrous.[16]

In this respect France was by no means unique in the sixteenth century.[17] In the absence of institutions able to control access to the nobility and, perhaps even more importantly, of records which could be examined to check claims to noble status, a combination of wealth, preferably landed wealth, patience and the right social connections could open many doors and transform the son or at least the grandson of a rich farmer, a merchant or a lawyer into a nobleman. In the first half of the sixteenth century conditions seem to have been particularly favourable for this sort of social mobility. A growing population produced a corresponding growth in the size of the noble elite, and rising prices for agricultural products created new wealth among landowners which could provide the foundation for new noble dynasties. In Protestant countries the redistribution of landed property after the Reformation was also an important factor. Moreover, the growth of the state bureaucracy and the replacement of clerical by lay officeholders opened up new chances for a career in the service of the state which could be a stepping stone to social advancement and the rise of commoners into the nobility, even in countries where offices were not in themselves seen as a sort of property which could raise their owners to noble status, as in France.[18]

These very tendencies, however, provoked a backlash as the traditional social hierarchy seemed to be threatened by ambitious upstarts. Older families as well as those who had just managed to establish themselves among the nobility were now eager to close the road to social advancement to others.[19] Not only in France but also in many other European countries, lineage as a criterion for social status was increasingly emphasised. Paradoxically, the criticism levelled by humanists as well as theologians against the nobility, namely that they lacked virtue as well as true piety (below, pp. 55–6), helped to create a concept of noble identity, which defined nobility exclusively in terms of lineage or even blood and race. If such a definition was accepted noblemen whose claims to social superiority rested primarily on their ancestry could no longer be accused of forfeiting their claim to noble status when they failed to display military prowess or did not support the allegedly true Church and faith, not to mention their lack of education and manners.[20]

The tendency to emphasise the exclusive character of the old nobility was therefore to some extent an attempt to limit the rise of new families which had been such a widespread phenomenon in the sixteenth century.[21] Of course, in many ways an ideology which saw nobility founded on race and lineage opposed not only social mobility, but also the widespread tendency to grant – or even worse, to sell – new titles of nobility to royal or princely servants, officeholders, in particular, or even financiers.[22] Such patents of nobility did not necessarily confer noble status as such on the recipient but rather a higher rank within the nobility to persons already accepted as noble. These, in particular, threatened the traditional hierarchy of status and honour, and could create considerable resentment among older families, as the example of the English peerage demonstrates. Elizabeth I of England had been very reluctant to create new peerages. However, her successor, James I (1603–25), was much more liberal; ruling a foreign kingdom where he encountered a great deal of hostility against his own country, Scotland, and its allegedly impoverished and greedy nobility, he tried to assuage such animosities by liberally granting new titles and honours to his English subjects. Facing severe financial problems, he also saw the sale of titles as a means to raise money. His son Charles I (1625–49) followed his father's policy and created many additional peerages during the first years of his reign and again in the 1640s, primarily to bolster support for his controversial policies in the House of Lords. Between them the two monarchs almost doubled the size of the peerage. Whereas there had been about 55 peers in 1602, there were 138 persons at the outbreak of the Civil War in 1642. Admittedly further expansion was much slower. There were no more than 153 peers in 1688, and 173 in 1700.[23] Moreover, by the standards of wealth and local power many newly ennobled families were the equals of the older established families. Others, however, owed their ascent more to the favour they found at court, or to massive cash payments which allowed them to buy new titles, payments from which royal favourites benefited at least as much as the Crown itself. This was even more true for titles in the Irish peerage, where all restraints were abandoned and new peerages sold freely to the deserving and the undeserving at bargain prices in the early seventeenth century.[24]

Downright venality may have played a less prominent role in the grant of princely titles by the Emperor in Germany. Nevertheless we find a similar inflation of honours in the seventeenth century as in England under the early Stuarts. Between 1582 and the end of the Empire in 1806 the Emperor bestowed the title of *Reichsfürst* (prince) on 160 new families, including grants to Italian, Polish and other foreign noblemen. After 1618 it often went to families from his hereditary dominions who had served him in war or in an administrative capacity, or to carefully selected counts of the Empire who belonged to the imperial clientele.[25] In this case, comparatively few of the new princes ever attained a seat in the imperial diet as one had to hold a fief directly from the Emperor to be eligible for this privilege and the chamber of princes was very reluctant to admit newcomers. Nevertheless the large number of new titles was sufficient to put considerable pressure on the older families to join the race for new honours and imperial favour.[26]

Matters were not very different in other European countries. In France the grant of the dignity of *duc et pair* to the house of Montmorency in 1551 marked the beginning of an age when simple *gentilshommes* (as opposed to princes of the blood or foreign princes of sovereign status) increasingly became members of the French peerage. In fact, Henry III's favourites, such as Anne de Joyeuse, the King's 'archimignon' (see below, pp. 90–91), created a duke in 1581, held a prominent place among those raised to the peerage. At the end of Henry's reign there were a total of 25 *ducs et pairs* in France and a further 11 simple dukes, whereas in the Middle Ages there had not been more than six secular peers in the kingdom.[27] This policy was continued under the Bourbons in the seventeenth century. During the period 1589 to 1723 the number of families which held a peerage and/or dukedom and who had originally belonged to the simple nobility (*gentilshommes*), however ancient, rose from 11 to 38. Most of this expansion occurred before 1661 (there were already 34 families of mere *gentilshommes* within the peerage in 1661), when royal authority was often weak and other sources of patronage to reward loyal supporters of the dynasty or to buy off potential rebels were limited.[28] Admittedly, the fact that as a rule new titles had to be registered by the *Parlement* in Paris – unregistered titles were much less prestigious – limited the expansion of the French peerage to some extent.

In Italy, where not only the king of Spain (who ruled Naples, Sicily and Milan) and the pope but also the emperor and other foreign sovereigns granted new titles to noblemen or commoners, the inflation of honours was even more marked. In Naples, the number of titled noblemen was three times higher in 1620 than in 1558 and was doubled once again in the following 130 years. In the end there were far more dukes and princes than simple counts. In Lombardy, the kings of Spain granted 276 new titles of *Conte* or *Marchese* between 1554 and 1706 to members of the elite.[29] The grant of new titles (some were in fact simply sold to the highest bidder) was an expression not just of the financial problems the Spanish monarchy faced – titles were a cheap way to reward the king's loyal servants and patient creditors – but also of a deliberate policy to integrate the Italian provinces into the Spanish Empire. A new hierarchy of titles granted by Spain replaced the ancient regional definitions of nobility. The process was completed by granting the status of *Grande* to a select number of loyal families and by rewarding others, primarily those who served in the Spanish armies, with a knighthood in one of the great military orders of Salamanca or Calatrava.[30]

In Spain itself we can observe a similar development. Whereas there had been only 28 marquesses and dukes in 1530, there were 113 dukes who also held the position of *grande* and 334 marquesses in 1700, after a century in which honours were often among the few rewards the Crown could bestow on its servants. Although individual titles necessarily lost some of their prestige because of this multiplication of honours, it has been argued that this process did not really undermine the traditional social hierarchy. Rather, according to I.A.A. Thompson, 'it was ... a clarification of existing social distinctions and economic power'.[31] Nevertheless, even Thompson admits that the growth of the titled nobility devalued the status of simple noblemen who owed their claim to honour, not to the Crown's favour but only to their descent and the way in which they lived.

Attempts, however, to defend this 'natural' inherited nobility against the forces of social and political change, had little chance of success without the prince's support. More often than not it was the prince himself who had to check the pedigrees which those claiming to be noble produced as proof of their status. An ideology which tried to limit the ruler's ability to determine and change the status of his subjects in some ways had the effect of actually increasing his power to act as arbiter of social aspirations, as has already been pointed out.[32] Equally ambivalent was the rise of the discipline of genealogy and the proliferation of printed genealogical works in the sixteenth century. The increasing number of published family histories and genealogical works made families more conscious of their ancestry and made it easier to identify and, possibly, to exclude parvenus.[33] But at the same time many tracts published by professional genealogists provided new families with a respectable lineage of ancestors going back in some cases many centuries.[34] Regardless of whether such pedigrees were consciously invented, or somewhat naively based on unreliable documents and hearsay, in practice they concealed the extent to which the nobility as a social group was changing, and thus responded to an obviously deeply felt social need to believe in an immutable social order.[35]

Nevertheless in the later sixteenth century there was clearly a changing perception that noble status was based primarily on lineage, and this perception was particularly visible in France. Here the Wars of Religion posed a greater threat to the traditional social order than elsewhere, not least because warfare offered – in the form of military careers, but also through the general chaos it produced – chances for social mobility which did not exist in quite the same way elsewhere. On the other hand France also had a tradition of strong royal government and a comparatively highly developed fiscal and legal bureaucracy staffed by university trained officeholders. These men tried to impose their own ideals of a society governed by clear legal principles upon the existing social hierarchy.

Quite clearly in France two conceptions of social order confronted each other in the late sixteenth century. In the words of Arlette Jouanna:

> [On the one hand was the idea] that society was a self regulating body which raised those to positions of eminence who were most admired by the standards of a collective social judgement and on the other hand the idea of an all powerful king, who like God whose counter-image and lieutenant he was, exalted the humble and meek and put down the mighty according to his will.[36]

The old concept of a self-regulating social order never quite disappeared, but the idea of a hierarchy of honour depending on the king's will certainly gained ground in France, or as James Wood has put it:

> The nobility ... moved from a situation, in which their status was defined in a purely customary way ... to a situation in which they were forced practically every generation to defend their nobility anew, on ever narrowing grounds, to the financial officers of the Crown.[37]

Royal officials undertook so-called *recherches de noblesse*, investigations to weed out from the ranks of the nobility those who falsely claimed noble status. In some provinces they took place as early as the fifteenth century, in others not until the later seventeenth century. Such investigations remained fairly unsystematic until *c.*1660. Only after this date were the *recherches de noblesse*, which enjoyed a first great wave in 1666–67 and continued intermittently until about 1718, undertaken in a much more systematic way.[38] Membership of the nobility either had to be derived from a formal royal act ennobling the family or person in question – a patent of nobility or the grant of an office that ennobled its possessor – or it had to be proved by demonstrating that one's ancestors had been noble, and had enjoyed all the relevant prerogatives and privileges for at least 100 years. The ever increasing tax burden made it imperative to push those who wrongly claimed noble status back into the Third Estate among the commoners. At the same time Louis XIV wanted to reinforce the traditional royal claim that the Crown alone could adjudicate disputes over rank and precedence.

The number of families permanently excluded from the ranks of the nobility because they were unable to produce the necessary documents or because they pursued commercial activities incompatible with the status of a nobleman may in most provinces have been limited, although initially the percentage of claims to nobility which were rejected could be much higher, ranging from about 30 per cent in Brittany or the *generalité* of Orleans in the 1660s (or even 40 per cent in Paris in 1696) to a more moderate 10 to 15 per cent in Normandy or Beauce.[39]

Those who were excluded during the investigations were often readmitted at a later stage. However, they not only had to pay special fees, but they also had to acknowledge the king's right to have the last word in all controversies regarding status and social prestige. As long as a family had enough local support – that is, was considered noble by local society – royal officials were apparently reluctant to reject its claim to noble status.[40] Nonetheless the *recherches* undertaken under the direction of Louis XIV's minister of finance, Colbert, after 1660 did change the prevailing concept of nobility. A concept of status triumphed which was based on the assumption that the king was the sole font of honour, however much he was forced in practice to accept pre-existing informal claims to status.

The *recherches* were a specifically French phenomenon but there were parallels in other countries. In the southern Netherlands, part of the Spanish Empire until 1700, statutes were enacted between 1595 and 1616 which put an end to the silent usurpation of noble status by commoners that had been common practice until this date. From now on the sovereign, the King of Spain or Archduke Albert (d. 1621) and Archduchess Isabella (d. 1633) as regents in his stead, had all claims to noble status checked by their heralds. Admittedly families which had already obtained a social position similar to that of nobles were rarely forced to abandon their social pretensions entirely. But instead of silently insinuating themselves into the nobility they now had to petition for a royal patent to raise them to the status they coveted, thereby acknowledging the fact that they were not part of the ancient nobility. This was a clear disadvantage as from the late sixteenth century membership of the Provincial Estates, for example, was increasingly limited to titled families which belonged to the ancient nobility that had already been noble in the late Middle Ages.[41]

In France and the southern Netherlands the Crown tried to create clear criteria for membership of the noble estate. In other countries, however, and this clearly represents an alternative model, noble corporations themselves undertook this task. Thus we observe the same tendency to transform the nobility into a closed and legally defined estate, but at the same time the nobility retained a greater degree of autonomy and did not become dependent on the monarch to define its identity. Italy offers a good example of this second model. Here almost every city had a patriciate of its own, and certainly every region had its own standards for defining noble status. In Venice, for example, the nobility had been closed to new entrants at around 1300. After some new admissions at a time of political crisis, in 1381, only very few new families, which the Venetian government wanted to honour in a special way, were admitted until the 1640s, when renewed financial problems forced the Venetian nobility to open its ranks to a number of wealthy newcomers prepared to pay vast sums for the privilege. In the final resort, however, the Venetian nobility as the collective sovereign of the city-state was able to decide which families to accept as equals and which to reject. Even in Florence, which had come under princely rule in the early sixteenth century, matters were not very different. Most families belonging to the Florentine nobility in the early eighteenth century had already been in place as officeholders before the end of the republic in 1532, as the Medici refrained from creating new noble families through patents of nobility, and the old families showed a remarkable talent for biological and social survival.[42]

Thus the specifically patrician and republican traditions of some Italian cities survived in the seventeenth century and beyond. At the same time at a national and regional level, the military orders of St John and San Stefano (the latter particularly in Tuscany) served to transform local elites, whose origins lay in the often quite heterogeneous patriciates of the more important cities, into more homogeneous provincial nobilities, and ultimately an Italian national nobility. In the late Middle Ages – until the mid-sixteenth century – the Knights of St John, whose principal seat in the early modern period was in Malta and which owned numerous priories and *commende* (commanderies) in Italy, had accepted proofs according to the local definitions of nobility valid in the place of origin of candidates when admitting new members. Gradually, however, more exacting standards were applied, and in 1599 a statute was passed by the Order which required all candidates who wanted to be admitted as knights within the Italian tongue to prove that their families had been noble for at least 200 years. Moreover, not only the candidates themselves but also their ancestors must not have indulged in any 'vile', that is, for example, mercantile activities. Only for the four cities Genoa, Florence, Sienna and Lucca were more lenient standards applied which continued to make the admission of candidates from merchant families possible.[43] Although generally opposed to nobilities engaging in commerce, the Order saw membership of an urban elite, clearly separated from the other citizens, as an essential criterion of noble status. This was considered more important than the possession of fiefs and landed estates, and certainly more important than patents of nobility granted by monarchs and princes. The Order thus supported the exclusive and self-recruiting urban elites of the Italian cities against all royal or princely pretensions to reshape them. To be accepted as a Knight of St John was tantamount to a public confirmation of noble status and the patriciate of the candidate's home city was also implicitly acknowledged as collectively noble.[44] Towns which failed to defend the exclusiveness of their elite against the lower strata of the population or against the monarch could no longer hope to have their candidates accepted by the Knights of St John.[45] Like the Knights of St John, the Order of San Stefano, created by the Medici and based mainly in Tuscany, also provided – at the regional level – a common standard for noble status. However, it remained open to new families able to buy their way into the Order, and was used by the Medici to create a unified Tuscan nobility out of the various urban patriciates of the Duchy.[46]

Varieties of noble status in the Holy Roman Empire

Although divided politically, Italy was united in religious terms, and the rules governing the admission to the Order of St John provided to some extent a common legal reference point for the various regional nobilities. In Germany, where most of the northern and eastern territories as well as some areas in the south-west were Protestant, military orders or similar ecclesiastical institutions were unable to play a similar role. Legally the emperor was the ultimate arbiter of all claims to nobility in Germany until 1806. In his hereditary dominions, Austria in particular, but also in Bohemia, the emperor used his right to bestow or confirm titles of nobility for political purposes, in particular to weaken the position of the old established Protestant families and to strengthen the influence of his own Catholic supporters in the assemblies of the estates.[47] Outside his hereditary dominions, however, the emperor's influence on the definition of noble status was more limited. In theory at least he alone could create new noble titles. The monopoly was only gradually eroded after the mid-seventeenth century, when German princes acquired sovereign principalities and kingdoms outside the Empire, as in the case of the Hohenzollern in Prussia (1613–60), the Wettins in Poland (1697), or the Hanoverian branch of the house of Brunswick in England (1714), or claimed, rightly or wrongly, exceptional privileges for their territory, entitling them to create their own nobility, as for example in Bavaria.[48]

Nevertheless, the tendency to define noble status in narrower legal terms, stressing lineage as the principal qualification, was apparent in many regions of the Holy Roman Empire in the later sixteenth and seventeenth centuries as much as in France or Italy. In Germany, it was often the wish of noble corporations themselves to exclude social climbers from their ranks that led to the enforcement of stricter standards of lineage and status. This trend was particularly pronounced among the Catholic cathedral and collegiate chapters. Here social exclusiveness held special attractions. Because the number of benefices in the chapters was limited, the old established families had a strong interest in excluding all newcomers to reduce the competition for the canonries. Most cathedral and many collegiate chapters in Germany were already closed to mere commoners in the late Middle Ages, although non-noble clergymen who had acquired a university degree still managed to gain access to some chapters. In the later sixteenth century standards for admission to benefices became even stricter. Increasingly, candidates were required to prove that all of their 16 great-great-grandparents, both male and female, had been noble. Thus not only commoners, but also newly ennobled families were excluded. This principle was officially established in many Catholic dioceses between *c.*1550 and the 1620s. The chapter of the bishopric of Hildesheim in northern Germany, for instance, enacted a statute of this kind in 1602.[49] Soon the territorial estates of the prince-bishoprics and in some cases also the estates in the neighbouring territories followed suit and also excluded all those who did not belong to ancient noble families. The new restrictive rules applied even to old established urban patrician families which had considered themselves a part of the nobility, but now saw their claims rejected. The requirement to prove the noble status of 16 great-great-grandparents was introduced for the knighthood of the bishopric of Münster in 1640 and also applied to other provincial diets in the Catholic regions of northern and north-western Germany.[50] Even in the south, chapters such as Constance and Passau, in which canons from patrician or even middle-class families had once been quite numerous (as late as the early sixteenth century), acquired an ever more aristocratic character in the seventeenth century, until they were virtually closed to candidates who did not belong to the old nobility.[51]

Implicitly this tendency of Catholic noble corporations to close ranks and exclude not only non-noble, but also newly ennobled families ran counter to the emperor's right to create new nobles, who were thus relegated to the rank of a second-rate nobility. In fact, in the competition for ecclesiastical benefices the Habsburgs tended to favour the imperial knighthood which, by and large, had followed less strict admission practices than the Catholic territorial knighthoods.[52] However, in both cases – the imperial policy of ennobling new families and the desire of many cathedral chapters to admit only noblemen of ancient lineage – an idea of nobility which stressed certain legal requirements as opposed to a tacit social consensus now shaped the identity of the nobility as an estate.

Admittedly, German noble corporations which were predominantly Protestant often took a more relaxed attitude. In electoral Saxony, for example, some legal claim to noble status – no matter whether this claim rested on inherited privileges or on a recent patent of nobility – and the possession of an officially acknowledged noble manor house or castle were sufficient to be admitted to the knighthood at the local level. Matters were, however, more difficult for those who wanted to attend the Diet of the Electorate claiming a personal hereditary privilege (as *schriftsässige Adlige*: the vast majority of all noblemen present during the sessions) as opposed to those who merely elected delegates to the assembly of the estates. For the former group the Elector enacted a law in 1700 which required 16 noble ancestors, both female and male, in the generation of a nobleman's great-great-grandparents, and these regulations were by and large strictly enforced in the eighteenth century.[53]

In neighbouring Brandenburg the Elector had promised in 1653 that non-nobles should not be allowed to buy noble estates, except under special circumstances.[54] In practice, however, in the later seventeenth century merchants and urban patricians were still in some cases able to buy estates which had belonged to noblemen. They benefited from the severe economic crisis caused by a fall in prices for grain, the Thirty Years War and high taxation which spelt doom for many noble families.[55] Not infrequently the new owners were later ennobled themselves. Not until after 1740, under

Frederick the Great, did the Prussian Crown systematically try to exclude commoners from the possession of noble manors and estates, making the knighthood, in theory at least, a closed corporation.[56] Other German principalities, however, such as electoral Hanover, remained much more liberal even at this late stage. Here non-noble or newly ennobled families continued to buy noble manors and at least the latter were in due course, after one or two generations, accepted by the knighthood as full members of their corporations.[57]

In some countries there was a tradition of keeping exact records of all noble fiefs and manors. For example, in Bohemia only those persons who owned an estate which was registered in the *Landtafel* (land register) could take part in the sessions of the diet, although in practice a family which had sold its estate was not necessarily excluded if it had been admitted at an earlier period. Moreover, the estates had first to bestow a *Ius Incolatus* or *Indigenatus* on new members, thereby granting them the status of a denizen of the kingdom, before they were fully accepted. In Bohemia the king exercised this right after 1620, but further to the east, in the Baltic provinces of Sweden and Poland, noble corporations managed to exclude all outsiders by making it impossible for prospective buyers without the status of an indigenous nobleman to acquire any noble property. The specific character of the German nobility in these countries (Estonia, Livonia and Courland), as an ethnic group clearly separated from the rest of the population was thus deliberately preserved.[58] In central Europe there were also areas where Protestant noble estates were reluctant to accept new members because they wanted to limit the number of candidates for ecclesiastical benefices which had, after the Reformation, been reserved for noblemen and -women (for example, canonries in Protestant chapters or benefices reserved for women from noble families in former nunneries). Here the Protestant knighthoods sometimes displayed a tendency to exclude outsiders rather like the Catholic ones. This holds true not only for some German principalities, as for the *Ritterschaft* (the corporation of the knighthood) of Hesse which gradually closed its ranks after 1532,[59] but also for the provinces of the Dutch Republic. Here a contemporary observer aptly remarked: 'it is more fun to distribute the spoils among few than among many'.[60]

This policy explains to some extent why the knighthoods in the provinces of the northern Netherlands became ever more exclusive in the seventeenth and eighteenth centuries; some had almost become extinct by the late eighteenth century. Admittedly, in practice no institution in the Dutch Republic claimed the right to create new noble titles, although the highest governing councils of the provinces might theoretically have done so. But it would have been natural enough to accept families with titles acquired abroad, in particular, in Germany. However, in most provinces this was a fairly rare exception.[61]

The populous nobilities of the European periphery: Poland and Castile

France, Germany and the Netherlands offer – in different ways – an example of a widespread tendency, apparent since the late Middle Ages but clearly gaining momentum in the later sixteenth century, to transform the nobility into a legally defined estate and make noble status dependent on some sort of proof of noble lineage or, alternatively, a patent of nobility. However, in some parts of Europe older, less formal notions of noble status did survive well into the seventeenth century and beyond. In Poland, for example, neither the king nor the nobility itself as an estate had sufficient power to exert any real control over claims to noble status. Those who could display some of the outward signs of nobility – for example, by bearing arms and serving in war – and were able to buy noble estates often managed to pass themselves off as nobles, even if they were the sons of peasants or merchants. There were occasional protests against this practice, and from time to time king and diet enacted laws which tried to restrict access to the nobility, but by and large they were ineffective.[62] In a country where the percentage of noblemen among the population was much higher than in those parts of Europe which had once belonged to the Carolingian Empire, and where even Jews automatically achieved noble status when they converted to the Christian faith, the nobility remained a comparatively ill-defined social group which included a large number of impoverished rural smallholders. Perhaps for this very reason, however, individual and collective freedom was cherished all the more highly as a mark of noble status. The right of individual noble deputies to veto majority decisions of the diet, the *liberum veto*, was not just a means to counter the influence of the overmighty magnates. It was also a symbol of the essential equality of all noblemen, and demonstrated that the poorest gentleman was as much a member of the noble estate as the greatest magnate. Many noblemen were as poor or poorer than the peasants they claimed to rule, but unlike the peasants they were citizens of the Polish Commonwealth, that, in its way, unique republic of noblemen, with all the rights this entailed.[63]

Like Poland, Castile had a comparatively populous lower nobility. Until the eighteenth century in some, admittedly exceptional, regions it comprised a majority of the population, or even, in the Basque Country, for example, all the inhabitants. One would therefore assume that nobility – if nobility is taken to mean *hidalguía* – was as loosely defined in Castile as in Poland. However, this was no longer the case in the later sixteenth century. Although the Crown continued to play a limited role in conflicts which arose from controversial claims to belong to the privileged group of *hidalgos* – patents of nobility raising a commoner to the status of *hidalgo* were only rarely granted – stricter legal standards were increasingly applied to determine whether a family belonged to the *hidalguía* or not. Normally individuals whose status as *hidalgos* was in doubt, for example, because the relevant town council was not prepared to grant them the exemption from direct taxes which *hidalgos* as opposed to *pecheros* (commoners) enjoyed, appealed to a royal court of law: the chancellery of Valladolid or that of Granada. If they could produce enough witnesses to support their claim, the court acknowledged them as *hidalgos*. Increasingly in the second half of the sixteenth century courts demanded proof that not only the applicant's parents but also his grandparents and more distant ancestors had been accepted as *hidalgos*. Such proof now had to be provided for maternal as well as for paternal ancestors, and on both sides there had to be absolute purity of blood. That is, those who had Jews or Muslims among their ancestors were now practically excluded from the *hidalguía*. At the same time the military orders became more demanding in their requirements of membership. To be granted the habit of one of the great orders of Santiago, Calatrava, Alcántara or Montesa was a cherished mark of noble status and clearly worth more than a mere judgement (*ejecutoria*) by the courts. These orders now excluded all those whose direct ancestors had been involved in non-noble activities such as manual labour, money-lending or trade.

Whether all this amounted to a closure of the nobility, however, is more doubtful, for the legal procedures which led to the acceptance or rejection of claims to noble status could be manipulated, at least by those who had enough money to do so. Noble ancestors could be invented, and rich and powerful men could always find suitable witnesses among their clients. The fact that only very few lawsuits involving claims to the status of *hidalgo* ended in rejection – the claims being quashed by the court – should not be overemphasised, as applicants for noble status who realised that they would fail, apparently broke off their lawsuits before a final judgement. Yet the social and legal approval of status claims by the *cartas ejecutorias* of the courts was as much a reflection of the wealth and power of the litigants and of their ability to convince not just their social equals in the town they came from, but also their inferiors of the justness and plausibility of their aspirations, as of their true genealogical ancestry.[64] Nevertheless, the process by which status claims were investigated, however open to manipulation, demonstrates an increasing preoccupation with an idea of nobility defined in terms of lineage, purity of blood and legal documentation, while upholding at the same time the old concept of a nobility which was defined by the social consensus of the entire local community, that is the urban community of which the would-be *hidalgo* and his family were a part or hailed from. For it was among the local community that the witnesses had to be recruited. In fact for claiming noble status in society a *carta ejecutoria* granted by a court was rarely sufficient in itself; it had to be supplemented by *actos positivos*, for example the ability to show that oneself or one's ancestors had held public offices which were normally reserved for noblemen or that one's family owned a suitable town house in a city known to be a seat of a numerous and prestigious *hidalguía*.[65]

While the status of *hidalgo* did not, as a rule, depend directly on royal grants – the Crown granted few patents of nobility, and those who had only a royal patent to prove their *hidalguía* were more often than not seen as mere parvenus – the influence of the Crown on membership of the higher ranks of the nobility was much more pronounced. The kings of Spain granted an ever increasing number of titles to prominent noble families in the seventeenth century (see above, p. 16) and they also controlled the military orders, which saw one of their principal purposes as confirming and elevating the status of individual *hidalgos*, often men who held an insecure position in the social hierarchy. This brought the new knight not only the title of *Don*, but also protection against those who questioned the purity of his blood or the immemorial age of his noble lineage – both were officially examined before anybody was granted the habit of a military order. The military orders were also used to assimilate the non-Castilian elites of the Spanish Empire, in the dominions of the Crown of Aragon, but also in Italy, with their different definitions of social status, to the Castilian nobility.[66] Thus Castile (in spite of its numerous lower nobility), unlike Poland, is no exception to the general trend towards applying stricter legal standards to claims for noble status, although the rank of *hidalgo* was essentially seen as something a man inherited and not as something the king could or should grant.[67] In this respect, the way in which membership of the lower ranks of the nobility was defined was at least superficially similar to notions of noble status in England.

England: a special case?

England was one of the few European countries in which the nobility with the exception of its highest ranks, the peerage, never became a legal estate. The gentry was always a much more informal social status group. Essentially, a certain degree of landed wealth combined with the appropriate lifestyle was sufficient to be accepted as a member of the local gentry in the sixteenth century.[68] However, there was certainly a considerable difference between those on the outer margins of the gentry and the leading families which, as a rule, were not only wealthier, but could also take pride in their ancient lineage. Sometimes the major families were even – however distantly – related to the peerage. As the younger sons of peers had no seat in the House of Lords and did not inherit their father's title, cadet branches of aristocratic families formed an essential part of the gentry. On the other hand, members of the urban elite were also addressed as 'gentleman'; leading merchants and aldermen were sometimes even knighted by the king. The gentry was certainly, unlike the patricians of northern Italy, a rural elite, but there was no clear line dividing it from the richest and most powerful urban families. Prima facie, therefore, the English gentry was not only a comparatively open elite in the sixteenth century, but it continued to be so in the seventeenth century. However, a closer look reveals that before the late seventeenth century the difference between the English gentry and, for example, the French *noblesse d'epée* was not as great as one is inclined to assume.

In countries such as France and Spain there was a powerful rhetoric of social exclusiveness in the late sixteenth century: descent, blood and race were stressed as the principal legitimations of noble status. But this rhetoric by no means always corresponded to the social reality, which still left room for a certain degree of social mobility. In fact, as far as the rhetoric of status is concerned, a renewed emphasis on ancient lineage – similar to what is found in France or Castile – was certainly not absent in England in the late sixteenth and early seventeenth centuries.[69] As in France, this may have been a conservative response to the pressure which demographic and economic change exerted on the traditional social order, but also perhaps to the more radical manifestations of a religious enthusiasm critical of all traditional secular authorities which refused to submit to the exacting moral and confessional standards set by God's elect.[70] On the other hand, legal mechanisms which restricted access to the gentry were almost totally absent in England. Although the heralds of the Court of Arms still undertook occasional visitations of the counties until the late seventeenth century, they had little power to exclude new families, whatever their pedigrees might be. In fact, in England there were few reasons for such exclusiveness. The status of gentleman might entail a certain prestige, but it conferred few legal privileges, and, in particular, no tax exemption. The Crown was therefore not really interested in defining gentry status more precisely, although some half-hearted attempts to do so – not entirely without a view to creating new sources of fiscal revenue – were undertaken during the Personal Rule of Charles I in the 1630s when the jurisdiction of the Court of Chivalry was revived by its presiding officer, the Earl of Arundel, in his capacity as Earl Marshal. Arundel took great pride in belonging to an ancient family and took a decidedly dim view of those who thought that mere wealth was sufficient justification to display a coat of arms and adopt the manners and status of a gentleman or esquire.[71] But such attempts were short-lived, and the Civil War further blurred the distinctions between old established families and newcomers.

Ill-defined as the gentry might be in legal terms, there was nevertheless a clear pecking order among the gentry families of a given county, expressed not least in the allocation of local offices. The leading families considered the most prominent places on the bench – that is among the Justices of the Peace, the most important local officeholders – their rightful property. They also tried to obtain positions as Deputy-Lieutenants – the Lord-Lieutenant, the military governor of a county, was normally a noble magnate – and sought election as Members of Parliament, preferably as Knights of the Shire. As the king appointed officeholders – only the representatives of the county in Parliament were elected – he could exert some influence on the local hierarchy of honour. However, he was well advised not rashly to exclude old-established and powerful families in favour of more loyal new-comers or outsiders, as this inevitably led to conflicts and could make a county virtually ungovernable. This was to become all too obvious in the late 1680s when James II tried to exclude most members of the established county elite from local government.[72]

In England, honour and status were based on a complicated compound of wealth, lineage and merit, that is, the ability to serve the Crown in positions of eminence in war or peace. Some families, in particular those who were for some reason or other excluded from holding offices – for example the Catholics – put more emphasis on lineage; others stressed their 'virtue', demonstrated by the offices they held.[73] All this may have been much more informal than the patents of nobility, or the documentary proof which royal commissioners, courts of law or noble corporations demanded on the Continent, but until the mid-seventeenth century the difference was more one of degree than of substance. It was not really based on a contrast between two totally incompatible notions of nobility.

As we have seen, other European countries increasingly developed a conception of nobility defined in legal terms as a group privileged by the sovereign. England, however, never took this path, at least as far as the gentry was concerned. Before the Civil War and even after 1660 the Crown had still been able to check or support claims to a more prominent social position by granting or withholding offices and other honours. In fact, during the 1680s Charles II and James II undertook systematic purges of the local and urban administration. These not only excluded all those deemed unreliable on political or religious grounds, but also posed a serious threat to the social status of those so excluded, as their positions were now taken by others, often social outsiders of Catholic or Dissenting leanings.[74] After the Glorious Revolution this radical experiment was not to be repeated. In fact, with the shift of political life to London, where Parliament was now the permanent focus of politics, local offices became less important.[75] Increasingly the urban as well as the landed elite were defined by property and by shared tastes, values and manners.[76] Those who did not have sufficient property and could not afford the necessary education to participate in the life of the elite were almost automatically excluded. No patent of nobility could protect them against the risk of social decline.

Thus England at the beginning of the eighteenth century presented an example of an elite which, precisely because it was not legally defined beneath the ranks of the peerage (and baronetage), was culturally and socially more homogenous than the various groups which formed the French nobility.[77] At the same time, the core of the governing class, that is the peerage and the highest ranks of the political elite, apparently displayed a comparatively high degree of family continuity not necessarily less pronounced than in France or other continental countries after 1660. At the same time the lower echelons of the elite remained open to new entrants, not just from a landed but also from a mercantile background.[78] Thus it has been calculated that of the *c.*900–1,100 families which formed the English parliamentary elite between 1520 and 1780 (defined as families with a seat in either House of Parliament at a given moment, and which had held a total of at least three seats in either House over the course of time),[79] new families never accounted for more than 6 per cent in any given period of 20 years between 1560 and 1780, with the exception of the two decades from 1640 to 1659 (6.3 per cent) when the turmoil of the Civil War created greater chances for newcomers. Only during the early sixteenth century, when the agricultural *hausse,* the Reformation and the redistribution of land offered particularly good chances, was the number of new entrants decidedly higher, reaching an all-time peak immediately after the Reformation between 1540 and 1560, when new entrants made up 14.1 per cent. The size of the elite itself fluctuated, reaching its highest level at about 1,100 families between 1640 and 1700 (holding about 80 per cent of all seats in the House of Commons). Later it declined to about 900 families in 1760–79 still holding about 80 per cent of seats in the Commons, which is the same level as in the 1520s. Therefore the number of families dropping out of the elite does not correspond exactly to these figures, with a comparatively high percentage (more than 10 per cent) of established families disappearing from the elite every two decades during the early eighteenth century (1700–19) and again after 1760. Even here, however, the really powerful families which sent a total of six or more members to either House of Parliament over time, had a better chance of survival than the families with fewer members. In fact, of this narrower elite group, most had established themselves in the gentry either in the Middle Ages or during the early sixteenth century, and the small number of families which can be described as grandee dynasties, because they were able to exert political influence on a national scale via patronage and government offices over many decades or centuries, had almost always already been members of the gentry in the late Middle Ages.[80] Thus, although it might have been easy enough to be accepted as a gentleman in England provided one owned enough property and had the right manners, it was far more difficult to gain admission to the charmed circle of really powerful families.

Conclusion

If the comparative openness of the lower echelons of the social elite in England was not as exceptional as it may appear at first glance, even countries such as France, were, as we have seen, slower to create clear legal standards for noble status than is sometimes acknowledged. However, once some sort of legal definition of nobility had been achieved, and all or most noble families had been registered, the families which had been acknowledged as noble had a sort of insurance policy against the adverse social consequences of economic decline. They were now, at least to some extent, immune to the vagaries of economic or political fortune. Even if they lost their estates and wealth, they still remained noble, as this status had been officially certified in the royal investigations. The problem of a poor nobility with aspirations to status and prestige which did not correspond to its actual economic and social situation, had already existed at earlier periods, but it was nevertheless exacerbated by a definition of nobility which put so much emphasis on legal criteria, birth and lineage.[81]

Thus attempts to create a legally more homogeneous elite actually produced even greater social, economic and cultural differentiation within the ranks of the nobility. In France, at the end of the *ancien régime* two very different groups of noble families confronted each other: one group with wealth and access to offices, honours and royal patronage, living at court, in Paris or at least in the major provincial capitals, faced another group which was impoverished and often badly educated, confined to its villages or small market towns, and lacked any access to the benefits the Crown might distribute.[82] In other countries where the French model of the nobility as an estate defined in legal terms by the monarch's lawyers and officeholders was less prevalent, such conflicts may have been less acute. Nevertheless, the identity and coherence of the nobility as a social group was as much of a problem in the eighteenth century as it had been in the sixteenth despite, or in some ways because of, the attempt to replace customary with statutory definitions of nobility.

2

The changing landscape of noble society

Introduction

As we saw in the preceding chapter, definitions of nobility in Europe varied greatly. The comparatively open elites of England, Poland, Hungary or Spain provided a clear contrast to the French nobility and even more to the narrowly defined and most exclusive corporations dominating many German prince bishoprics and some Dutch rural provinces. In what follows we shall first look in greater detail at the differences between the populous nobilities concentrated at the European periphery and the less numerous elites in other parts of the Continent. We shall then briefly examine the relationship between nobilities and the urban world and the enormous differences in wealth and power within the national nobilities, in which magnates who were almost sovereign princes lived next to poor country gentlemen who could barely employ a single servant. Finally we shall look more closely at two very distinct noble elites: the high aristocracy of the Habsburg monarchy and the English gentry. In depicting the development of these very different noble groups we will address topics which are further developed in later chapters: the relationship between the nobility and the Crown, the importance of local authority for noble power and the economic foundations of noble lordship. In addition to regional and national differences in the structure of noble society, we shall also concentrate on the social and economic changes which affected the various nobilities in our period, changes in particular which have often been seen as part of a wider-ranging crisis of the aristocracy.

Numbers: the size of noble elites in Europe

As has already been emphasised, the heterogeneity of noble elites in early modern Europe is in many ways quite striking. To start with, the number of nobles per head of population varied considerably. On average nobles made up between 1 and 1.5 per cent of the population – numbers in France, Germany, Northern Italy and England corresponded roughly to this pattern – but some countries had a far more populous nobility. This held good in particular for the European periphery, that is Spain, Poland and Hungary. In Poland noblemen and their families may have made up between 6 and 7 per cent of the population in the late seventeenth century, but some areas such as Masovia, for example, had a far higher density of noble families, as much as 25 per cent.[1] The situation was similar in Spain, where the northern provinces of the kingdom of Castile had a particularly high proportion of noble families. In the provinces bordering on the Atlantic, Asturia and Cantabria, up to 80 per cent of the population claimed the status of *hidalguía* and in the Basque provinces the entire population was, theoretically, considered to be noble. This privilege may have had some impact on the mentality of the inhabitants but little real meaning otherwise as these noblemen had nobody they could rule or dominate. In the whole of Castile *hidalgos* and their families constituted about 10 per cent of the population in the late sixteenth century, with a high concentration in the north and much lower figures of about 2 to 5 per cent in the south. In the east, in the provinces of the Crown of Aragon, figures were lower still at about 1 to 2 per cent of the population, which was about the European average.[2]

Another country with a numerous lower nobility or gentry was Hungary, where nobles of all descriptions – some belonging to special ethnic groups such as the *Hajdu* or *Haiduken* who were collectively considered as noble – comprised about 5 per cent of the population in the early eighteenth century. Here again, regional differences were marked. Areas which had long been under direct Turkish rule had, in general, only a small nobility whereas in the north-eastern regions, comparatively safe from Turkish attack even in the sixteenth and early seventeenth centuries, noble families made up 10 to 15 per cent of the population as a whole.[3]

In northern Spain, the almost permanent warfare against the Islamic states in the early and high Middle Ages, which had involved almost the entire population and not just the traditional elite, accounts to some extent for the high number of *hidalgos*. By doing military service men who would otherwise have been simple peasants could claim noble status. Similar factors had been at work in northern Hungary when the southern and central regions of the country had been occupied by the Ottoman Empire in the sixteenth century, although the percentage of nobles may already have been comparatively high before this date.[4] Although in Hungary many noblemen in fact had German or other foreign ancestors, they tended to consider themselves the real descendants of the erstwhile Magyar conquerors. The nobility saw itself as a distinct ethnic group and in many parts of Hungary and Transylvania the peasant population did indeed belong to different ethnic communities (e.g. Slovakian or Romanian) from the landed elite.[5] The idea that the nobility was a distinct ethnic or national group was also alive in Castile and Poland. In Castile *hidalgos* deemed themselves the descendants of the Germanic tribes, in particular, the Visigoths who had ruled the country before the Arabian conquest in the eighth century. In Poland the idea that noblemen, and only noblemen, constituted the nation, being the real citizens of the Polish *Res Publica* – to the total exclusion of all peasants and the entire urban population – was even stronger. It was increasingly based on the idea that all noblemen were descended from the ancient tribe of the Sarmates, a people which, in late Antiquity, had lived outside the borders of the Roman Empire to the North of the Black Sea. The idea that all noblemen shared a common ethnic origin may have been a mere myth, but it nevertheless deeply influenced the outlook and mentality of noblemen.[6]

While Poland, Hungary and Castile were classic strongholds of a populous though often impoverished nobility, Bohemia and Moravia (treated at greater length below) were dominated by a comparatively tiny elite of noble magnates. During the early modern period the lower nobility gradually disappeared almost completely. Noblemen with a seat in the estates probably comprised, with their families, not more than 0.1 per cent of the population in the late eighteenth century, and even if families of nobles who were not represented in the estates are included, the figure would probably not be much higher than about 0.5 per cent.[7] The situation in Scandinavia was not very different. In Denmark the noble estate had become increasingly exclusive during the course of the sixteenth century. The king's right to ennoble commoners was severely curtailed during the period of aristocratic ascendancy in the sixteenth and early seventeenth centuries. The nobility hardly comprised more than 0.25 per cent of the population in the old Danish heartlands around 1600, although the situation was different in the Duchies of Schleswig and Holstein – the latter was part of the Holy Roman Empire. In the 1660s, when the king became strong enough to break the noble monopoly of power in the central administration, it became easier for commoners to be elevated to noble status, but even so, the Danish nobility always remained a comparatively small elite.[8] The same more or less holds true for Sweden where noble families represented about 0.5 per cent of the population in the early eighteenth century.[9] Here the strong position of an independent peasantry may to some extent account for the fact that there were never very many noble families.

Both in Denmark and Sweden many noble families were of foreign origin, often German, although in Denmark this trend was more marked in the period before 1660 than later. That Schleswig and Holstein were part of the Danish monarchy and that the dynasty was closely related to the German counts of Oldenburg partly accounts for this fact. In Sweden, which also held dominions in Germany and the Baltic (Estonia and Livonia) between 1648 and 1721 and the small province of *Vorpommern* until 1815, the status of the country as a major military power in the seventeenth century was more important. Many of the officers serving in the Swedish armies were foreign noblemen or ennobled commoners who later settled in Sweden.

Town and country: rural and urban nobilities

The various European nobilities were distinguished not just by the different criteria for defining noble status, their relative size and their wealth and power; perhaps even more fundamental was their relationship with urban society. Outside the Mediterranean countries the lower nobility was predominantly an elite of rural landowners. Often the average *gentilhomme campagnard* or country squire lived a life that was not very different from that of the richer peasant farmers. At least, this was true until the seventeenth century, when gradually a process of cultural differentiation and refinement set in which created a wider gulf between the world of the manor house and the village. The exact social position and cultural outlook of this landed elite, however, depended on a number of conditions which gave the various national or regional nobilities in Europe their specific character. First there was the position of the state. In regions where the Crown or princely authority had been weak in the late Middle Ages, even members of the lower nobility often enjoyed extensive rights of jurisdiction. In the sixteenth century they ruled their tenants almost as sovereign lords. This was the case, for example, in north-eastern Germany and east-central Europe in general. In other countries the state, relying on a bureaucracy of salaried officeholders, was already capable of controlling the localities more closely, as for example in seventeenth-century France. In England the gentry (see below, pp. 49–55) monopolised the commission of the peace, which exercised jurisdictional and administrative rights at the local level in the king's name. However, gentlemen had few jurisdictional rights of their own.[10]

The social position of the urban elite was a further factor which indirectly determined the outlook and character of the rural nobility. In areas such as the Low Countries or south-western Germany, but also to some extent in France, powerful urban elites posed a challenge to the ascendancy of the rural landowners. In eastern and east-central Europe, on the other hand, the position of the towns and cities was generally quite weak, with the exception perhaps of major port towns such as Danzig or Königsberg, for example. In politics the nobility could largely ignore the interests of the urban elites. This holds true for areas such as Brandenburg as much as for Poland.

Finally, the structure of agriculture must be taken into account when looking at the position of the rural nobilities. In eastern and east-central Europe noble landowners tended to farm large demesne lands themselves or through their stewards, often relying on the unpaid labour services of unfree peasants, their hereditary subjects.[11] In north-western Europe, on the other hand, but also in the western regions of the Holy Roman Empire, noblemen may have owned a small home farm, but were otherwise content to collect the rents and other revenues from the land which they let to peasant farmers. Although there were areas of France, for example, where medieval labour services (*corvées*) survived well into the early modern period and in fact were sometimes exploited more energetically in the eighteenth century than in the preceding period, most French *seigneurs* derived a much smaller proportion of their income from such feudal dues than their counterparts in eastern Europe.[12]

On the other hand, although land and labour never quite became mere commodities, to be bought and sold in a capitalist market at the most advantageous prices, in the early modern period, this trend was certainly much stronger in the economically advanced areas of north-western Europe than in the east. This process necessarily affected the position of noble landowners in the local community and in society in general. While long-term leases were often replaced by short-term ones from the late sixteenth century, this sort of 'rack-renting' tended to undermine the loyalty of tenant farmers and threatened to transform the relationship between tenants and lord into a predominantly commercial one. This was bound to weaken the authority of noblemen in the local rural community.[13]

In fact, across large areas of Europe the country squire was by no means the typical nobleman. In Italy, in particular in the north, the old established urban elites had gained a position which often gave their members the status of nobility. Aristocratic merchant republics like Venice and Genoa present the foremost example of this type of nobility. Whereas in the north of Spain, which had comparatively few towns, the *hidalguía* was traditionally more rural in character, in particular in those regions which had a particularly high number of *hidalgos* per head of population; noblemen in the south lived in the cities, but so did most of the rest of the population. Of course the small towns of the south were often, in economic terms, dominated by agriculture rather than by trade or commerce. Even in the rural north, however, many noblemen abandoned their castles and manors in the sixteenth century and bought or built town houses in which they lived for most of the year, if they could afford to do so. In fact, in most Castilian cities at least half the seats on the bench of urban aldermen were reserved for *hidalgos*, and the representatives of the principal cities in the *Cortes*, the assembly of estates, were almost invariably *hidalgos* themselves. In Castile the town was the natural focus of noble life, both socially and politically.[14] In the seventeenth century the same increasingly came to be true of other areas of southern Europe where in the past noblemen had tended to live on their estates, for example Catalonia or southern Italy. The ever more important role of cities as administrative, economic and financial centres, combined with the closer co-operation between nobility and state, but also between rural elites and urban patriciates, all contributed to making towns and, in particular, capital cities, more attractive to noblemen.[15] Often they formed their own highly exclusive urban corporations, such as the *Seggi* in Naples, which gave stability to the cultural and social identity of the nobility as an estate, and tended to replace the traditional parliament or diet as the monarchy's partner even in matters relating to the entire kingdom.[16] While in southern Italy the old 'feudal' aristocracy moved into town, the traditional urban elites of the north increasingly acquired rural estates and fiefs with the relevant rights of lordship. In fact quite a number of patrician families from the north, in particular from Genoa, bought fiefs in southern Italy and thus became part of the rural elite in the Kingdom of Naples and in Sicily. The same held good for numerous cadet branches of dynasties ruling a sovereign principality elsewhere in Italy such as the Medici or Farnese, or for the Roman aristocracy which dominated the papal court. Often a fief in Naples was an assurance policy against the vagaries of commercial and political fortune.[17]

In Tuscany, as opposed to Sicily or Naples, the fiefs urban families acquired were often quite small. Their importance lay in the title and status they gave their owners rather than in the revenues or the power one might derive from them. Nevertheless the acquisition of fiefs and noble titles by patricians and former merchant families signified a deeper social and cultural change. The urban elites became, in a manner of speaking, 'feudalised' and adopted the manners and values of the rural nobility, often abandoning at the same time any visible commercial activities, while investing their money primarily in real estate or government bonds, although some patrician families in the major commercial centres such as Venice, Genoa or Florence continued to maintain an interest in trade and banking.[18]

While the patricians of northern Italy tried to 'look and sound' like nobles and courtiers in the seventeenth century,[19] the rural elites of other European countries were affected by a process of urbanisation. In Normandy and other French provinces where the nobility had originally been a predominantly rural elite, wealthy noblemen increasingly lived in town for most of the year in the later seventeenth and eighteenth centuries.[20] Those who could afford it wanted to gain access to the urban markets for fashionable consumer goods and the amenities of city life, not least perhaps because their wives and daughters wanted to escape from rural boredom.[21]

In spite of this widespread tendency for noble life to become more urban in the later seventeenth century, relations between the rural nobility and urban elites were more complicated in northern Europe than in the south where the two *milieus* merged more easily. In Germany many important cities were ruled by a hereditary urban elite, the patriciate. In other cities this elite had been forced to share power with the representatives of the great livery companies in the late Middle Ages, but nevertheless still held a dominant social position. The patricians often tried to emulate the ideals of the rural nobility. In some cities, such as Nuremberg, ruled by a particularly proud and exclusive patriciate, they held their own tournaments in the fifteenth century. And in the later sixteenth and seventeenth centuries they increasingly abandoned any active participation in commerce, living instead on the income from their landed estates and the capital they had invested or lent against interest. They bought noble lordships and served in war just like noblemen.[22] Nonetheless, noble corporations in Germany, such as the *Reichsritterschaft* (knights who recognised only the emperor as their lord) were reluctant to accept patricians as members unless they abandoned citizenship rights in their home city. The reason for this was not so much a feeling that a rural knight was superior in status to an urban patrician, but rather that the political power of the cities was seen as a threat by many noblemen. Such fears were particularly pronounced in south-western Germany where most great cities were *Reichsstädte* – that is, politically independent – and had acquired extensive rights of lordship outside their walls in the late Middle Ages. Only Strassburg in Alsace was a clear exception. Here the corporation of the knighthood of Lower Alsace and the patriciate of the city of Strassburg merged almost completely in the sixteenth century.[23]

In Germany the imperial free cities and other towns dominated by old established patrician families were an exception in a feudal world which was ruled by its own laws. In the seventeenth-century Dutch Republic the urban elites of the great mercantile cities, such as Amsterdam, held a much more powerful position than their German counterpart. In the central province of Holland with its numerous cities, this urban elite, the *regents*, dominated politics and not the small rural nobility which held only one seat in the provincial estates.[24] In other provinces which were more rural in character, such as Gelderland or Frisia, the balance of power was different and rural noblemen managed to hold their own or more than that. Nevertheless, the *regents* everywhere were a proud and politically powerful elite. Although some were merchants, they were not a class of great merchants as such. Most had either originally engaged in local trade and commerce – such as brewing – or had derived their income from the urban and provincial offices they held and from investments in bonds and capital ventures. When Dutch colonial expansion set in, after about 1600, many acquired shares in the great colonial trading companies, in particular the Dutch East India and West India Company. In the seventeenth century they slowly became a rentier class and began to imitate the ways of the rural nobility with its country houses and specific sense of honour and status.[25] As manors and lordships could as easily be acquired by commoners as by noblemen in the Republic, many *heerlijkheiden* (rights of jurisdiction, etc.) were owned by regents in the late seventeenth century. Intermarriage between rural and urban elites was not entirely unusual in the Dutch Republic. In the early eighteenth century the eldest son of the Count of Limburg-Stirum, a member of one of the highest ranking Dutch noble families, wooed – unsuccessfully – the daughter of a rich postmaster, whereas other noblemen married into wealthy regent families to bolster their financial position. Amsterdam was the most important marriage market for such matches in this period. Nevertheless, they continued to be frowned upon by many families and the more fastidious provincial noble corporations were reluctant to admit noblemen whose mothers or grandmothers had been commoners from regent families.[26]

Whatever their later aspirations to lead a life unsoiled by business activities, the Dutch regent families had often risen to their position of eminence as wealthy retailers or merchants. The high route to noble status in France, however, was a different one. There were still a number of great merchants in late sixteenth-century France who managed to acquire noble fiefs, thereby silently gaining access to the Second Estate. A prominent example was the famous mayor of Orleans, François Colas des Francs, who, under Henry IV, held nine *seigneuries* in 1599. This path to social advancement was increasingly barred in the seventeenth century. With the *Ordonnance* of Blois (1579), the heirs of commoners who had bought noble fiefs no longer became noble as a matter of course (see above, p. 13).[27] The easiest way to rise from the Third into the Second Estate was now through a legal career. Like other monarchs, the King of France recruited his officeholders among lawyers willing to serve the Crown to his and their own advantage. In France the venality of offices was a very widespread phenomenon in the late sixteenth and seventeenth centuries. To sell offices was not only a means of reducing the deficit in the royal budget, it could also serve to reduce the influence of noble magnates on appointments. A man who had been appointed to an office because he had paid the Crown the official price out of his own pocket was, as a rule, no mere client of an influential nobleman.[28]

Particularly in the supreme law courts, the *parlements* or other so-called *cours souverains* such as the councils exercising rights of jurisdiction in fiscal disputes (*chambres des comptes* and *cours des aides*), and also the royal chancellery, many of the senior offices sold ennobled those who held them, or at least their heirs, although their position as members of the Second Estate was not officially acknowledged until 1715. However, even before this date a new noble elite, the *noblesse de robe* emerged. Initially, many members of this group came from merchant and professional families. When royal commissioners examined claims to noble status in Paris in 1696, they discovered that 76 per cent of all noblemen came from families newly ennobled after 1560, and that of the 460 new families 51 per cent owed their status to the acquisition of a royal office.[29] However, the principal period of social mobility was probably the sixteenth and early seventeenth centuries when the number of royal offices greatly increased from about 4,000 in 1515 to more than 45,000 in 1665.[30] In the later seventeenth century access to the new elite became increasingly more difficult. When the hereditary nature of proprietary offices was officially recognised in 1604, the *noblesse de robe* slowly became a closed estate.[31] In the early eighteenth century the *noblesse de robe* tended to merge with the upper echelons of the *noblesse d'epée*, the erstwhile military nobility,[32] but relations had not always been so harmonious. At the meeting of the Estates General in 1614, the Second Estate had vehemently protested against the sale of royal offices which virtually excluded members of the ancient military nobility from most positions in the central and regional civil administration.[33]

However, it is doubtful whether the conflict between robe and sword was really a clash between two distinct social groups in the early seventeenth century, rather than between different ways of life chosen by men who often shared a similar social background. Noblemen who had chosen a military career resented the social superiority claimed by lawyers and officeholders because they were better educated and often wealthier as well. They saw the councillors of the Parliament of Paris and the provincial courts as 'those little rogues who because of their positions, want to strut around and pretend they know everything' or as 'those beggars the councillors, [who] have no hesitation about condemning soldiers to hang, even if they don't deserve it.'[34]

Such animosity among the military nobility against men who had risen to positions of eminence as lawyers and bureaucrats was certainly not limited to France. It can be found in Germany as well, for example, in the late sixteenth century.[35] The entire academic world, the breeding ground of professional officeholders, was still seen as potentially hostile by many noblemen at this period. This was perhaps to some extent the case even in England, where conflicts between 'arms and letters' were less pronounced than elsewhere but where peers such as the second Earl of Essex nevertheless acted as self-appointed spokesmen for military valour and chivalry against mere 'penpushers' at the end of the sixteenth century (see below, pp. 113–15).

At the same time one needs to bear in mind that in some countries the new administrative elite was mostly recruited from among families who could already claim noble status and, vice versa, officeholders with a legal training were accepted as members of the nobility (at least the lesser nobility) without any major reservations. Such was, by and large, the case in Spain, where the *letrados* formed the monarchy's administrative elite. Almost all members of the Council of Castile in the period 1621–1746 came from families which belonged at least to the *hidalguía,* the lower nobility. Moreover, up to 40 per cent were from the middling or higher nobility. Their fathers had been *caballeros,* or, in some cases, even members of the titled aristocracy. Perhaps because the Spanish or at least the Castilian nobility was in many ways an urban elite and more than capable of dominating the towns anyway, it was less reluctant than other traditional nobilities to acquire the knowledge and skills taught by universities.[36]

Rich and poor: magnate and country squire

It has already been emphasised at the beginning of this chapter that noblemen all over Europe tended to share a common ethos and were attached to similar ideals and values. Nevertheless, actual differences in economic power and social status necessarily created divisions within the nobility which were often as pronounced as that dividing noblemen from commoners. In those countries where the proportion of noblemen exceeded the average of 1 or 2 per cent which was normal for France, Germany and many other countries, it is not surprising to find many simple gentlemen leading a life not so different from that of moderately wealthy, or perhaps even not so wealthy, peasants. In countries such as Poland with its numerous *szlachta* many noblemen had to till their fields themselves – if they were not, in fact, entirely landless. These landless noblemen could count themselves lucky if they found employment in the service of a magnate as estate stewards, soldiers or even as simple domestic servants. Others, despite the strong aversion of the Polish nobility to the cities, which were often dominated by merchants of German or Jewish origin, settled in towns where they lived in poverty, trying to eke out a living in the most humble occupations such as toll-keeper or boatman.[37] Matters were not very different in Castile, where simple shoemakers or water-carriers claimed to be *hidalgos*, and where, in the northern provinces, many rural *hidalgos* were in effect peasants 'living in mud cottages distinguished only by the coat of arms externally surmounted on a brick or stone portal'.[38]

Castile, Poland and Hungary all offer examples of deep divisions between a comparatively small, wealthy nobility – the *bene possessionati* as they were called in Hungary – and a large number of simple gentlemen who retained the ethos and pride of the nobility, but few of the rights and none of the possessions which normally accompanied noble status. But even in a country where there were fewer noblemen, such as France, poor or impoverished noblemen were by no means exceptional figures. In Brittany, for example, with its numerous nobility, at least a third of all noblemen found it extremely difficult to live from the proceeds of their estates in the seventeenth century. In fact, two-thirds of all noblemen paid no more than 20 livres tax (10 was the absolute minimum) at the end of Louis XIV's reign, when a new tax, the *capitation*, was introduced which was imposed on all three estates, not just the *roturiers*.[39] In Brittany many noblemen had to seek employment in trade or commerce – officially this led to a loss of noble status, or at least to the temporary abandonment of claims to such status which became dormant. Even in other provinces, where the problem of noble poverty was less pressing than in Brittany, the average provincial nobleman did not live in a castle or great country house, but generally in a large farmhouse not very different from those inhabited by great tenant farmers. What distinguished the nobleman's way of life from that of a peasant may have been the possession of more valuable dishes (made of pewter and in the eighteenth century perhaps of bone china, rather than stoneware or wood), a few paintings and similar 'luxury' furnishings. But such provincial noblemen often had only one domestic servant. This was true of about 50 per cent of the nobility in Normandy in around 1700, and in the area examined by

Jonathan Dewald, 10 to 15 per cent had no servants at all. In fact, some rural squires had to collect the manure for their fields themselves, although such manual labour was certainly highly unusual even for impoverished *hobereaux*.[40]

Noblemen who did not own substantial estates or some other source of income – and this was clearly the majority – were often too poor to serve in war as officers or to equip themselves adequately when the king raised the provincial feudal host the *ban et arrière ban*. Thus they were unable to maintain the major justification for the privileges they enjoyed as members of the French *noblesse d'epée*, active military service.[41] From the late seventeenth century on, the king tried to support poor noblemen by creating military academies and similar establishments where their sons could receive an adequate education. But such attempts often remained half-hearted or benefited those who were not so badly off after all rather than the really destitute.[42]

In France, as in other countries, it was largely the prevailing customs governing inheritance that created a large impoverished nobility. Although these customs ensured more favourable treatment for the eldest son in many French provinces, the younger sons nevertheless retained a claim to noble status and some part of the ancestral estates. This was often too small to sustain their social pretensions, but large enough to keep them from sinking outright into the Third Estate.[43] The best way to escape from this situation was often to marry the daughter of a wealthy commoner, a merchant, financier or officeholder. Such marriages were sometimes frowned upon, but the French definition of nobility, which concentrated on the male line, left considerable leeway for matches which elsewhere would have been considered simply as unforgivable *mesalliances*.

Changing cultural expectations and standards undoubtedly exacerbated the situation of the less well-off provincial gentry in France and in other countries from the late seventeenth century onwards. Education, culture and manners (see below, pp. 56–61) became more important than in the past. To meet the standards set by the court and metropolitan society was costly and often impossible for those who lacked the means to undertake a grand tour, to study at an academy in their youth or to attend the court. Increasingly such mere country gentlemen were despised by the court nobility or those who could afford a town house in the provincial capital.[44]

In the second half of the seventeenth century and even more so in the eighteenth century – with the increasing tendency of noble magnates and of many wealthy provincial noblemen to spend more time at court, in the capital or in military garrisons outside their own home province (cf. below, pp. 138–9) – simple country gentlemen often lost the patronage and direct support which they had received from their superiors in the past. In France, for example, the Religious Wars and the tensions between rivalling aristocratic factions had moved many magnates to increase the number of noble officeholders and retainers on their payroll considerably in the late sixteenth century. This process was now reversed.[45] Some ties of clientage did survive into the eighteenth century or were revived in new forms, but in countries such as England or France, or even many provinces of the Habsburg monarchy, wealthy noblemen – with the exception perhaps of the greatest among the magnates such as the princes of the blood in France – no longer needed to maintain large numbers of household servants of noble status let alone armed noble retainers after the mid-seventeenth century.[46] At the same time, to serve a member of the aristocracy as an estate steward or even more as a domestic servant was increasingly frowned upon and could be seen as potentially demeaning. Increasingly lesser nobles tried to defend their status not as a magnate's client, but in opposition to a distant court nobility. However, this was an arduous and not necessarily successful undertaking.[47]

If the impoverished country squire was sometimes not much more than a peasant farmer with social pretensions and a real or fictitious list of ancestors, the status of many noble magnates was not far removed from that of reigning princes. In fact, in some parts of Europe, in particular in the Holy Roman Empire, they actually were reigning princes. Elsewhere even dukes and marquesses were subject to royal authority, but nevertheless their wealth, rank and power gave them a special position. Often the most prominent members of the higher nobility were related to the royal dynasty, as in France, where the princes of the blood formed the core of the upper echelons of the nobility. Traditional accounts have depicted the magnates – the quintessential 'overmighty' subjects – as the natural opponents of a strong monarchy. However, in many countries the members of this noble elite owed their status as much to royal favour as to inherited wealth and authority; conflicts with reigning monarchs were therefore more often the result of adverse circumstances than of inherent structural tensions (see below, chapter 5). In fact, in many ways members of the higher aristocracy were better placed to benefit from the process of state formation in our period than less powerful and wealthy noblemen.

However, historians have often depicted the late sixteenth and early seventeenth centuries as a time of crisis for the aristocracy, in England as much as in France or Spain and even in the Habsburg monarchy.[48] The price inflation of this period, the conspicuous consumption which the new court culture demanded, the seeming erosion of the aristocracy's traditional military role and not least the direct or indirect fiscal exactions of the Crown all apparently contributed to a reduction in the aristocracy's economic power and political influence.[49] In the English case which has been more thoroughly studied than others, a 'rising' assertive gentry benefited from these developments, or so it seemed to many historians.[50] Recent research, however, has become much more sceptical with regard to this thesis. For England it may indeed be true that members of the peerage faced serious economic problems in the early seventeenth century (although the economic data are much less clear than some historians have assumed). But then a tendency to overspend was fairly widespread among noblemen all over Europe, and not just at this period but almost throughout the ages. Because of their social position noble magnates were not only under considerable pressure to spend liberally in the service of the state or to maintain their own prestige, they were also considered to be much more creditworthy than other debtors, and, in some respects, than the Crown itself. To incur huge debts – in the early seventeenth century more often short-term than long-term debts – could, up to a certain point, therefore, seem a rational strategy; it was certainly an ever-present temptation. The fact that it became easier to raise credit in many European countries in the late sixteenth century was bound to increase this temptation. Besides, noble families which were already heavily indebted sometimes tried to bolster their creditworthyness by spending more not less as to do otherwise might have been perceived as a sign of impending financial doom.[51]

However, as long as total economic collapse and the large-scale sale of assets, that is real estate, could be avoided, the power and influence of a noble magnate was not necessarily reduced by economic problems.[52] This was true for England as much as for Spain and France, where in the late sixteenth and early seventeenth centuries great noblemen were able to compensate for their partial loss of independent military power by placing their clients and 'creatures' in important positions at court or in the civil administration.[53] Even in purely economic terms the problem of aristocratic indebtedness – which undoubtedly existed – could coexist with a gradual concentration of great estates in the hands of a few particularly wealthy families which intermarried among themselves. This seems to have been the case in Spain where the disparity in wealth between the highest rank among the nobility, the dukes, and the rest of the aristocracy became greater rather than smaller during the late sixteenth and early seventeenth centuries.[54] Historians have nevertheless pointed out that the juridification of social and economic conflicts – the fact that such conflicts could no longer be resolved by force of arms but only by persuing one's claims by litigation in the law courts – did not favour noble landowners. In fact, as Yun Casalilla has demonstrated for Castile, litigation was not only costly, it also restrained the tendency of powerful noble families to extend their power at the cost of Crown and peasants alike. In the new age, under the rule of law, noble power, both economic and political, could only prosper in close co-operation with the state and such a co-operation had its own price, heavy investment in conspicuous consumption at court or in the capital for example, or the burdens which loans granted to the Crown placed on the aristocracy. An accumulation of debts was often the necessary consequence of such a policy.[55]

On the other hand, the introduction of special legal rules which limited the right of great noblemen to sell or otherwise alienate their landed property or to distribute it at will between their various heirs was a major factor contributing to the consolidation of aristocratic power and wealth in this period. In most countries there had always been special laws of inheritance for fiefs and noble estates in general,[56] but earlier customs now became part of a coherent legal system designed to ensure that the interest of the aristocratic lineage or house prevailed over all individual interests, be they those of daughters and younger sons or the first-born principal heir himself. In Spain the first entails (*mayorazgos*) were established in the late Middle Ages, but the system was not completed and refined to cover the bulk of all major aristocratic estates until the sixteenth century. In theory, estates which were part of a *mayorazgo* could not be mortgaged; in practice, noblemen were able to obtain licences from the king to contract mortgages all the same, although the property remained largely secure against any direct action a creditor might take. Creditors could and did distrain rents in certain cases, however, when the debtor had defaulted on the interest payment. In general, however, the fact that families who owned *mayorazgos* were secured against the worst consequences of bankrupty increased the temptation to incur enormous debts. In fact, the entail system in itself led landowners to borrow on a massive scale, as junior members of the family, who could not inherit any of the entailed estates, often received huge stipends and other payments in compensation, which could rarely be financed out of current income alone. Dowries for daughters were a further drain on resources. Younger sons also received land not included in the entail and in some cases separate *mayorazgos* specifically created for them. These might include rights of clerical patronage which could be used to provide for future generations of younger sons.[57] Thus the *mayorazgo* did not necessarily work against the interests of younger sons, but undoubtedly increased paternal authority. Fathers could deny their children the customary annuities or even disinherit them completely if, for example, they contracted a *mesalliance*.[58] Here, as in other areas, the Crown supported and reinforced paternal power which was also true for similar patterns of inheritance in other countries, as for example the *Fideikommiß* in Germany.[59]

In the Habsburg monarchy ruled by the Austrian branch of the dynasty individual families began to emulate the Spanish *mayorazgo* as early as the late sixteenth century. The close ties between the two branches of the Habsburg dynasty meant that the details of the system were familiar to them.[60] Such *fideicommissa* formed an essential basis for the preservation of the enormous aristocratic fortunes which characterised the social structure of the Habsburg monarchy and which will be discussed in more detail below.

In England primogeniture had always been the prevailing inheritance custom among the great landowners. In fact, noble titles as such could be inherited by only one person, as a rule the eldest son. This ensured that the English peerage was and remained a comparatively small and compact group.[61] In England, younger sons were legally no more than simple commoners. Although they might be addressed as 'Lord', this was no more than a courtesy title. Strict primogeniture ensured that the holder of the title found it easier to maintain his social position than in countries where younger sons were co-heirs with equal or almost equal rights. On the other hand, providing marriage portions for daughters could pose serious economic problems, and even the strict settlement, increasingly popular after 1660, which was intended to ensure that the main bulk of the estates could not be sold, did not stop owners from contracting high mortgages. In fact, long-term borrowing seems to have increased after 1660, as peers wanted to make sure that their daughters found high-ranking marriage partners and therefore spent enormous sums on dowries. This was a problem that had already almost ruined the Spanish titled aristocracy in the early seventeenth century.[62]

It needs to be stressed again, however, that such financial problems did not necessarily undermine the political power of the nobility and the higher nobility in particular, although they could force noblemen to seek a closer co-operation with the Crown, as in Spain or in France after 1660 (see below, pp. 133–8, 144–6), as the Crown could grant them protection against their creditors. Both in seventeenth-century Castile and (after the Thirty Years War) in many German principalities this was an important element in a process which created new bonds between noblemen and their rulers. By regulating the repayment or permitting the partial cancellation of outstanding debts and interest payments the ruler could make or unmake the fortunes of entire families.[63] Whatever their economic situation, much more than other strata of the nobility, the high aristocracy was defined by its political role and the position it held as the partner or opponent of the ruling dynasty. Nowhere is this more apparent than in the Habsburg monarchy in the seventeenth century.

The quintessential magnate class: the Habsburg titled aristocracy

There are many examples of noble magnates among the nobilities of Europe: The French *Grands*, the English peerage and the Spanish *grandes* all in different ways fit this image. But hardly any European state was dominated as much by a small group of magnate families – while the lower nobility was excluded from all real power and socially marginalised – as the Habsburg monarchy, or, to be more precise, its heartlands in Bohemia, Moravia and, to a slightly lesser extent, the Duchies of Upper and Lower Austria around Linz and Vienna in the later seventeenth century. The religious and political conflicts of the early seventeenth century deeply transformed the nobilities of the Habsburg dominions. After 1648 the high aristocracy was an elite which had, in many ways, been created and fashioned by the dynasty. But once the turmoils of the early seventeenth century had been overcome, it was also well able to defend its interests against the dynastic state if necessary. The transformation of the traditional elite was particularly visible in the provinces just mentioned (Bohemia, Moravia, Austria) where Protestantism had been strongly entrenched in the late sixteenth century and the Counter-Reformation had triumphed after 1620. Social and political changes were much less pronounced outside these heartlands of the Habsburg monarchy. In Hungary, but also to a lesser extent in Silesia, Protestantism survived and in Tyrol and the *Vorlande* (the scattered Habsburg possessions between Lake Constance and southern Alsace) it had never really taken root.

The social structure of Bohemia and Moravia, in particular, had always differed from that of other parts of the Holy Roman Empire to which the two countries nominally belonged. In most parts of the Empire the titled nobility had managed to create its own autonomous territories, however small. As a consequence, the diets of the greater principalities lacked a separate estate of lords and barons, while many of the diets in the Habsburg lands had their own *Herrenstand* (estate of barons), rich and powerful magnates who ruled their own lordships and dominions not much smaller than many of the semi-sovereign lordships (for example the *Reichsgrafschaften*) in the Empire. Some of these magnates were spectacularly rich. In fact in Bohemia a mere 1.7 per cent of all noblemen in the kingdom (both lords and mere knights) ruled over 40 per cent of all subjects under noble jurisdiction in the mid-sixteenth century.[64]

However, the tendency to overspend combined with the price inflation of the late sixteenth century and the bad harvests of the same period, undermined the position of many magnates. The fact that the great noble lords found it difficult to deny the Emperor Rudolf II (1576–1612), who almost permanently faced bankruptcy, the loans and financial support he insistently demanded (a problem they shared with great aristocrats in other countries) may also have contributed to their economic decline.[65] But the rank and file of the lower nobility fared much worse during the difficult last decades of the sixteenth century and were much less well equipped to survive the upheaval caused by the rebellion of the estates in Bohemia, Moravia and Upper Austria and its subsequent suppression. With the defeat of the Protestant rebellion against the House of Habsburg in 1620 (see below, chapter 5, pp. 111–112) Catholic converts from native families on the make or noble immigrants from outside Bohemia and Austria – from Germany, for example, or the Piccolomini from Italy or the Taaffe from Ireland – replaced the native Protestant elite which was expropriated and driven into exile. This process accelerated the shift in power and wealth from the lower nobility, the *Ritterstand*, towards the titled aristocracy, the barons, counts and princes, which had already been under way before 1618.[66]

In the 1740s, the order of knighthood (*Ritterstand*) in Bohemia comprised no more than 238 members who still owned their own estates. There were a further 530 who counted as members of the lower nobility although they had lost all their land, whereas at the beginning of the seventeenth century there had been almost a thousand landed knights in Bohemia.[67] Some families had, of course, risen into the ranks of the titled nobility in the seventeenth century. To be precise 555 members of the *Herrenstand* belonged to this group of families in 1741, not counting minors and noblemen in clerical orders, but many others had succumbed to the pressures exerted by economic and political changes. The Habsburgs favoured a comparatively small group of loyal Catholic families who served them at court, in the army or as regional officeholders. Some were native, while others were immigrants from all over Europe. Those who had no access to the Emperor's favour found it difficult to compete against the great courtiers or successful military entrepreneurs. Moreover, in the sixteenth century the households of the greater noblemen had been places where simple gentlemen could find employment and patronage, not to mention the fact that their children were often educated in these noble households. In the later seventeenth century many rich noble families moved to Prague or Vienna for at least part of the year, leaving their former clients, who lacked the means to acquire urban residences or lead the life of courtiers, without support. The demographic decline of the lower nobility was compounded by the fact that newly ennobled families who rose in the service of the reigning dynasty found it difficult to be admitted to the assemblies of the estates unless they acquired property which gave them the right to claim a seat in the diet.[68] In fact, after the turmoil of the 1620, in Austria as well as Bohemia, opportunities for social advancement became much more limited; the gulf between the well-established court aristocracy and non-noble or newly ennobled officeholders was simply too great.[69]

The Habsburg dominions – in particular Bohemia and Moravia, but also to some extent the two Austrian duchies – were a paradise for the titled nobility. (The situation in Hungary which did not come under full Habsburg control until the early eighteenth century and where a very numerous lower nobility continued to thrive was a different matter.) Titled noblemen – some of them of course from families who had in the past belonged to the order of knighthood themselves – benefited from the decline of the knights, but also from the generally weak position of the urban elites and the fact that the peasants, who were subjected to a strict regime of high rents and labour services, enjoyed few rights and liberties. The wealth of these aristocratic families rested on more secure foundations in the later seventeenth century than in the past. Most of them had created entails which privileged the eldest son, thereby ensuring that the estates of the family remained undivided in one hand.[70]

There were few areas in Europe where the lower nobility was pushed aside as radically as in the central provinces of the Habsburg monarchy, Bohemia, Moravia and the Austrian duchies. However, as has already been pointed out, spectacularly rich families such as the Liechtensteins or Schwarzenbergs (in the mid-eighteenth century the Schwarzenbergs' income from their Bohemian estates alone amounted to 329,000 fl., whereas among the mere knights only a minority had an annual income from real estate exceeding 800 fl.)[71] did not really form the core of the *Herrenstand*, the estate of barons in Bohemia and Austria. Rather the well-to-do middling ranks of the *Herrenstand* who ruled over more than 100 but less than 900 peasant subjects dominated political and social life. In Bohemia this group owned about 50 per cent of all noble property in 1656. In neighbouring Moravia on the other hand, the ascendancy of a very small circle of families was more pronounced. About 20 per cent of all Moravian peasant farmers were tenants or serfs of the house of Liechtenstein in the late seventeenth century. The Liechtensteins had done spectacularly well out of the confiscations and currency manipulations after 1620. A further 5 to 7 per cent of all arable land was owned by the Dietrichsteins. As the Church was also an important landowner in Moravia, almost 50 per cent of the land in Moravia was in the hands either of these two richest families or of the Church. Moreover, the most powerful prelate in Moravia, the Bishop of Olmütz (Olomouc) was often a Dietrichstein or Liechtenstein in the seventeenth century, if he was not a Habsburg archduke or a member of the house of Lorraine, closely allied to the Habsburgs.[72]

The richest of the Bohemian and Moravian magnates tried to achieve the rank of 'prince of the Holy Roman Empire'. In fact, many of the newly created *Reichsfürsten* of the later seventeenth century were Bohemian aristocrats (see above, p. 15). Of the 17 new German princes created between 1620 and 1740, who managed to obtain a seat in the imperial diet, nine owned substantial estates in Bohemia or Moravia, among them the Liechtensteins, Schwarzenbergs, Lambergs, Piccolomini, Dietrichsteins and Auerspergs. However, these princes did not necessarily form the real core of the Habsburg court nobility in the later seventeenth century. They were sometimes ill at ease at court, where they did not always receive the respect their rank deserved, or at least that was what they felt. Prince Karl Eusebius von Liechtenstein advised his son and heir in around 1680 not to visit the imperial court more often than twice a year, once in summer and once in autumn, each time for about a month. This should be enough to pay homage to the emperor and gain the support of his most influential advisors.[73] Of course, junior members of these princely families were often much less reluctant to accept high-ranking office at court or even in the army in the mid-eighteenth century. The princely families as such were therefore well represented in the service of the Habsburgs.[74] Nevertheless, until the early decades of the eighteenth century the heads of princely houses tended to emphasise their independence and sometimes spent long periods on their own estates where they maintained extensive household establishments.[75] Thus Prince Karl Eusebius von Liechtenstein employed a household staff of 108 in 1655 and more than double this number in the late 1670s, including a troop of 25 armed retainers (*Gardisten*) and 130 equerries and other staff working in the stables. His successor, Johann Adam Andreas, spent between 110,000 and 140,000 fl. on his court and household. This was an enormous sum, given that even among the Bohemian noblemen who ranked as counts few had an annual income of more than 10,000 fl.[76]

However, these counts provided the rank and file of the court nobility, or, to be more precise the nobility capable of serving at court ('der hoffähige Adel') because of their wealth, education and the connections with the imperial dynasty they had managed to establish. Many also held important offices at the regional level.[77] Thus the counts of Waldstein (Wallenstein), the relations of the imperial commander-in-chief killed as a traitor in 1634, provided the Habsburgs with a whole series of diplomats and of Lord High Chamberlains – one of the highest officers at court – in the later seventeenth century. The Waldsteins were originally a native Czech family, as were the Slavata and Martinic – two officeholders belonging to these families were thrown out of the windows of Prague Castle at the beginning of the 1618 Bohemian rebellion, but miraculously survived. Between them these two families held a disproportionately high share of the highest offices in the Kingdom of Bohemia. Thus Bernard Ignác Martinic (1615–85) served for 30 years as Lord High Burgrave (Oberstburggraf) in Prague. The Burgrave was the highest ranking official in the Bohemian administration who governed the kingdom for the emperor but also acted as a representative of the Bohemian aristocracy. Only the Bohemian chancellor, resident in Vienna, could match his power in domestic Bohemian affairs and none of the two offices ever went to a real outsider who was not a member of the established aristocracy in the seventeenth century.[78] In effect the highest domestic offices of the kingdom remained firmly in the hands of families which had already been prominent before 1620 in spite of the undeniable influx of foreigners during the Thirty Years War. Although the Habsburgs had successfully suppressed the attempt to create a sort of Protestant aristocratic republic in Bohemia and Moravia (and possibly even Austria) in 1620, the power structure of the state they ruled remained dominated by the aristocracy. As one prominent historian has put it referring especially to Bohemia: 'The Bohemian state coach was now [after 1620], indeed, heavily stacked with Habsburg luggage; but the ruling house provided no new equipage to draw it.' In fact, they had to rely on the old horses, that is the aristocracy. Some families had indeed failed to survive the purges of the 1620s and others, who were newcomers, had been endowed with vast estates as a reward for their loyalty. But even the new families after one or two generations tended to identify with their new 'patria'. The fact that they now spoke German, Italian and French instead of Czech was probably more a sign of the impact of a cosmopolitan court culture than of a betrayal of native traditions. In fact, many families, including the newcomers, took great pride in their long line of real or imagined ancestors among the local nobility.[79] The more a family owed its rise to fame and fortune to the favour of the reigning dynasty, the more its genealogists tried to construct lines of descent leading back to the earliest historical ages and mythical heros, although few went as far as the Hungarian Eszterhazy – Hungarian magnates who

successfully co-operated with the Habsburgs – who considered Attila, King
of the Huns as their real ancestor.[80] The nobilities of the Habsburg monarchy had indeed been transformed by the events of the 1620s and the
Counter-Reformation. A new, much more coherent nobility representing a
unified elite dominating all core provinces of the monarchy, which took its
cultural lead from the court, had been created. Although firmly Catholic
and politically loyal, the families of this new elite were by no means the sub-
servient henchmen of princely absolutism as which they have often been
portrayed. In fact, until the 1740s they managed surprisingly well to preserve local power and autonomy within a state which often lacked the
administrative and financial means to implement its policies in the
provinces.

The triumph of the squirearchy? The English gentry

In Bohemia and Moravia, but also to a lesser extent in the Austrian duchies,
the once politically important lower nobility had virtually disappeared by
the end of the seventeenth century, leaving the field to a small class of magnates and wealthy noble landowners often closely connected to the imperial
court. In England, on the other hand, the gentry thrived in this period. Some
historians have even maintained that it achieved social and political promi-
nence at the cost of the aristocracy and the Crown alike (see above, pp. 41–2
and note 50). Most historians agree that the number of gentry families grew
from the end of the Middle Ages to the late seventeenth century. Although
exact figures are not available, reliable estimates assume about 5,000 heads
of families who were gentlemen and esquires for the 1520s and perhaps as
many as 20,000 for the late seventeenth century (in a population numbering
then about 5.5 million as against 2.5 million in the early sixteenth century).
Moreover, the estates held by the gentry, which had constituted about a
quarter of all arable land at the end of the Middle Ages, made up between
45 and 50 per cent in around 1700, whereas at that time the peerage held
about 15 to 20 per cent of all land, much the same as 200 years earlier.[81]
The land which the Church had lost through confiscations and sales, and
which the Crown had been forced to sell for financial reasons, accounts for
the gains made by the gentry.

The richest gentry families were almost the equals of lesser members of
the peerage. Often the heads of these families had been knighted by the king
– a non-hereditary title which had a strong correlation with wealth – and
were the leaders of the gentry community in their counties. In the early seventeenth century they often enjoyed an income of £1,000 or more. Members
of the minor gentry, in particular in areas with less fertile soil and less efficient methods of agricultural production, were much poorer. In areas such
as Wales or Cheshire their annual revenues did not necessarily exceed £50
p.a., whereas £200 was considered a minimum income for a gentleman in

some richer regions.[82] The status of esquire – a title assumed by members of the upper echelons of the gentry who were not knights – was less clearly defined than that of knight. But again wealth, ancient lineage and the possession of offices on the local level, in the royal household or the central administration, were important criteria for the social esteem a man had to command if he wanted to be accepted by society as an 'esquire' and thus a member of a select elite among the gentry.

The 'multiplication' of the gentry in the sixteenth and early seventeenth centuries changed the structure of landed society. More villages were now dominated by a resident member of the gentry whereas peers, often concentrating on career prospects at court, found it more difficult to influence local politics. The mainstay of the gentry's local power was the office of Justice of the Peace. Created in the late Middle Ages, the commission of the peace was responsible for punishing a wide variety of offences such as thefts, assaults and trespasses, but also minor robberies and riots, while the most serious felonies, punishable by death, were reserved for the higher courts. The Justices also licensed alehouses and fixed wages, and generally sought to maintain order and peace. Although more serious business was dealt with by the commission *in corpore* at the quarter sessions, a smaller number of Justices met locally on a monthly basis at petty sessions to deal with minor misdemeanours and to oversee the work of local officers such as constables. Gradually, during the course of the seventeenth century, the tasks dealt with by the petty sessions increased. After the mid-seventeenth century they debated and decided issues such as bastardy, settlements, apprenticeship and local taxation. Individual Justices on their own could also arrest and examine suspects; often such examinations took place in the hall of the local manor house.[83]

The authority bestowed on the Justice by the Crown and the social authority he enjoyed thanks to his status and local power were visibly fused on such occasions. In fact, on the one hand, membership in the commission of the peace was an official confirmation of the status of the county's natural rulers; on the other, the gentry also provided the state with the power to implement its policies in the localities. Although the office of JP was specifically English, this close co-operation between local elites and the central state, with all its inherent tensions, was not and can be found in many other countries as well. The state lent legitimacy to the power and social position of the local noble elite, and this elite in turn provided the state with the clout it needed to enforce its policies. As there was no paid royal bureaucracy in the counties apart from those officeholders who administered the royal demesne and forests, to be supplemented by tax officials responsible for the excise and related revenues in the late seventeenth and eighteenth centuries, only the prestige and influence of the landed elite could ensure compliance with royal commands.

In the late sixteenth and early seventeenth centuries it had been of the utmost importance for gentlemen to obtain a position on the bench of the

Justices, and the competition for the most prestigious positions as *custos rotulorum* (head of the commission) or as a member of the *quorum* (a select minority of which at least one member always had to be present at all judicial sessions) had been fierce. In fact, membership of the commission constantly increased between the mid-sixteenth and the early eighteenth centuries. Whereas the average county commission had had about 40 members before the Civil War, this had increased to 70 or 80 or even more around 1700. Altogether there may have been about 3,500 justices in 1700.[84] But at this time many Justices sought only a nominal appointment, and they no longer took part in the real business of the commission. In the early eighteenth century this trend became even more pronounced. This may have been a reaction to the fact that the commission had been overburdened with so many administrative duties that to be an active Justice involved too much hard and boring work. Moreover, the attractions of London persuaded many leading gentlemen to reduce the amount of time they spent in their own counties of origin. To the extent that membership in the commission of the peace lost its importance as a status symbol, status had to be demonstrated in other ways. Because the gentry enjoyed few clearly defined legal privileges, informal social prerogatives assumed a greater importance than elsewhere and were sometimes even belatedly confirmed and extended by new statutes. Thus harsh legislation directed against tenant farmers and rural freeholders barred these social groups from hunting after 1660. The legislation against poaching – defined in effect as all or most hunting activities by those who were not gentlemen – culminated in the Black Act of 1723.[85]

The hunt, to which only gentlemen were admitted, thus became an important status symbol, quite apart from the fact that it offered gentlemen a chance to practise horse-riding and shooting – an opportunity which was perhaps all the more welcome in England as only a minority of gentlemen had a chance to serve in war.[86] In fact, the gentry was not strictly speaking a military elite, although some gentlemen did pursue military careers and military traditions influenced the ethos of the gentry at least until the late seventeenth century. But as England lacked any clear distinction between urban professional and landed elites, the career patterns of English gentlemen, and even more of their sons, were more varied than those of noblemen in many continental countries. In France members of the *noblesse d'epée* forfeited as a rule their status if they engaged in trade or similar activities. Although an English gentleman was well advised not to engage in menial work, as a shopkeeper, for example (although here standards became more lenient in the eighteenth century when an urban pseudo-gentry developed and the expression 'gentleman' gradually lost any clear meaning), trade and in particular long-distance trade was by no means despised by gentlemen and their sons in the sixteenth century. Of the *c.*8,000 apprentices who were bound to members of the 15 most prominent London livery companies between 1570 and 1646, 12.6 per cent were the sons of knights and gentlemen,[87] a far higher proportion than that of gentlemen among the population as a whole. At least until the mid-seventeenth century it was still acceptable for a wealthy rural gentleman's son, especially a younger son, to become a merchant.[88]

Even at that stage, however, a professional career, in particular as a lawyer, may have been more popular with the sons of the gentry.[89] In England the world of the law courts was closely linked to the material and moral world in which the gentry lived, and not just because litigation was one of the favourite activities of the gentleman of means and leisure in the late sixteenth and seventeenth centuries – few ages were as litigious as this period. In England the law was much less of an academic and theoretical discipline than in countries where the Roman Law had triumphed. This may have been one reason why the mentality of the common lawyer, with his empirical frame of mind, was closer to the outlook of the landed gentleman than that of the university-trained civilian in other countries.[90]

The political power of the gentry found its expression not merely in their position as local officeholders, but also in the fact that members of the landed elite dominated the House of Commons, as we have already seen (chapter 1, pp. 27–8). Not just the knights of the shire – who represented the counties in parliament – but also many of the burgesses who represented urban constituencies belonged to the gentry. In the late sixteenth and early seventeenth centuries smaller boroughs – and the number of populous and prosperous towns among the parliamentary boroughs was quite limited – increasingly elected not their own citizens as burgesses but members of the landowning elite. Often these were men who, to a greater or lesser extent, controlled local politics as major landowners.[91]

Before 1640 the Crown had increasingly threatened the local authority of the country's natural rulers by imposing new fiscal burdens on the counties, sometimes relying on unpopular outsiders such as Catholics to implement its policies in the localities. The Civil War brought even greater turmoil. Politically the gentry was split during the war, often along religious lines; gentlemen with Puritan leanings sided with Parliament, while those who identified with a less Calvinist religious outlook, which left room for example for the traditional rural culture with its May dances and pre-Reformation social rituals, supported the King. During the war, and even more so after the abolition of the monarchy in 1649, men from the lower margins of the gentry, or even from social strata below the gentry, who had served in the parliamentary army, replaced members of the old-established elite in positions of authority, although the traditional social order was never really threatened as such. Nevertheless, many gentlemen felt that the world they knew was falling apart.[92]

After 1660, however, the traditional order was restored and the House of Commons, which played an increasingly important role in politics, was more than ever the political voice of the gentry as a social class. The Revolution of 1688 was seemingly the triumph of the gentry,[93] but in actual fact a high price had to be paid for the victory over 'absolutism'. Higher taxes on land which directly affected the gentry were one problem; another was the greater influence of the 'moneyed interest' on politics and the tendency, already visible before 1688, for Members of Parliament to lose their independence. Placemen dependent on the government and men who had found their way into the House of Commons as clients of the aristocracy became ever more numerous in the eighteenth century. National politics had less and less room for the simple country squire, who had been such an important figure in the sixteenth and seventeenth centuries. And in the second half of the eighteenth century, with the biological extinction of many older families, a new urban 'pseudo-gentry' replaced the old established elite in many counties.[94]

Conclusion

The Habsburg aristocracy and the English gentry offer two contrasting examples of the development of noble elites in our period. On the one hand we have a small group of wealthy families who closely co-operated with a dynasty ruling a vast composite monarchy in which each kingdom and principality had originally had its own national and regional elite which was only gradually replaced by a more unified court nobility. On the other hand we have a comparatively ill-defined class of rural landowners who lacked many of the legal privileges of continental nobilities (such as exemption from taxation or extensive rights of jurisdiction) but who nevertheless adhered in many ways to the same ideals and values as other European nobilities, at least until the mid-seventeenth century.

Dominating local administration, the gentry managed to hold its own in the seventeenth century against the centralising policies intermittently pursued by the Stuarts and the Commonwealth. In spite of the continued importance of patronage networks maintained by members of the peerage, only a minority among the gentry were likely to define their political and social role primarily or solely by reference to such ties. Few gentlemen were prepared to act merely as a great magnate's 'creatures' or clients. The lack of legal privileges, which might have allowed impoverished gentlemen or younger sons to maintain their status, ensured that the problem of a poor nobility or gentry hardly existed in England. Those who had neither land nor capital lost their status within one or two generations. Without a large reservoir of impoverished gentlemen, magnates in England found it more difficult to recruit clients who were totally dependent on the goodwill of their master than for example in Poland with its numerous impoverished *szlachta*.

In the Habsburg monarchy, on the other hand, the predominance of the high aristocracy in state and Church was so pronounced in the later seventeenth century that most magnates could afford to neglect the lower nobility altogether. Even as mere clients they were now superfluous. The co-operation with the confessional dynastic state created in the 1620s was the real basis of their power. Only by serving the ruling dynasty could the magnates maintain their own status and power, although some of the greatest continued to act and live as princes in their own right. For their part, the Habsburgs were largely content to leave the magnates to their own devices in local affairs after 1648 as long as religious conformity and political loyalty were guaranteed.

Nevertheless both the English and the Austrian–Bohemian example demonstrate that the traditional noble elites were profoundly transformed in the late sixteenth and early seventeenth centuries, not least by the need to meet the challenges posed by new standards of education and religious loyalty. Our next chapter will examine how the nobility managed to adapt to this changing cultural and religious environment, and how new ideals of urbanity and politeness gradually replaced the more violent ideal of the heroic warrior and independent lord or *seigneur*.

|3|

Education, religion and civility

Introduction

In 1578 a Swabian poet and humanist teaching at the university of Tübingen, Nikodemus Frischlin, gave a speech in Latin in praise of rural life. An innocent enough subject, one might think, but Frischlin's speech was anything but innocent. Long passages of his oration were a violent invective against the nobility in general and the imperial knighthood, the *Reichsritter,* in particular. Brutal and uneducated, lacking all civility and even the rudiments of good manners, these men, Frischlin argued, thought that a long line of ancestors gave them the right to treat their peasants like slaves. More beasts than men (*centauri*) they immediately closed ranks when criticised for their boorish manners, brutality and tyranny, so that all opponents were soon outmanoeuvred. Officially they pretended to serve their prince loyally in war and peace, but in reality they were only waiting for the right moment to commit treason. In effect, according to Frischlin, nothing more preposterous than noble status had ever been invented.[1] It comes as no great surprise that this speech created an uproar and that the Duke of Württemberg decided to dismiss Frischlin from his service. Some years later Frischlin was arrested and died during an escape attempt.[2] Not all men of learning necessarily took such a dim view of noble life and noble culture – or rather the lack of it – as Frischlin. In fact, in his less polemical moments Frischlin himself got along well enough with noblemen who were prepared to listen patiently to his poems and speeches and to employ him as an academic teacher. But in the later sixteenth century the Tübingen professor of poetry was by no means alone among European intellectuals in criticising the nobility for its lack of culture. One may with some plausibility see in such attacks the 'typically jaundiced views of poorly paid academics looking

down their long intellectual noses at men who were richer and more powerful'.[3] Nevertheless, there is little doubt that in many parts of Europe noblemen found it difficult to compete with the new elite of university-trained
lawyers and humanists in the late sixteenth century.[4] Their way of life and
education failed to meet the standards set by the new elite. Only by developing their own ideas of culture and good taste did the nobility gradually
manage to beat the university-trained elites at their own game. Suddenly the
learned humanists looked like mere pedants lacking the social graces and
elegance expected of truly educated men.

Like the new humanist cultural ideals, the more exacting standards of
piety and morals emerging in the process of confessionalisation posed a
challenge to traditional noble attitudes. Again, most noblemen coped with
this challenge surprisingly well in the long term. By the end of the seventeenth century the Churches were either more predominantly aristocratic in
character than ever before, like the Catholic Church, or had made their
peace with the ethos of aristocratic society, like most Protestant religious
communities, a few sects excepted. Nevertheless, cultural and religious
changes did transform the traditional noble elites all over Europe in our
period. The following section can deal only with selected aspects of this
transformation. We will look at changes in noble education, at the impact
which confessional loyalties and religious ideals had on the nobility and,
finally, we will examine in greater depth a particular aspect of noble culture,
the decline of noble violence, but also its persistence, albeit in more muted
forms such as the ritualised duel.

Education

When the English traveller Fynes Moryson visited Germany in the early seventeenth century he soon discovered that he was well advised to conceal his
knowledge of Latin and not to mention his degree of Master of Arts when
speaking to German noblemen. They were convinced that anybody who had
taken a university degree could not but be a 'pedant', a man who erro-
neously thought that learning was more important than courage, military
virtue and lineage.[5] This attitude was fairly widespread at the time among
members of the nobility, not only in Germany but also in France and other
countries of northern and eastern Europe (less so, however, in Moryson's
native England). In fact in Poland where, admittedly, standards of education
were generally lower than in northern Italy or the Netherlands, for example,
more than two-thirds of all noblemen were probably virtually illiterate in
the late sixteenth century.[6]

But the first signs of change were already visible. Traditionally, noblemen
had only attended a university when they wanted to pursue a career in the
Church; laymen were educated at home or in the household of another
nobleman and tried to gain military experience at an early stage. Mere book

learning was of little help in winning battles or fighting a feud and therefore was regarded with considerable scepticism. However, for many noblemen education was not least a financial problem. Law, the most prestigious course of study at university after theology, was quite expensive – often too expensive for the sons of simple country gentlemen in the sixteenth century. Wealthier noblemen's sons however, who could afford to spend several years at university, found a career at court or in the army more attractive than life as an officeholder.[7] Nevertheless, a university education attracted more and more young noblemen in the late sixteenth and early seventeenth centuries. In England attendance at university among sons of peers increased threefold between 1603 and 1640, and figures for the wealthier gentry appear to be comparable. Before the Civil War a majority of the wealthier members of the gentry, that is those with an annual income of £500 p.a. or more had probably been to university.[8] In Ingolstadt in southern Germany, a university dominated by the Jesuits and popular with Catholic noblemen, about 18 per cent of all students were of noble status at the end of the sixteenth century, and the figure was not much lower for some Protestant universities such as Heidelberg. In Lower Austria about one-third of all noblemen had been to university around 1620.[9] However, noblemen were often reluctant to take a degree. In England this seems to have been slightly less of a problem, at least for the mere gentry (the peerage was a different matter), and the same holds good for many regions of southern Europe. But in Germany nobles often felt that to submit to a formal examination for an MA or a doctorate would detract from their social status and jeopardise their superiority over mere lawyers and non-noble officeholders.[10] Even in Castile, where the university-educated *letrados* were generally acknowledged to be members of the ruling elite, nobles felt, at least until the mid-seventeenth century, that for a nobleman of ancient lineage (unless he was a clergyman) a regular university education was problematical. Thus it was often the less well-to-do members of the nobility, or the younger sons of greater noblemen who chose to study law, not the wealthy first-borns.[11] In fact, the argument which we have already encountered that a standard university education was more suitable for pedantic scholars than for gentlemen remained influential in the seventeenth century.[12] Noblemen of high status therefore tried to combine a university education with wider ranging social experience. The *Kavalierstour* (nobleman's tour), as it was called in Germany, or the grand tour, was designed to give young noblemen an opportunity to visit foreign universities, but also to attend the leading European courts, to see the more important urban centres of Italy and western Europe and, if possible, also to observe or even take an active part – as an *aventurier* – in military conflicts.[13] The military aspect of the *Kavalierstour* certainly remained important until the mid-seventeenth century, and some travellers such as the Brandenburg nobleman Matthias von der Schulenberg, later recorded the many opportunities for a career in foreign armies which they had been offered while on tour.[14]

It has been argued with some plausibility that travelling was such an important part of a nobleman's education because young men of noble status were expected to develop an independent character at a comparatively early age. To be educated abroad – far away from parents and home – it has been suggested, could help in shaping the sort of personality which a future military commander or courtier had to possess. Or, in the words of Jonathan Dewald:

> Such emphasis on individuality, with all the discomforts and conflicts that it generated, gave aristocratic education its principal colouring. In contrast to nobles destined for careers in the magistracy, young men preparing for military careers received educations that allowed considerable freedom of personal development and that regularly placed them in situations of moral ambiguity.[15]

Italy was in many ways the most attractive country for noble travellers from all over Europe for most of the early modern period. It was the centre both of Renaissance and Baroque culture and moreover no country north of the Alps could match its riding academies and fencing schools before the seventeenth century.[16] Nevertheless, in the late sixteenth century Protestants were still somewhat reluctant to visit the centre of the Counter-Reformation; there was a certain risk of getting into trouble and being charged as an heretic. Only Venice and its *terra ferma* provided a religious climate which was more tolerant. Those who did visit the seat of the papacy, however, were often deeply impressed.[17] Gradually, as religious tensions declined, an increasing number of Protestants were drawn to Italy's universities, academies and works of art. For English travellers the most important part of a grand tour was always a visit to Italy, especially in the eighteenth century, when the enthusiasm for classical antiquity was stronger than ever. Visiting the ancient monuments of Rome and other cities provided noblemen – and now sometimes noblewomen as well – with a shared experience which reinforced their feeling of cultural superiority.[18]

Other countries, however, also had their fair share of visitors. The Netherlands, known for its cultural and economic achievements as well as its universities (Leiden in particular), attracted many noble travellers, primarily Protestants, whereas England, in spite of a number of high-ranking princely visitors from Germany in the Elizabethan and early Stuart ages, remained to some extent outside the standard educational itinerary until the eighteenth century. Germany was visited by Protestant noblemen from eastern and east-central Europe (Hungary for example), while Spain attracted few foreign nobles even from Catholic countries. Scandinavia as well as eastern Europe were hardly visited at all, whereas Vienna for example – next to Paris – was particularly popular with Italian travellers who did not look abroad for a culture superior to their own, but who nevertheless wanted to gain the experience necessary for a future courtier or diplomat.[19] France held attractions for Protestants and Catholics alike and was visited by Italians just as much as by German and English nobles.[20] For Protestants the academies in Saumur and in Sedan, on the border between France and the Spanish Netherlands, were particularly important.[21] But other places, like the university in Orleans, for example, which offered a legal education in Roman law based on modern methods of scholarship, also had their share of foreign visitors. Thus Sir Thomas Wentworth, son of a rich landowner in Yorkshire, visited Paris, Orleans, Bordeaux and Saumur in 1611–12. He learnt not only French but also, to a lesser extent, Italian and Spanish, and read a number of works fashionable at the time, such as Justus Lipsius's letters.[22]

In the later seventeenth century, France and the French court culturally dominated almost all of Europe, and to have seen Paris and Versailles therefore became an indispensable part of many noblemen's education. For Austrian or German noblemen, unable to visit France at times of war, Turin provided an alternative. Its court was inspired by French cultural ideals and the town boasted a famous academy for nobles closely linked to the princely court in the late seventeenth century.[23] At this time, however, the *Kavalierstour* was already beginning to decline in importance in some European countries. Many rulers were not pleased to see noblemen's sons spend enormous amounts of money abroad and preferred to train their nobility at home in special socially exclusive academies or military schools. Some monarchs, such as Frederick William I of Prussia in 1714, even enacted laws which declared travelling abroad for purposes of education illegal.[24]

The *Kavalierstour* or grand tour had always been costly. Some Austrian noblemen spent as much as 12,000 or 18,000 fl. on the tour in the seventeenth century. This was the price of a manor house complete with an estate of moderate size, and much more than many ordinary noblemen could afford. However, whatever the price, for a long time Italy and France offered advantages which no education at home could really provide, not least an opportunity to master foreign languages, an essential prerequisite for those who aspired to a career at court or as a diplomat.[25]

However, in the long run the disadvantages of foreign travel were difficult to ignore. The sexual experience a young nobleman might seek while abroad may have been useful for the gallant behaviour expected of a courtier, but parents, and the private tutors who accompanied the young men on their travels were often less than enthusiastic about these aspects. The dangers of contracting a venereal disease or of marrying the wrong girl abroad were too obvious. The risk of being financially ruined by spending too much or by gaming was another drawback of the grand tour.[26] As early as the late sixteenth century the idea was therefore conceived of providing at home at much smaller cost and even lesser risk most of the amenities which the voyage abroad was designed to offer: a good education in modern languages, fencing, riding and dancing lessons, and generally all those skills which a true courtier needed. To meet these needs special academies for noblemen were founded. They tried to offer a programme of education which was genuinely suitable for gentlemen and not just a watered down version of classical humanism. Originally inspired by the reforming ideas developed by French noblemen such as François de la Noue, who were shocked by the violent if not barbarous manners of many members of their own class, as well as by their lack of education, the idea of educating nobles in separate institutions which taught young men the necessary social graces soon became popular in France and Germany as well as in Scandinavia.[27]

Admittedly by no means were all these academies a great success. In France they received little or no official support and therefore depended on the ability of their founders to attract a wealthy clientele to keep them going.[28] German academies were far more frequently founded by the territorial princes, but as many new educational establishments were founded in the last decades before the outbreak of the Thirty Years War, they often declined after a short period of success. After 1648 the universities of Central Europe tried to incorporate some of the educational ideals of the noble academy.[29] The fact that universities, like many other institutions of higher education, were accessible to commoners still irritated young noblemen and their parents, which led to the foundation of new, more exclusive establishments, catering only for noblemen, in the late seventeenth and the eighteenth centuries.[30] Nonetheless, some accommodation between the social ideals of the nobility and the world of learning had been achieved. During the Baroque period the noble contempt for the scholarly pedant had to some extent become the common currency of the prevailing culture.[31] Elegance and gallantry were now more important than mere booklearning. On the other hand, noblemen had themselves adapted to the world of learning. In Germany, noble academies often boasted lectureships in civil law.[32] Moreover, a knowledge of ancient mythology and antiquity in general were now widely seen as an essential part of the intellectual equipment of the nobility, and not just of a few aristocrats.[33]

Admittedly, a certain disdain for too much scholarship and learning continued to characterise the noble outlook on life. Thus many noblemen felt that they had to abandon any serious academic pursuits once they attended the court or served in the army, even when they had learnt at school or at university to read and speak Latin as well as many scholars.[34] In France, where even in the later seventeenth century the *robe* and the sword remained culturally separate groups, noblemen who belonged to the *noblesse d'epée* tended to complete their formal education at a Jesuit college, for example, in their mid-teens. Two or three years at an academy might follow, where, however, in contrast to similar German institutions, law and seriously scholarly subjects were rarely taught. Essentially, to travel, to serve in the army or to attend the court at a comparatively young age was more important than an academic education in the strict sense of the word.[35]

Whatever the shortcomings of the education many noblemen had enjoyed in the late seventeenth century, they were now much better equipped than in the past to compete with the non-noble officeholders who had studied law or the liberal arts. In fact, in some way the noble disdain for mere book-learning and pedantry had triumphed over the aspirations of non-noble scholars and learned intellectuals who had aspired to the first place in state and society in the age of humanism. In good society it may have been much more important to be well educated in the early eighteenth century than 150 years earlier, but it was also important to pretend that education and intellectual superiority had been achieved without any great effort, in accordance with the courtier's pre-eminent virtue, nonchalance or, as Castiglione had called it, 'sprezzatura' (see below, pp. 82–3).

Religion and piety *c.*1550–1660

The second half of the sixteenth century was a period when confessional values and principles increasingly pervaded all areas of society. The growing confessional conflict provided a decisive frame of reference not only for politics but also for education and culture. How did noblemen and -women react to this process of confessionalisation? As we have seen, the nobility was severely criticised at this time for its lack of education and culture, but its apparent lack of religious fervour was equally a point of criticism. Nikodemus Frischlin, the Württemberg humanist who depicted the knights of Swabia as ignorant ruffians, as we have seen, took an equally dim view of noble piety. For Frischlin, noblemen were basically guided by their own worldly interests and not by the quest for religious truth. Moreover, many, in his opinion, favoured religious sects. One example was provided by the followers of the Silesian nobleman Caspar Schwenckfeld (1489–1561) who saw a non-confessional piety and a *via media* between the various religious denominations as their true ideal.[36] Frischlin may have been more outspoken in his criticism than other authors, and because he was not a clergyman he could more easily be called to account by his noble opponents, but in the later sixteenth century he was by no means alone in his attack on the religious and moral shortcomings of the nobility. The Lutheran theologian Nikolaus Selnecker wrote in his interpretation of the psalms:

> As far as – after the lords and princes – noblemen are concerned, we have almost reached a stage where all Christians know ... that they despise God's word ... their law is violence ... their ornament is syphilis, bad breath, dirty hands and feet, puffing and snorting; ... no wonder that the common man despises them almost everywhere.[37]

At the end of the sixteenth century some of the pamphlets published by the supporters of the Catholic League in France were even less flattering and more radical in their attack on a nobility which either held heretical views or was lukewarm in its support for the true Church (see below, p. 110). The leaders of the Scottish Presbyterian Kirk were equally outspoken in their indictment of the 'insatiable, sacrilegius avarice of earles, lords and gentle-men' who were all to a lesser or greater extent defiled by 'sacrilage, swear-ing, blasphemie, blud, adulteries, reafe, and oppresseioun.'[38] Such polemics give at best a partial picture of the relationship between the nobility and the confessional Churches. Nevertheless it is true that for clergymen of all per-suasions, be they Catholic priests or Presbyterian ministers, the fact that noblemen were powerful enough to ignore their spiritual advice was often annoying and sometimes a cause of profound anger.

Some noblemen even took pleasure in openly flouting the values and ideals preached by clergymen. In France the early seventeenth century *lib-ertins* who rejected the moral and religious norms of the Catholic Reform were often noblemen; the Restoration rake in England played a similar role in his provocative reaction to the religious enthusiasm of the Puritans who had dominated England during the interregnum before 1660. Anti-clerical aristocratic libertinism was an important element of noble culture both in England after 1660,[39] and in France during the entire seventeenth century. To some extent it fed into the anti-clericalism of the Enlightenment, although figures such as the French Marquis de Sade or the aristocratic members of the English hell-fire clubs (devoted to an anti-clerical neo-paganism, involving secret rites and sexual licence) were extreme cases, and not representative of the eighteenth-century nobility as such.[40] It is never-theless no coincidence that Don Juan, the literary figure who became the anti-hero of several famous plays and Mozart's opera, was a nobleman. The combination of sexual libertinage, violence and a heroic contempt for all authorities both in this world and the next was certainly an 'ideal' which held some attractions for noblemen in the seventeenth century, especially for young men who wanted to prove their personal courage and manliness by provoking their elders and established authorities.

At a more practical level the widespread tendency among noblemen to consider the property of the Church as their own but for the asking, and the Church itself as the nobility's natural almshouse, could also create problems with the ecclesiastical hierarchy, both Protestant and Catholic. In Protestant countries noblemen had often benefited from the dissolution of the monas-teries, at least indirectly by buying former monastic estates which Protestant rulers had confiscated and then sold at bargain prices. In England many peerage and gentry families had, in fact, acquired extensive landed estates in this way in the sixteenth century.[41] In parts of Germany and some other Lutheran countries, however, estates dominated by the nobility had rather tried to defend ecclesiastical property against wholesale confiscation by the prince. A number of wealthy nunneries survived as ecclesiastical communi-ties for unmarried noblewomen in northern and north-eastern Germany, thus partially solving the problem of providing dowries for the daughters of impecunious country squires.[42]

Moreover, some Protestant cathedral chapters also provided an additional income for members of the rural nobility. In many German territories, once Lutheranism had been firmly established as the dominant religion, clergy and nobility – the former's political vision inspired by a slightly modernised version of the medieval theory of the three estates – soon discovered that they shared a wide range of interests which they stubbornly defended against political and religious innovations promoted by the territorial rulers. Brandenburg provides a good example of this alliance between Protestant clergy and nobility in the seventeenth century. Thus the Prince Elector's attempt to impose Calvinism on his Lutheran subjects after 1613 largely had to be abandoned in the face of noble resistance.[43]

In other Protestant countries, however, the Reformation had left a Church whose resources were much diminished and sometimes, in fact, insufficient to provide the clergy with an adequate income. In Ireland, in particular, where the wealth of the Church had primarily been in the hands of monastic corporations before the Reformation, the Protestant bishops and ministers of the Church of Ireland – many of them hard pressed to make ends meet – presided over an institution which had lost almost all its wealth to ruthless adventurers and property speculators such as Richard Boyle, first Earl of Cork (1566–1643). Men like Cork, who took great pride in being an ardent Protestant and enemy of popery in all its forms, had by highly dubious methods acquired the estates of entire bishoprics.[44] Churchmen who saw the alienation of ecclesiastical property as sacrilege managed with royal support to force Cork and other noblemen who had grown rich in a similar way to return some of these former ecclesiastical estates to the Church in the 1630s.[45] Similar attempts were made at the same time in Scotland and even, to a lesser extent, in England.[46] In all three Stuart kingdoms the new Protestant clericalism created considerable resentment and apprehension. Many of those who fought against the King in Scotland after 1638 and in England after 1642 did so not least because they saw any plans for a re-endowment of the Church as a threat to their own property. The hatred which faced lordly prelates such as William Laud, Archbishop of Canterbury (1633–45) and his Scottish and Irish brethren was partly motivated by worldly interests which were all too obvious.

In Catholic countries ecclesiastical property was more secure against outright confiscation by princes and noblemen. The real problem facing the Church was more subtle in nature. Powerful noble families had always been accustomed to provide for their younger sons by having them elected or appointed as bishops or as abbots of wealthy monasteries. The Counter-Reformation did little to diminish this tendency as long as aristocrats did not try to secularise Church property by becoming Protestants – which would have enabled them to marry and pass on their bishoprics and benefices to their sons.

Once such attempts – widespread until the Thirty Years War in Germany, for example – had been suppressed in many Catholic countries, the higher echelons of the ecclesiastical hierarchy became more than ever a preserve of the nobility. Canonries and bishoprics were reserved for those who could submit proof of a long line of noble ancestors (see above, pp. 20–21) to the exclusion of possibly more gifted and highly motivated non-noble clergy-men.[47] It was no easy task to transform men who had initially chosen a career in the Church for worldly reasons – or had been told by their family to pursue such a career – into shining examples of Tridentine piety. Nevertheless bishops such as Carlo Borromeo in Milan (d. 1584) in the six-teenth century, Pierre Cardinal de Bérulle, the General of the Oratorians (d. 1629), and François de Salignac de la Mothe Fénelon, Archbishop of Cambrai (d. 1715) demonstrated that, as leaders of the Church, aristocrats could be as saintly as men of lowlier origin.[48] And although a shrewd politi-cian such as Cardinal Richelieu undoubtedly used his benefices for political ends and to further his own and his family's financial interests, he took a decidedly dim view of fellow bishops who neglected their pastoral duties.[49]

In fact, whatever the misgivings of many noblemen about the more egali-tarian varieties of religious enthusiasm, the fight for the true faith in its dif-ferent forms also provided the nobility with a new chance to justify its political role and its social authority. It created a new form of legitimisation which, it seemed, was badly needed at a time when older noble role models such as the knightly warrior had become less and less convincing and plau-sible. Moreover, in the sixteenth century noblemen could invoke religious arguments when justifying their resistance to a ruler they considered a tyrant (see below, chapter 5, pp. 102–12).[50] Furthermore confessional loyal-ties could reinforce existing ties of patronage and friendship and could tame, or at least divert into worthier causes, the endemic violence which was such a widespread phenomenon in the later sixteenth century by persuading nobles to fight for God's cause and not just for their personal honour and power.[51] In fact, both the renewed idea of a crusade against the Turks and infidels, popular in Spain but to some extent also in other Catholic countries such as France and Lorraine, and the revival of chivalry, in late sixteenth-century England for example, tried to redefine noble honour in such a way that godliness and a nobleman's honour became virtually inseparable.[52]

The nobleman as godly fighter for Church and king or – perhaps even bet-ter in this context – queen had a chance of regaining the respect of society which the competition with non-noble elites, better educated and often closely allied with the state, had considerably diminished in the sixteenth century. The appeal which Protestantism initially held for many noblemen was at least to some extent based on the opportunities it offered them to prove their valour and virtue. At the same time it also appealed to noble-women, a fact which should not be forgotten. A form of piety which put so much emphasis on the role of the family as a godly community in which prayer, meditation and Bible reading reinforced the true faith gave a new and more important religious role to women, not least in the religious edu-cation of children.[53] Moreover, wherever Protestants were persecuted, or at least frowned upon, women who could not pursue a career at court or as officeholders found it easier than men to follow the dictates of their conscience.[54]

It is difficult not to be struck by the fact that Protestant Churches which were not yet fully established or which faced the threat of persecution, often found their real strongholds among the urban population and among the rural nobility. This holds true, for example, both for France before 1598 and for the Habsburg dominions before 1618.[55] In France, Protestantism seems to have found its greatest support among regional noble elites which were for some reason or other at odds with the centralising tendencies of the state, and felt that their social status and economic power were under threat.[56] Thus the populous and often impecunious nobilities of south-western France certainly played a particularly prominent part in the Huguenot struggle. Moreover, religion could often be an important element in reinforcing existing bonds of loyalty among noblemen, or between a nobleman and the magnate or prince he had chosen to serve. Thus Fabian von Dohna, a nobleman from Eastern Prussia who served Johann Casimir, the Count Palatine of Pfalz-Zweibrücken and regent of the electoral palatinate in the 1580s, emphasised in his autobiography that many noblemen who favoured Calvinism were prepared to serve Johann Casimir – at that stage the only Calvinist among the German princes – without pay and fought for him out of religious enthusiasm.[57]

In the case of Calvinism the important position which lay elders held in Presbyterian churches could provide noblemen with new opportunities to reaffirm their authority in the local community with the blessing of the Church (unless the presbyteries were staffed by officeholders dependent on the Crown or prince). In Scotland the lairds – the Scottish equivalent to the English gentry – were often closely allied with the Presbyterian Kirk in which they acted as elders at the local level. The Kirk increasingly directed its moral and religious zeal against the misdeeds of the lower orders and this certainly facilitated the alliance between the secular and the ecclesiastical elites. Moreover, their position in the Church gave noblemen a feeling of being part of an international community, uniting Calvinist nobles everywhere in Europe.[58] Nevertheless, the question of clerical patronage remained controversial throughout the seventeenth century. The right of landowners to nominate ministers was officially abolished after the Glorious Revolution in 1691, but reintroduced by the British Parliament in 1712 in the face of strong resistance by strict Scottish Presbyterians, and remained a bone of contention throughout the eighteenth century.[59]

Rights of patronage and advowsons could be a problem for relations between Protestant clergy and the local laird or squire, but throughout Europe it was primarily the noble magnates who had problems in finding their place within the new Protestant Churches unless they were sovereign or semi-sovereign rulers. Pro-Protestant noble magnates sometimes sought to establish ecclesiastical structures of their own making within the lordships they controlled, not very different from the territorial churches founded by the semi-sovereign princes in Germany.[60] However, within the framework of a larger, centrally organised national Church, powerful aristocrats found it much more difficult to submit to the moral and religious discipline which the Protestant – and in particular the Calvinist – ministry tried to impose on all laymen regardless of their status. In fact, even if they had managed to muster the necessary religious fervour, to do so would probably have undermined their prestige and authority in regional or local society.[61]

In some ways an accommodation or co-operation with Roman Catholicism was easier for such magnates. The bishoprics, prince bishoprics and canonries which the Church could offer aristocrats who espoused its cause were an ample reward for her loyal sons. Both in Germany and in France there were a number of noble and princely families who, with great consistency and considerable success, pursued a policy in which religious fervour and the pursuit of place and profit within the Church became indistinguishable. The Dukes of Lorraine – both the principal branch in Nancy and the junior line, the Guise, in France – offer an example of such a combination of the crusading spirit with more secular motives.[62] There is no denying the fact that once they had decided to back the Counter-Reformation their religious fervour, like that of other ultra-Catholic leaders of the League, was genuine enough.[63] The Duke of Mercoeur (1558–1602), the former leader of the League, for example, entered the Emperor's service after the end of the French religious wars in 1598 to fight against the Turks.[64] On his way back to France he died the death of a perfect Christian nobleman in Nuremberg. In his funeral sermon François de Sales, who saw his mission in converting the nobility to the true Catholic faith, extolled Mercoeur as a man whose life and death perfectly combined the noble ethos of honour and glory and Christian humility.[65] Another Catholic magnate, Charles de Gonzague, Duke of Nevers (1580–1637) pursued similar ideals before the Thirty Years War, when he tried to organise a great crusade to liberate Jerusalem. He even founded a new military order, the *Ordo Militiae Christianae* in Olmütz in Moravia in 1618, with the support of the King of Poland and the Austrian count and imperial courtier Michael Althan.[66]

Some French noblemen brought up as soldiers rejected and denied the world and its temptation altogether. They entered religious communities after a life on the battlefield, or wondered whether to choose the life of a warrior or that of a monk and saint. Henri de Joyeuse (1563–1608), for example, younger brother of Henry III's favourite, the Duc de Joyeuse, and one of Henry's leading courtiers, took holy orders and became a Capuchin after the death of his wife in 1587, as Père Ange de Joyeuse. He returned, however, with the necessary papal dispensations, to the world of politics and the battlefield to lead the League's troops in the final phase of the Wars of Religion, only to become a simple monk again in 1599. An eloquent and ardent preacher, he died nine years later in the convent of the Capuchins in Paris.[67]

In Germany the princely house of Wittelsbach, allied with the Dukes of

Lorraine by marriage, pursued an uncompromising Counter-Reformation policy both in its own Duchy of Bavaria and the Empire as a whole. This policy bore fruit. In the seventeenth and early eighteenth centuries, many of the richest and most powerful prince bishoprics in Germany were ruled by Wittelsbach princes. But it is clear that genuine religious conviction and calculated political decisions dominated by more worldly considerations could well co-exist. Like many other Catholic princes and noblemen, Maximilian of Bavaria (1573–1651) believed in miracles and the protection of the saints with almost the same passion as the simplest peasant in a remote Catholic village.[68]

Other noblemen, for example many members of the *noblesse de robe* in France, may have preferred a more refined form of spirituality, as developed by Jansenist theologians, for example, and further removed from popular religious practices. But for the majority of noblemen the rigours of Jansenism and similar purist ideas were too demanding.[69] However, in the seventeenth century the papacy and the Catholic religious orders such as the Jesuits and the French Oratorians, both active in developing an educational programme which met the needs of the social elite, managed to create an image of Roman Catholicism as a religion fit for a gentleman – in fact, as the only religion fit for a gentleman. Baroque court culture with it roots in Italy seemed to be imbued with the spirit of the Counter-Reformation. More so than Protestantism, in particular in its Calvinist or Puritan form, Catholicism made sufficient allowances for the existing social hierarchy and the specific social expectations that a nobleman or courtier had to fulfil. Preachers and theologians such as the Bishop of Geneva and Annecy, François de Sales, who has already been mentioned, encouraged men and women of whatever status to fulfil their religious duties in the position which society had assigned to them. There was no need to question the God-given structure of society or one's inherited duties and privileges, he argued, to be a good Christian.[70] Jesuit confessors, sometimes to the disgust of more rigorous priests, such as the followers of Jansenism, even employed all their considerable intellectual powers and a wide arsenal of theological casuistry to interpret the moral principles of their Church in such a way that a man of high status, or for that matter, a woman (although there was clearly a tendency to be stricter where women were concerned) could feel that they were good Catholics without changing their lives too profoundly.[71]

Religious change in the late seventeenth century

In any case, in many European countries the appeal of Catholicism and its capacity to recruit converts among the nobility increased during the seventeenth century. In France and the Habsburg monarchy political pressure helped to convince Protestants that there was no salvation outside the Roman Church (there were certainly no career prospects for those outside it). But after a century of religious controversy and growing scepticism many noblemen may also have been attracted to the seemingly simple answers which the monolithic Roman Church could provide.[72] Religious uniformity and a faith based on tradition and authority now seemed the best guarantee for the existing social order and against the corrosive force of a religious individualism which could undermine the deference and obedience of the lower classes. The English Civil War had provided an example of such dangers which had not passed unnoticed in the rest of Europe.[73] Many Protestant noblemen – like other laymen – had begun to harbour doubts about the more extreme demands of rigid Protestantism in the later seventeenth century, with its potentially dangerous political or possibly even social implications. They had turned away in disgust from the theologians' fanaticism and their dogmatic pedantry and from the religious enthusiasm which had caused such bitter conflicts and political turmoil. Many had come to prefer a tamed and watered-down version of the reformed religion, such as the Arminian variety of moderate Calvinism or the ritualised and, in moral terms, rather undemanding piety of the established Church in England after 1660. Given the right political circumstances, however, an equally low-key variety of Catholicism (in terms of its moral or religious demands on the individual, not necessarily in its attitude towards heretics) could be even more attractive, once rigorous Protestantism had been abandoned. In France, the Marshall Turenne, one of the most famous French military commanders after 1660 – originally a Protestant who later converted to Catholicism – offers an example of such an attitude.[74] In Germany, where political pressure on Protestants was much less pronounced after 1648, we also find a large number of conversions to Catholicism both among princes and simple noblemen in the late seventeenth century. Among the greater princely dynasties only the principal branch of the house of Brunswick and the Hohenzollern remained staunchly Protestant (the latter Calvinist) in the early eighteenth century.[75]

However, a rejection of the sterile dogmatism of traditional orthodox Protestantism could also move noblemen to support new religious reform movements such as Pietism at the end of the seventeenth and in the early eighteenth century. Here the emphasis was on a truly Christian life, and the personal – possibly mystical – experience of faith, which was defined much more in emotional than in dogmatic terms. In fact one of the leaders of this movement was Count Zinzendorf (1700–60) a nobleman whose family had – like so many others – been exiled from Austria during the Thirty Years War. Zinzendorf, who was married to Countess Reuß from Thuringia, while his stepfather was the Prussian General Dubislav von Natzmer and a strict Pietist himself, became the head of the Moravian brethren, and was even elected as bishop of this small religious community in 1737. Few noblemen played such a prominent part in the history of Pietism as Zinzendorf, who went to America and England to preach and win new disciples. But the movement soon found lasting support among the nobility of eastern

Germany, and of Prussia in particular. Some historians have claimed that by embracing Pietism Prussian nobles became 'defeudalised' and bourgeois, as frugality and self-control were quintessentially bourgeois values. This interpretation, however, is doubtful, as the history of the Prussian nobility demonstrates sufficiently that a way of life which was shaped by a movement for religious renewal could go hand in hand with more traditional noble ideals such as those of military valour.[76] Outside Prussia some members of the higher nobility, such as a number of imperial counts (*Reichsgrafen*), in particular in the Wetterau near Frankfurt, espoused the cause of Pietism, for example, the counts of Ysenburg or Wied. For these aristocrats, who could not but realise that they had lost out to the more powerful princes in the competition for status, this frustration may have been an important psychological motive behind their decision to seek personal fulfilment in religious experience and good works rather than in more secular pursuits.[77]

Nevertheless it would be wrong to assume that with the exception of a few individuals, noblemen had an innate tendency to avoid any deeper religious commitment. Like early modern critics of noble attitudes, some modern historians have claimed that ultimately most nobles 'had always attached too much importance to family pride and personal honour to be very consistent Christians whether Protestant or Catholic.'[78] Undoubtedly there were tensions between the traditional noble ethos and the demands of religious reformers, be they followers of Luther and Calvin or the Council of Trent. Such tensions became particularly apparent at moments of crisis, such as the French Wars of Religion or during the later 1640s and the 1650s in England. But if many noblemen turned to a fashionable, rather flexible form of Catholicism deeply embedded in the international court culture of the later seventeenth century, or, as Protestants, became more secular in their outlook and attitude to life, these changes to some extent only mirrored the more general intellectual and cultural trends of the time. Like other social groups and classes, nobles had been transformed by the impact of the Reformation or the Catholic reform and Counter-Reformation. In spite of some reservations one may have about the idea of a new and stricter social discipline being imposed as a result of the process of confessionalisation, education was certainly influenced by the ideals preached by reformers.[79] As we shall see in the next section, the new self-restraint which the reformers had demanded is apparent not least in noble attitudes to violence, bloodshed and death.

Nevertheless, in order to survive, both Protestantism and Tridentine Catholicism had to accommodate themselves to what the social elite and, in particular, the nobility expected from a socially acceptable form of religion. Ranting hell-fire sermons preached by mere tinkers predicting the imminent reign of Christ on earth when everything would be turned upside down appealed to few noblemen, and the arrogance of lordly prelates who were themselves the sons of mere peasants or butchers – such as some seventeenth-century English bishops – was in general equally unpalatable. The Catholic Church of the later seventeenth century was certainly more than ever an aristocratic Church – with all the problems this was to cause in the Age of Enlightenment. And most Protestant Churches had also long found their place within a society governed by deference and a pre-existing social hierarchy and had accepted the rules this entailed.

Civility and the decline of noble violence

Both Protestantism and Counter-Reformation Catholicism, with their emphasis on higher standards of self-discipline, undoubtedly changed noble attitudes and noble behaviour, but this was a slow and tortuous process. In France the manners of the nobility at the beginning of the seventeenth century were so unrefined that a later generation, during the early years of Louis XIV's reign, recoiled in horror when it contemplated them. A writer who wrote down his anecdotal tales from the age of Henry IV and Louis XIII in the late 1650s, Tallemant de Réaux, repeatedly emphasised not only the brutality and physical violence which prevailed, especially among the *grands* of the recent past – it was common practice to beat one's servants and companions of inferior status – but also the complete sexual licence, a sort of indiscriminate fornication unrelieved by any aspirations to gallantry and love and extending even to incest, allegedly practised in aristocratic circles. Tallement certainly exaggerated to some extent, but his writings indicate, as Jonathan Dewald has argued, that sensibilities and mentalities did change in the mid-seventeenth century, and that even the manners of the quite recent past now appeared barbarous.[80] This change, however, 'the retreat from an unqualified emphasis on courage and military reputation,'[81] and the greater weight given to modesty, self-restraint and a certain familiarity with the world of arts and letters, was by no means simply imposed from above. Rather, they were part of a wider process which gradually changed the values and ideals of the nobility, a process whose focal points were, in France, Jesuit colleges, the salons of the capital and noble academies as much as the court.[82] If true nobility was redefined in France and in other countries in the seventeenth century, this was largely because noblemen themselves came to recognise that the unrestrained military prowess which they had traditionally cultivated was ultimately self-destructive and made it impossible for them to compete successfully with rival elites.

The next chapter will look in greater detail at the impact which the new norms of conduct, developed for life at court or in urban society, had on the mentality and culture of the nobility. Here we shall concentrate on one particular aspect of this change, the slow but steady decline of noble violence. The social position of noblemen in late medieval society was based to a considerable extent on their capacity to use physical force if their legal claims or their honour were challenged. Unless they entered the Church noblemen defined themselves as warriors and all noblemen were expected to follow the profession of arms at least in younger years. The increasing importance of mercenaries and of the infantry in general reduced the number of nobles actively engaging in warfare in the sixteenth century. This is certainly true for Castile and England, for example. Neither country was directly affected by warfare, although Spain was almost permanently at war outside its own borders. Perhaps more surprisingly, even in France where the Wars of Religion offered ample opportunities for those eager to prove their military valour, only a small minority of noblemen served, it seems, for more than a short time in one of the opposing armies. The others preferred to live, if possible, the more peaceful life of a country squire, partly of course because they simply lacked the economic means to pursue a military career.[83]

But if at least in western and central Europe the nobility became more reluctant to participate in warfare in the later sixteenth century, although the following century was to reverse this trend in many countries, violence nevertheless remained an essential part of a nobleman's life at this period. In many ways violence was endemic in sixteenth-century society. Brawls in alehouses which left many wounded, if not dead, were an everyday occurrence; simple craftsmen or peasants felt that insults of whatever kind – and they tended to be particularly touchy where their masculinity or their role as husbands and fathers was concerned – had to be avenged immediately, otherwise they lost face and their claim to honour and status.[84] If this was true for peasants it was all the more true for noblemen. But noblemen were also accustomed to resolve disputes about property or rights of lordship by taking up arms against their opponents – hence the custom of feuding. Although ecclesiastical and secular authorities, in particular urban magistrates (the attitude of territoral princes in Germany, for example, was often more ambivalent), had long tried to stamp out the feud and the small-scale warfare characteristic of these disputes, the violent habits of an earlier age were slow to die. They often survived well into the second half of the sixteenth century and, in some countries, beyond.[85]

One of the last major feuds in Germany, where feuding had been widespread during the fifteenth century, and one of the most spectacular, was conducted by a Franconian nobleman and mercenary leader, Wilhelm von Grumbach.[86] The Franconian knight had once served the King of France as a colonel, and there were few major German mercenary leaders and noble cavalry captains whom Grumbach did not know personally. He could thus to some extent rely on a network of noble military entrepreneurs, who had found themselves without work once the Peace of Cateau-Cambresis put an end to the wars between France and the Habsburgs in 1559. As in France, where many of the violent conflicts of the Religious Wars were rooted in regional feuds between rival noble factions (cf. below, pp. 108–9), these unemployed noblemen, dissatisfied with their position in civilian life, created a potential reservoir for armed conflict.

Grumbach was involved in a long-standing conflict with the Bishop of

Würzburg and in 1563 he took the bishopric's capital by force. Grumbach knew how to appeal to the resentments harboured by noblemen all over Germany against the princes and their legal and financial experts of non-noble origin, as well as against the prelates grown rich at the cost of their noble vassals.[87] Although Grumbach had first enjoyed strong sympathy among noblemen all over Germany, his support dwindled once the Emperor turned against him in earnest and the territorial princes combined forces against his rebellion. Only the Duke of Saxony, Johann Friedrich, supported him to the very end. In 1567 Johann Friedrich's capital, Gotha, where Grumbach had retreated, was besieged and had to surrender to the enemy forces. Grumbach was captured and quartered in the market square of Gotha. His princely ally, Johann Friedrich, spent the rest of his life as the Emperor's prisoner in Austria.

Grumbach's undoing was not just the superior power of the territorial state but the fact that the majority of his own noble companions ultimately preferred to make their peace with the princes and the political *status quo*.[88] The foundation and consolidation of the *Reichsritterschaft* (imperial knighthood) as a confederation of the independent lower nobility under the Emperor's protection was one of the principal reasons for the end of the feud, and consigned spectacular acts of violence such as those committed by Grumbach to the past. Thus in Germany the end of the feud was rather a result of an increased noble self-discipline than of a domestication of the nobility imposed by the princes, who in the past had themselves used feuding noblemen, often high-ranking officeholders, for their own purposes of territorial expansion, but now no longer saw any need to do so.

Noble manners and procedures of conflict resolution also changed in other European countries. In Scotland the Crown's authority had always been rather limited in most regions of the kingdom. The long period during the fifteenth and the sixteenth centuries when the reigning kings had been minors did little to make the country more peaceful. Moreover, the particular kinship structure of Scottish society meant that all members of an extended family, a clan, felt under an obligation to take revenge if one of their relations was insulted or killed. And unlike in other European countries, where feuding nobles treated their enemies with a certain respect if they belonged to the same status group, whereas the peasants often bore the full brunt of the brutality such warfare entailed, no such rules seem to have obtained in Scotland. In 1619 a laird (William Buchanan) who had won a court case against a family he was in dispute with, the MacFarlanes, was captured by them. They 'stripped him, tied him to a tree, slashed him with dirks, cut out his tongue, slit open his belly, took out his entrails, entwined them with those of his dog, and then cut his throat.'[89] Such unmitigated cruelty would have been difficult to find in most European countries outside full-scale warfare, in particular religious warfare. However, even in Scotland the violent ways of an earlier age slowly died during the reign of James VI (1567–1625). The influence of the Kirk and its moral discipline, James VI's political shrewdness in managing his aristocracy and the fact that the union between England and Scotland (1603) had made the borders far easier to police all ensured that at least in the Lowlands the rule of law replaced the bloodfeud, but also the customary informal means of arbitration and conflict resolution which had by no means always been inefficient.[90]

In fact while the late sixteenth century – at least in western and central Europe – saw a clear decline of the traditional feud and related 'crimes' such as the hiring of paid assassins to get rid of enemies, a form of resolving problems quite popular in parts of Italy, for example,[91] other forms of interpersonal violence among noblemen were on the increase. The duel as an ideally strictly regulated combat between two noblemen, sometimes supported by seconds, became increasingly popular in this period. In France and temporarily even in England, the popularity of the duel assumed endemic proportions at the beginning of the seventeenth century.[92]

The rise of the duel was at least to some extent the result of the increasing influence of courtly ideals and values on noble culture. This holds true in particular for Italy where the first systematic treatises teaching noblemen how to defend their honour in single combat were written. These handbooks were clearly part of the general literature which sought to instruct noblemen on how to behave in polite society in general and at court in particular. Most tracts of the 'perfect courtier' variety genre emphasised the importance of speech and gestures and of polished manners in general. But the same tracts which taught noblemen to pay proper respect to superiors also taught them to pay close attention to the smallest slight they might receive from others who did not address them as their status and honour required.[93]

Thus many duels – whatever their deeper cause – were triggered off by one of the two opponents 'giving the other the lie', that is calling him a liar, which according to the prevailing code of behaviour was an unforgivable insult.[94] Admittedly, the ritualised *mentita* as it was called in Italy or *démenti* in French (giving the lie) was often only the answer to an earlier insult, which could often be serious enough, such as telling somebody he was a coward or a cuckold. But the essential final step towards actual physical combat was nevertheless the *mentita*.[95] In Italy itself the intricate rituals of honour seem to have been so highly developed at the end of the sixteenth century that actual duels were not often fought. To arrive at the point where no other solution but physical combat was possible was just too complicated for many would-be duellists. In fact, the prohibition of duels by the Council of Trent in 1563 may also have been more effective in Italy than elsewhere, and the Italian nobility was, by and large, less warlike than for example its French counterpart.[96]

In France however, where public order had almost totally broken down in many provinces during the Wars of Religion, matters were different. Recent estimates reckon that about 350 noblemen were killed each year in duels in

France at the beginning of the seventeenth century. An official French list for the years 1656–60 gives the names of 218 duellists, but is almost certainly incomplete as it does not mention a single case from the south of France.[97] Numbers were certainly lower in most other European countries. In England, for example, newsletters reported up to 35 duels annually between 1610 and 1620 (the real number was presumably higher), but the social impact of the duel was nevertheless considerable.[98]

In the late sixteenth and early seventeenth centuries one duel often triggered off the next, as the kinsmen and friends of the man who had died in the first combat felt a temptation if not an obligation to take revenge. Thus in his *Memorials of the Holles Family*, Gervase Holles mentions a fairly typical case from the 1590s. His ancestor, Sir John Holles, had fallen out with a powerful local magnate, the Earl of Shrewsbury, as he had married the daughter of a man Shrewsbury considered his enemy. Tensions had mounted and one day one of Holles's retainers, one Roger Orme, killed Shrewsbury's Gentleman of the Horse, by the name of Pudsey, in a duel. Holles was now accused by another local gentleman, one of Shrewsbury's clients, Gervase Marcham, of having been responsible for Pudsey's death, whereupon Sir John sent Marcham a challenge including the crucial words 'I affirme that you ly and ly like a villaine'. However, no place to fight a duel acceptable to both sides could be found. Accused by Marcham of cowardice because he had allegedly avoided meeting him in combat, Holles sought an opportunity to restore his honour. Encountering Marcham by chance on a road, Holles attacked him, and 'ran him betweene the privities and the bottome of the gutts up to the hilt and out behinde towardes the small of his backe' with his rapier. Strangely enough, Marcham survived and Holles escaped safely under the protection of another local magnate, Lord Sheffield, one of Shrewsbury's rivals.[99]

Holles's story shows that although seemingly only conflicts between two individuals, duels were often the expression of deeper tensions between rival noble factions or kinship networks which poisoned the atmosphere of local politics, not just in England, in the late sixteenth and early seventeenth centuries. In France, the strict rules for fighting duels which were developed in Italy had been ignored for so long that some combats were difficult to distinguish from premeditated murder. This meant that local feuds and duels continued to interact for a long time. They were part and parcel of the same wave of noble violence which engulfed the country after the mid-sixteenth century, at one and the same time fuelling the Religious Wars and fomented by the religious conflict.[100]

Duels were not only fought in the provinces. Matters were not much better at the centre, at court, where personal and political animosities also frequently led to duels, not to mention conflicts about rights of precedence and status. In fact, the duel served to reaffirm the unity of the nobility in an age when newly created titles and rights of precedence were threatening to destroy this unity. As the contemporary theory affirmed, even members of the high aristocracy had to accept challenges from simple gentlemen. An earl or count refusing a challenge from a gentleman risked appearing ridiculous, or worse still, a coward. Even earls and barons were 'besides their dignitie none other then gentlemen, and gentilitie or nobilitie is hereditary and cannot be taken away but dignitie may.' On the other hand, non-nobles had no right to fight duels, unless they had served in the army, and had not later returned to civilian life, to their 'mestier mecanique'.[101]

Single combats became less frequent in most European countries not least in France itself in the later seventeenth century, although recent research has questioned the assumption that the state managed to stamp out this provocative protest against normal legal procedures or even seriously tried to do so. In fact, as far as France is concerned, some historians have argued that apart from the fact that duellists became more cautious when arranging their encounters, which were now kept as secret as possible, nothing much changed, and that there was indeed, after a slow decline under Louis XIV, a renewed rise in the number of duels in the second third of the eighteenth century. Nevertheless the number of persons killed may indeed have fallen as seconds now refrained from intervening actively in the combat and as the ferocity and sheer brutality of the contests was less pronounced than in the past.[102] The comparative decline of the duel or at least of its deadliness can to some extent be attributed to the greater degree of political stability during this period. Less was now at stake in power struggles and even those who were temporarily out of favour at court or politically outmanoeuvred in their own home province did not necessarily lose their status and honour altogether.

Frequently the decline of the duel, or at least the disappearance of the most spectacular and public manifestations of this kind of noble violence, in particular in France, is also seen as a result of the victory of absolutism. It is indeed true that Richelieu had pursued a relentless campaign against the duel. This could be seen as an attempt to stamp out a provocative ritual which defied royal justice and proclaimed a nobleman's right to be judge in his own cause where his honour was concerned. However, the Church had never approved of the single combat, and expressly condemned the duel at the Council of Trent in 1563. And Richelieu was not only a politician but also a conscientious clergyman. Moreover, he had himself lost near relations in duels.[103] His campaign against the duel should therefore not too rashly be seen as an absolutist attack on noble liberties. In fact, the Crown was not alone in opposing the duel. The *Societé de Saint Sacrement* which promoted the cause of Catholic Reform and was closely linked to devout aristocratic circles inspired by the ideals of Jansenism, strongly intervened against the duel from about 1646 onwards. Many of its noble members signed pledges that they would not accept challenges.[104] Although they did not hesitate to denounce those who issued challenges, the French *Dévots* were by no means ardent supporters of unlimited royal authority. Their doubts about official foreign and ecclesiastical policy were far too pronounced for that.[105]

They rejected the duel because too high a sense of personal dignity was incompatible with their ideal of Christian humility. Moreover priests and bishops who were part of the movement for the renewal of French Catholicism tried to persuade noblemen that it was erroneous to see a violent, heroic death as the only one acceptable for a man of honour. To die in one's bed, as a good Christian supported by the consolations and ministrations of the Church, was far more dignified. Gradually this idea of the good Christian death – we have already encountered it in the sermon preached by François de Sales after the death of the Duc de Mercoeur – replaced the idea of the glorious heroic death.[106]

The Catholic reform movement was certainly not the only factor in changing the manners of the French nobility. The new ideal of the *honnête homme* (to be examined in the next chapter) certainly helped in creating new modes of conduct. Heroism and personal glory now took second place after social grace, which allowed the perfect nobleman to shine in polite company, as a 'worldly gentleman who relied upon wit, grace and dissimulation to move with ease in society, pleasing all and offending no one.'[107] As opposed to the heroic warriors of the early seventeenth century, the *honnête homme* felt no need constantly to defend his honour in public against the slightest remark which could be taken amiss. A social hierarchy underwritten by the Crown and defended by the king against all mere gatecrashers and upstarts gave him a sense of security which his predecessors had lacked.

Thus even in France cultural changes and a new sense of what constituted social status and the identity of an individual were at least as important for the comparative decline in the number of duels fought as the growing power of the state. In fact, the state would not have been able to increase its power and authority without such cultural changes. Moreover, not to fight a duel could still have dire consequences for the reputation of a nobleman, especially when he was an officer serving in the army. Four years after Louis XIV's death, in 1719, a young aristocrat, Paul-Albert de Luynes, was forced by his mother to abandon his military career – at the age of 16 Luynes already held a commission as a colonel – and to become a clergyman because he had refused to fight a duel after having been insulted by a fellow officer. Luynes later became Bishop of Bayeux and eventually Archbishop of Sens, a position in which he seems to have been happy enough.[108]

As in France, in Spain the ability and courage to fight a duel when challenged by an opponent remained an essential part of the code of honour to which noblemen were expected to subscribe. But there had always been fewer duels in Spain than in France – partly perhaps because until 1640 many members of the social elite in Spain had had little direct experience of warfare, and certainly not of warfare at home. Over time the actual duel became much less important than the *ley del duelo*, the code of honour. In fact *duelo* became a byword for honour, and in this sense Calderón could call one of his plays *También hay duelo en las damas* (Ladies too have a sense of honour). The law of the *duelo* embodied the ideal of honour which noblemen and noblewomen had to follow. The actual duel was its supreme reference point (at least for men), but it was a distant, one might say transcendental, point of reference. The will and ability to fight a duel was sufficient to prove one's honour. One did not actually need to fight with real arms; words and gestures might be sufficient or, at worst, a feigned duel in which one went through the motions of meeting the opponent arms in hand, but where precautions were taken to avoid actual bloodshed (by alerting the authorities through maximum publicity, for example). On the other hand, spontaneous violent combats not regulated by the rules which applied to formal duels continued to play an important part in the life of the Spanish nobility.[109]

In the Netherlands in the seventeenth century, the duel was popular among military officers – who were often foreign noblemen – whereas the civil authorities dominated by the urban elite consistently rejected the specific ethos which found its expression in such combats. In the eighteenth century, however, when the urban *regents* adopted a lifestyle inspired to some extent by aristocratic ideals of conduct, town councillors or merchants themselves fought duels to defend their honour and claims to social prestige.[110] In England the duel survived well into the eighteenth century, especially as part of the specific culture of honour prevalent among active and former army officers.[111] Moreover, after 1660, fighting duels was an essential part of the anti-Puritan culture of the Restoration court. Quite a number of Charles II's courtiers were involved in such combats. Thus in 1670 the second Duke of Buckingham killed the Earl of Shrewsbury in a duel. Shrewsbury had unwisely objected to the love affair between Buckingham and his wife.[112] But other forms of aristocratic violence also prospered in the hothouse atmosphere of Restoration England. In London young men from the upper classes formed clubs whose members were called 'Hectors', and engaged in the 'sport' of 'scowring'. 'A group of gentlemen revellers and their hangers-on ... would forcibly clear a tavern of its other patrons and would then rush out into the street to smash windows and assault bystanders and the Watch.'[113] Such excesses were more than the expression of youthful high spirits. Through such violent behaviour members of the elite asserted their superiority, by mocking the law-abiding citizens of inferior status. Examples of such rituals can be found in other societies and periods as well, in Spain as much as in mid-sixteenth-century small-town Swabia.[114]

Ritualised tavern brawls and street fights may have been unpleasant enough for those who were unwittingly caught up in them, but more serious aristocratic violence also survived well into the later seventeenth century, even in such comparatively peaceful countries as France and England, at least in the more remote regions. In 1665–6 the Parliament of Paris had to send a special commission of judges to the Auvergne, a particularly badly policed province, to hold a special assize session, known as the *Grands Jours d'Auvergne,* to stamp out the endemic robbery and banditry in which

the nobility of this province was deeply involved.[115] Such measures had
some degree of success, but what has been said about northern England in
the Restoration period concerning widespread acts of violence and similar
outrages – 'renaissance concepts of aristocratic behaviour were evidently
late in spreading to South Yorkshire'[116] – could equally well be said of the
remoter provinces of France and southern and central Italy, where bandits
were openly protected and abetted by noblemen, and Spain in the later seventeenth century.[117] Only gradually, with the increasing urbanisation of
noble life and the concomitant assumption of more urbane manners and the
greater efficiency of law enforcement, did the problem of noble violence –
apart from the occasional duel – slowly recede. For noblemen who wanted
to prove their physical courage and prowess, war and, to a lesser extent,
hunting, still offered more than enough opportunities.[118]

Conclusion

A recent study of upper-class manners in early modern England has characterised the cultural changes of the sixteenth and seventeenth centuries as a
transition from a model of behaviour centred on the ideal of 'lordship' to
one best described by the catchword 'urbanity'. The model of lordship was
devised to impress social inferiors, vassals, clients and tenants more than the
members of the same social class. It led nobles, for example, to demonstrate
their authority by recruiting large retinues of servants – often armed – and
dispensing hospitality to social inferiors, but it also led them to emphasise
their power through displays of physical superiority and, if necessary, by
acts of violence. Urbanity, on the other hand, was more the mode of an elite
'whose members tend to vest their sense of social identity in their possession
of a shared culture principally expressed and elaborated in the conduct of
social relations with each other.'[119] Courtly manners, self discipline and
politeness were now more important in impressing one's equals than the visible signs of physical prowess or military power which had been so central
to noble identity in the past. Competition and rivalry for prestige and status
with their potential for political and social conflict, however, certainly did
not disappear from the world nobles lived in, though they did become somewhat more subtle. Moreover, to some extent the propensity of some noblemen to demonstrate their personal independence and their feeling that
normal standards of behaviour did not apply to them by embracing everything that was condemned and frowned upon by the advocates of civility
and higher moral standards, from fornication, serious drinking and violent
brawls to atheism, was perhaps a necessary concomitant of the 'civilising
process' that the nobility underwent during our period. Noblemen may have
been prepared to abandon old violent habits and manners which were now
seen as barbaric, but they certainly had no wish to be just like everybody
else, and when politeness and education were insufficient to demonstrate

one's status, then a premeditated affront to middle-class values could some-times serve instead. Civility and anti-civility were thus linked in noble culture.[120]

Nevertheless, to the extent that wealthy noblemen increasingly adjusted themselves to the new values of urbanity and literary culture, while succes-sully assimilating these values to older aristocratic traditions, they distanced themselves from their own tenants and peasants, and to some extent from the simple country squire as well, more radically than in the past. The per-manent presence of servants in the household for example – whose status declined as they lost their military functions and were now more likely to be female than male anyhow – was by the late seventeenth century increasingly seen as a matter of embarrassment; they were banished to the pantry and the backstairs.[121] The manor house was separated by large gardens or vast parks from the village; in fact, in some cases entire villages were razed or displaced to create such parks in the first place. Whereas in the past the manor house had been part of the village and had not tried to conceal its economic func-tion as the centre of a home farm, it was now, in the late seventeenth and the eighteenth centuries, much more likely to be the outpost of a sophisticated urbanised culture which looked to distant centres – Venice, Florence or Rome for example – for inspiration, not to the surrounding countryside and regional traditions.[122] Noblemen who had still seen cities as a potentially hostile environment in many parts of central and northern Europe in the early sixteenth century now rented or built palatial town houses where they lived often for longer periods than in their castles or country houses.[123] While adapting to an urbanised culture, wealthy nobles were careful to maintain their cultural hegemony by promoting a particularly sophisticated style in art, architecture and manners which those outside the charmed circles of aristocratic society found difficult to imitate successfully. Palladianism in eighteenth-century England, for example, or the varying fashions in dress, table manners and cooking patronised by French aristo-crats, set cultural standards which allowed the noble elite to judge men and women from newly established families who tried to emulate them as defi-cient in taste and breeding.[124] In this cultural and social competition the court often served as the laboratory where new images and ideals of noble behaviour were first developed and tried out. Our next chapter will there-fore look at the relationship between the nobility and the court, and at the influence which the ideal of the perfect courtier had on noblemen all over Europe.

4

The court

Prison or showcase of noble life?

Introduction

There had always been noblemen who had lived the life of a courtier, as a member of a prince's household, and 'courtliness' as a system of values, a way of life, had certainly influenced the behaviour and attitudes of some noblemen and noblewomen in the Middle Ages. However, it was the Renaissance which gradually transformed most noblemen into potential if not actual courtiers, first in Italy, then in other European countries as well. Whether one actually lived at court, or attended the court of a prince or not, not to have the accomplishments of a courtier was now seen as an unpardonable lack of style. From the sixteenth century onwards the virtues – and vices – of the court began to permeate noble life everywhere, even in the small provincial town or the remote country house. This was certainly a gradual process which probably did not really affect northern Europe until the late seventeenth century, but it was nevertheless of fundamental importance for the values and mentalities governing noble life.

Court culture has often been associated with absolutism, and has been seen as centred on the ideals of service to the monarch and the almost religious reverence due to him (or her). Recent research has, however, partly revised this image. Historians have emphasised that the traditional aristocratic cult of honour always remained an essential ingredient of court culture. Even when older aristocratic traditions were transformed or re-invented at court, as the late medieval tournament and the concomitant ethos of chivalry were used to express a new 'cult of personal allegiance to the prince', they never quite lost their older connotations.[1] For a nobleman to reassert and defend his personal honour and status within the context of the social and cultural world of the court was no contradiction. On the contrary, as has been shown, the origins of the duel – often taken as a symbol of the conflict between aristocratic notions of liberty and personal honour on the one hand and the absolutist monarch's claim to be the sole font of honour on the other – lay at least to some extent in the value system of court culture itself. This had created a heightened sensibility for a nobleman's personal prestige and status. In any case, the connotations of court culture remained ambivalent: personal loyalty to the prince and subordination to his authority loomed large, but at the same time it remained an expression of a specifically aristocratic ethos which left more than enough scope for conflicts with royal power.

The Italian *Cortegiano* as a social model for the nobility

It is certainly no accident that the new ideal of the nobleman as courtier was first articulated in Italy. In the history of the early modern princely households the courts of Renaissance Italy occupy a position of special importance. The Italian princes of this period set an example for other European courts by patronising poets, painters and sculptors and collecting works of art in a systematic way much earlier than other rulers – thereby creating a special cultural milieu for themselves and their entourage which developed only gradually outside Italy during the sixteenth and seventeenth centuries.[2] It could be said that the courtier and his specific way of life were invented in Italy in the early sixteenth century. It was an Italian nobleman, Baldassare Castiglione, who wrote the book which was to become the most famous treatise on the courtier and his life in the early modern period. Strictly speaking it was not a treatise at all but rather the – idealised – portrait of a living society, the *Cortegiano*.

Baldassare Castiglione, born in 1478 in Casatico near Mantua (his mother was related to the ruling family of the Marquesate of Mantua),[3] wrote the *Cortegiano* between 1513 and 1518–19, but continued to revise the text in later years. The final version was probably not established until 1524.[4] In the sixteenth century the Cortegiano was often read as a tract teaching would-be courtiers the skills and arts which they had to master to succeed at court. But in fact Castiglione had not written a manual for potential or actual courtiers – as many of his successors were to do – but a dialogue in which the court of Urbino during the last years of Montefeltre rule (the discussions were meant to have taken place in 1507) was presented to the reader as a model of the perfect court society. The reader was invited not so much to learn the principles of courtmanship – the very idea that one could become a successful courtier by reading manuals would have seemed ridiculous to Castiglione – as to participate in the conversation games of an ideal court society as represented in the dialogue. Because court society was essentially constituted by conversation it could only adequately be portrayed in such a conversation.[5]

Very few of the arguments advanced by the men and women participating in the discussion of the *Cortegiano* can lay claim to any great originality. In fact, it was not Castiglione's intention to develop novel arguments as such. One might rather say that he collected the relevant commonplaces with which one had to be familiar in order to participate in a discussion about life at court. The juxtaposition of often contradictory *topoi* – commonplaces – explains to some extent why the Cortegiano is such an ambiguous work. Contradictions between the various arguments often remain unresolved, as, for example, in the debate on the requirement of noble birth as a precondition for a career at court.[6]

In spite of the ambiguities, certain features which constitute the essential habits and accomplishments of the courtier do emerge in Castiglione's dialogue. The courtier should master the arts of war. In fact, as one of the participants in the discussion, the Count Canossa, states, 'the principall and true profession of a courtier ought to be in feates of armes.' At the same time, however, the courtier had to be familiar with the world of learning. He should be a humanist as well as a warrior, know both Latin and Greek, and should even be able to paint and draw.[7] Castiglione's courtier appears as a true 'uomo universale', a perfect human being, learned, civilised, elegant, well dressed, courageous and a good fighter both in battle and in duels. The courtier has to be a man of many parts, at home in war as well as in peace, a man who will cut a good figure in battle as much as in an elegant conversation or when courting a lady. Love is an important subject in the *Cortegiano* and women formed an essential part of court society, in spite of the fact that they did not enjoy the same status as men. But it is impossible to reduce the courtier to any of his many roles; the feature which really defines him is none of his individual accomplishments but the 'grace' (grazia) which is the hallmark of everything he does. In this respect the ideal courtier who emerges from the conversations at Urbino is defined as much by aesthetic as by ethical criteria. An essential part of the 'grace' or charm which marks the true courtier is that everything he does should appear natural and effortless. For this ease and naturalness in appearance and behaviour Castiglione coined the term 'sprezzatura', a catchword which was to become famous and which remained a key term in later tracts on the courtier. Indeed it was an ideal which deeply influenced the way noblemen in general tried to appear to society, their 'self-fashioning'.

Sprezzatura is not all that easy to translate,[8] but essentially the point Castiglione wanted to make was that the courtier had to conceal the effort which it might cost him to excel, to be witty, to appear elegant and to master the arts of war and peace. There is no greater fault in a courtier than to succumb to the temptation of ostentation. A certain nonchalance combining self-confidence with understatement but also spontaneity – or what would seem to be spontaneity – was necessary if the courtier's behaviour was not to appear laboured and contrived.[9] But there is also a social dimension to the ideal of seemingly effortless grace. To make it appear that everything the true courtier did was natural, it was helpful if his behaviour was based on habits acquired early in life, if they were the result of birth and breeding and not of conscious self-education and laborious learning. Thus the ideal of *sprezzatura* was much more of an obstacle to social climbers who wanted to succeed at court than the formal requirement of noble birth which the Count of Canossa pronounces indispensable in the *Cortegiano*,[10] not without being criticised by other participants in the discussion. If the ideal of a life lived in leisure and without working in any visible way was typical of the old-established noble elites of early modern Europe, then Castiglione's *Cortegiano* was indeed a perfect nobleman and would be inconceivable in a world where merchants, or for that matter, scholars set the tone.[11]

At the centre of the courtier's existence was his relationship with the prince, or as Castiglione puts it: 'the conversation which the courtier ought chiefly to bee plyable unto, with all diligence to get him favour, is the very same that he shall have with his prince.' But there is a problem here, for he adds, that the term 'conversation' may not be quite appropriate. Conversation presupposes equality but there can be no real equality between prince and courtier.[12] For Castiglione the relationship between courtier and prince nevertheless remained a reciprocal one; the courtier tries to gain the prince's favour but the prince's reputation also depends on the accomplishments of his courtiers.[13] They could therefore presume to be not only the prince's companions but also his teachers and instructors.[14]

Castiglione assumed that the prince was a member of the court society which was constituted by the conversation games of the courtiers, and no more, essentially, than the first nobleman among equals. But in the later sixteenth century this assumption became increasingly questionable. In later Italian tracts on the court, the relationship between the individual courtier, often depicted as a potential favourite, and the prince assumed an ever more prominent place: court society tended to fall apart because it could integrate neither the prince nor the ambitious would-be favourite. The individual courtier was no longer the prince's instructor – the sole objective of his actions was to win the prince's favour, to seduce him in a manner of speaking and to eliminate the other courtiers competing with him for influence and favour.[15]

The extent to which the coherence of court society was threatened under these circumstances is demonstrated, for example, by Lorenzo Ducci's tract *Arte Aulica* (1601). Ducci comes to the conclusion that there can be no real 'società' or society between courtier and prince because they both pursue only their own interests. There is no common good which they both accept as the norm governing their actions,[16] although the prince does owe rewards to the members of his entourage. Given the lack of coherence of court society, Ducci even wondered whether it was worthwhile for the courtier to gain access to the prince – normally the courtier's most important objective – for in conversation with the prince it was the ruler who could ask the questions and was therefore able to make his servants reveal their true thoughts much more easily than the other way round.[17] This was a remarkable insight but, in fact, Stephano Guazzo in his *Civil Conversation*, published several decades before Ducci's tract, had already come to the conclusion that princes were subject to no rules in their conversation with their subjects or courtiers. The actions of princes belonged to the sphere of the *arcana* and *occulta*, to the myteries of state, which remained incomprehensible to mere mortals. Not surprisingly, any conversation between the courtiers and the prince was problematic, given the enormous distance between the two sides.[18]

The French *honnête homme*

For the Italian authors of the late sixteenth and early seventeenth centuries a meaningful conversation between prince and courtiers, or even among the courtiers themselves, became increasingly difficult and the art of conversation had to seek refuge within the walls of learned academies or in the *salon*.[19] Nevertheless, the tradition of tracts on the court and the courtier survived, but manuals for courtiers often tried to teach their readers only the specific skills required for bare survival at court. The ideal courtier now was not so much the civilised, graceful and universally talented nobleman, but the prudent man who carefully planned every move he made in the battle for favour and influence and whose real thoughts and feelings were concealed behind the impenetrable facade of absolute self-control, as in the writings of the Spanish Jesuit Gracián.[20]

On the other hand, civility, the art of appearing graceful and elegant, increasingly became the focus of a debate which addressed not so much the world of the court but 'good society', the social elite as such.[21] Models of behaviour first developed for the court by Castiglione were applied to domestic and social life in general, or rather the life of the nobility. Grace, dissimulation, affability and a certain nonchalance became qualities which were required of every nobleman and noblewoman, even outside the court. 'The court of the princes is reproduced in the families of the nobility.'[22] Instead of courtly conversation games, the wider problem of a conversation among and between the various estates of society becomes the central problem of later tracts on civility.

This process, which made qualities initially required of the courtier part of the habit and lifestyle of every nobleman, and to some extent noblewoman as well, was more or less completed in Italy by the end of the sixteenth century. In France, on the other hand, the *noblesse d'epée* had long remained a warrior caste which had largely rejected learning and the arts as effeminate and beneath their dignity (see above, pp. 70–1). French noblemen were well known for their brutishness and ignorance as late as the reign of Louis XIII.[23] There is, indeed, no doubt that the norms governing the behaviour of French noblemen changed to a very considerable extent between the late sixteenth century and the 1660s and that this change was particularly visible at court. In the 1580s Henry III, the last Valois, had tried – not always successfully – to prevent his own courtiers from looking over his shoulder while he read letters addressed to him, or from sitting on chairs which were reserved for his own use.[24] Under Louis XIII, in the 1620s and 1630s, much stricter and more formal rules of conduct already prevailed and they were further refined under Louis XIV.[25] Admittedly, this was a two-way process. Courtiers were required to show the utmost respect to the monarch on all occasions, but on the other hand, the king was also expected to observe certain rules of decorum. According to Tallemant des Réaux, Louis XIII had the habit of beating his *valets de chambre* – admittedly these were normally of non-noble origin for the very reason that this gave the king the opportunity to beat them without causing a scandal – whereas Saint-Simon found it worth recording that Louis XIV, in a moment of extreme anger, once thrashed a servant with a cane because he had dropped a dish.[26]

The new ideal of the civilised, self-controlled nobleman – although its origins lay, as we have seen, in polite urban society and the cultural ideals of the Catholic reform movement as much as in the court itself – was initially put forward by many writers as a prescription for success at court. Probably the most influential treatise of the early seventeenth century propagating this new ideal was Nicolas Faret's *L'honnête homme, ou l'art de plaire à la cour*. The term *honnêteté* denotes a behaviour which is at once polite, civilised and unpretentious. The *honnête homme* is a man of a certain social rank and prestige, that is, normally a nobleman, but who combines this with a certain level of education.[27] When Faret published his tract on the *Art of Pleasing at Court*, he deliberately avoided describing his potential readers as 'courtisans'. This term had been largely discredited in France by writers who had vehemently criticised the court in the late sixteenth century. 'Courtisan' had become a byword for dissimulation, moral and sexual depravity, effeminacy and the betrayal of French cultural traditions to the artificial innovations both in manners and speech associated with Italy.[28] Occasionally Faret spoke of 'sage courtisan', not just *courtisan*, to denote the good and virtuous courtier, but in general he preferred the term *honnête homme*.[29]

Faret's treatise was hardly a work of great originality. Long passages are no more than slightly modified free translations of Castiglione's remarks in his *Cortegiano*, but the very fact that Faret took Castiglione as his model, and not the contemporary Spanish treatises on the court, is significant in itself. The world described by Spanish manuals for courtiers has little room for women or love, whereas for Faret, as for Castiglione, court society was inconceivable without a strong female element.[30] Moreover, in Spain Gracián's 'discreto' gained internal freedom by concealing his real thoughts and his real self,[31] whereas Faret's *honnête homme* seeks a compromise between virtue and the need to please the prince and other courtiers, between his own personality and social constraints. Ideally Faret's *honnête*

homme was born a nobleman, not least because a courtier of non-noble origins could never feel at ease at court but would blush in the presence of his
social betters. [32] Indeed, in France he could not even expect to be presented
to the king (see below, p. 87).

The *honnête homme* had to be a man of many parts; not to be familiar
with arms and horses was unforgivable, but at the same time a modicum of
education and learning was indispensable. [33] To be successful at court he had
to gain the friendship of the *Grands* and of influential ladies. However, the
court itself – and this is an interesting admission – was not necessarily the
ideal place for conversation and finding friends. The 'circles' in the Louvre
had the great disadvantages that they were dominated by some grander per-
sonage, perhaps even the king himself, or that they were infiltrated by spies.
It was therefore preferable to go to town ('descendre à la ville') and visit the
salons of the most famous ladies ('les plus honnestes femmes'), 'et se mettre
dans leur intrigues'. [34]

Faret identified the *honnête homme* with the courtier, but he was forced
to admit that to find friends – both male and female – and patrons one might
have to leave the court at times. In the following decades the ideal of the
honnête homme, refined in the salons of Paris and by the noble *Frondeurs*
whose political ambitions had been shipwrecked in the early 1650s, increasingly lost its connection with the court. The *honnête homme*, who had been
a courtier seeking social advancement and a career in Faret's treatise,
increasingly became a man of honour, though not necessarily of high morals
in any conventional sense, cultivating his own personality in polite conversation in order to drive away the boredom (*ennui*) which was the price he
had to pay for the life of leisure which was such an essential precondition
for his cultural achievements. [35] This new conception of the *honnête homme*
is visible for example in the writings of the chevalier Meré. A provincial
nobleman, he had failed to make a career at court and sought consolation in
the thought that the real *honnête homme* was a man without any clear occupation or task in life, a man without 'metier' who turned his life into a work
of art and thereby became self-sufficient. [36] Thus in France as in Italy, but
much later, a particular style of conduct developed at court and for the
court became an extremely influential model of behaviour for noble society
in general. At times its aesthetic or ethical implications would even make it
incompatible with the real life of a courtier.

The political culture of the court

Treatises on life at court and satires or sermons against lewd and corrupt
courtiers both belong to an important theoretical discussion. [37] But what
political and social function did the courts of the late sixteenth and early
seventeenth centuries really have? The political culture of the early modern
court differed in specific ways from those of medieval courts. In the Middle

Ages the royal courts had competed with the households of the nobility. Admittedly this competition between different courts survived in Germany and to some extent in Italy. Elsewhere, after the middle of the seventeenth century the royal courts increasingly absorbed the formerly independent or semi-independent noble magnates and their affinities, although some of them continued to maintain substantial household establishments. This process of concentration meant that it became more difficult to find a hierarchy of rank and status which was acceptable for all men and women attending the court. The seventeenth-century courtier's obsession with rights of precedence and status originated at least to some extent in the fact that there was no longer a unified system of criteria which could be relied upon to determine the status of each individual, so that one continually had to reassert one's rank. Of course, there were seventeenth-century authors who maintained that if one wished merely to gain access to court society ancient lineage and nobility were of no great significance. In particular, in a foreign court it was quite sufficient to proclaim 'Je suis un gentilhomme étranger'[38] (I am a foreign nobleman), and one would be accepted in society, as one German handbook on behaviour at court claimed.

Other authors, however, were not so sure. A book on the imperial capital and court in Vienna warned the prospective visitor to the Habsburg residence that he would immediately be asked at court and in the aristocratic households associated with the court: 'Sir, are you a count, are you a baron, do you belong to an ancient family, do you have money?' And the author of this book advised his readers only half jokingly that it might be good a idea to have one's genealogical table ready to hand to present to inquisitive courtiers. Noblemen from so many different countries with their own traditions of defining noble status congregated in Vienna, which made it difficult to assess the rank of people one met in society. Vienna was perhaps an exception as far as the outspokenness of such questions was concerned.[39] Even in the more liberal Versailles, however, the full 'honneurs de la cour', which included for men the right to accompany the king on his hunting expeditions and for women the right to be presented to the monarch, were reserved for members of the ancient nobility.[40]

In the seventeenth century the court was, as we have seen (above, 11–16), at the centre of a process which redefined the notion of honour in many continental monarchies.[41] The honour and status of a nobleman no longer depended primarily on the informal respect of his equals or his betters, as it had still done in the early sixteenth century and continued to do in the case of the English gentry, but rather on the formal recognition of his rank and title by the prince and his legal agents. No early modern ruler could overturn the existing social hierarchy, but sovereign rulers increasingly claimed the authority to define status groups within this hierarchy and to endorse or reject claims for privileged positions in the existing system. And the court more than anywhere else was the place where these claims for status were assessed.

At the same time the political culture of the early modern court offers a pronounced contrast with important political and administrative developments of the same period, which are often seen as specifically modern. The tendency to transform informal political and social relationships based on mutual trust into fixed legal structures based on contracts and laws, and the development of more bureaucratic administrative institutions – so important for the development of the state in the early modern period – never really affected the rules of political life at court. Here conflicts were resolved in a much more informal way than in the courts of law, the conciliar bodies of the central administration or the assemblies of estates. In fact, one of the most important features of the court's 'political culture' was the lack of formalised legal procedures – apart, of course, from the court ceremonial.[42] The relationship between prince and courtier was never a contractual one: the courtier could never confront his lord with legal claims if he wished to be rewarded for his loyalty. On the other hand, he did not, *qua* courtier, receive orders, but was expected to adapt all his actions to the wishes of the prince without any formal command. When he received gifts and grants these were not a reward for a specific service but for his loyalty and friendship.[43]

Many textbooks of early modern history still present the royal or princely court essentially as a place where a once independent nobility was domesticated by an absolute monarch. Certainly, even at the time there were voices warning noblemen against subjecting themselves to the servitude of life at court.[44] The Italian literature on the court was probably the first directly to address all these issues and their implications, as the Italian courts had anticipated many of the developments which were later to form a common European standard. The argument that servility was the only way to success at court gained extra weight from the fact that the social status and prestige of household servants generally declined. Whereas at the beginning of the sixteenth century it was still normal practice for members of the lower nobility to serve personally in the households of great aristocrats, this came increasingly to be seen as demeaning in the seventeenth and eighteenth centuries, at least for men.[45] The position of the sovereign prince, who continued to be served by noblemen, thus became ever more exceptional, and critics of the court who saw the entourage of the prince as a place of servitude became correspondingly more vociferous.

Against such arguments, defenders of the court replied that courtiers, by their nature, were the ruler's friends not his servants, because they benefited from their position at court and received grants and gifts as a reward for their loyalty. A mere slave or unfree servant could never expect any reward at all.[46] Gifts and grants were indeed extremely important for giving court society the coherence which other forms of social interaction, such as conversation and sociability, could no longer provide in the later seventeenth century, when the idea that courtiers could be the ruler's instructors had lost all credibility. The distribution of grants at court was therefore never exclusively a means to satisfy the desire of courtiers for material rewards. It was also a means of enhancing the status of the recipient and of creating a social bond between ruler and the noblemen attending his court.[47]

The perfect courtier: the rise and fall of the favourite

Patronage was undoubtedly at the heart of court politics. The rise of favourites at court can to some extent be explained in the context of the politics of patronage, giving the favourite an important place as the central patronage manager whose dominance put an end to the chaotic struggle of competing factions for a place in the sun.[48] The influence achieved by individual courtiers who acted as virtual prime ministers, or, vice versa, by principal ministers who dominated the court, reflected the much closer relationship between court politics and government, both central and local, in the late sixteenth and seventeenth century. This new relationship was expressed in the role played by favourites during this period. In Spain the position of royal favourite or *valido* was almost institutionalised. A whole series of favourites rose and fell at the Spanish court during the seventeenth century. In the reign of Philip III (1598–1621) the Duke of Lerma acted as the king's virtual alter ego for about 20 years until his fall from favour in 1617. Under his successor, Philip IV, the Conde-Duque Olivares held a dominant position, until a series of political and military defeats forced him to relinquish power in 1643. He was succeeded by his nephew Don Luis de Haro, who was officially addressed as 'primer ministro' and directed Spanish policy until his death in 1661. Less eminent figures continued to exercise a dominant influence at the court of the last Habsburg King of Spain, Charles II (1665–1700), although none had quite the standing and power of their early seventeenth-century predecessors.[49] Spain was unusual in giving favourites an almost official position as the king's friends and most trusted advisors. In fact, even political theorists wrote tracts on the favourite in which his role was acknowledged as a potentially legitimate one. In Spain, court ceremonial created such a vast distance between the almost invisible monarch and the outside world that the king almost needed an alter ego to govern. Moreover, the nature of bureaucratic administration in Spain with its strict legal procedures created the need for a more flexible and at the same time more efficient power structure based on patronage and influence, and it was the favourite who organised and supervised this structure.[50] The *valido* brought 'court patronage and local clientelism ... within a single system of control'. From his clients he could expect a degree of loyalty and obedience which the king often failed to find among his own officeholders.[51]

The semi-official position of the Spanish *valido*, at the same time the king's friend and his first minister, was rarely paralleled outside Spain, with the exception of the papal cardinal nephew in Rome.[52] Some contemporary French writers tried to legitimise the position of the all-powerful cardinal ministers in the mid-seventeenth century with similar arguments.[53] At other courts, the favourite's position was much more precarious and ambivalent. In England the Duke of Buckingham, who was assassinated in 1628, had become notorious first as King James I's favourite and possibly lover, and later, during the reign of his son Charles I (1625–49), as the latter's all-powerful councillor and personal friend. In and outside parliament, Buckingham had been strongly criticised for the corruption for which his name stood, the sale of titles and offices and the patronage from which even his most distant relations and most humble clients benefited. In 1626 a formal impeachment (criminal proceedings before the House of Lords) had been initiated by the House of Commons. Charles I dissolved Parliament before Buckingham could be called to account, but the proceedings had demonstrated how deep the resentment went against the dazzling parvenu – Buckingham had been born into an ancient but impoverished gentry family – both among the nobility and the nation at large.[54] Buckingham's rise to eminence, owed exclusively to the King, seemed to deny older notions of noble honour which emphasised lineage and virtue but also inherited power and wealth.

In France, the reign of Henry III (1574–1589) first witnessed the full development of the phenomenon of the courtly favourite. The embattled monarch confronted by both radical Catholics and Protestants sought to re-establish royal authority by creating a personal affinity throughout the kingdom led by noblemen who were members of his entourage. Most of these men came from the 'noblesse seconde', locally powerful families which were nevertheless placed well below the great magnates, the princes of the blood and the *princes étrangers* in the noble hierarchy. The members of this royal patronage network dominated the court and were known pejoratively as the King's 'mignons', and the most powerful among them as 'archimignons'. As his enemies accused the King of having homosexual leanings, the word also acquired a sexual connotation. A satire on the royal court by Artus Thomas Sieur d'Ambry, published posthumously in 1605 as *L'isle des Hermaphrodites*, in fact depicted the King's court as a stronghold of sexual licentiousness and libertinage at which Italianised and homosexual noblemen celebrated the cults of Bacchus, Cupid and Venus and despised all true religion.[55] Whatever the truth of these rather doubtful accusations, the favourites did embody a cultural refinement inspired by Italian manners and fashion, one which was seen as alien and decadent by those who defended a more traditional, more rugged ideal of nobility.

On the other hand, the King deliberately tried to groom and educate his favourites so that they could serve as a model for the ideal nobleman: perfect warriors, but at the same time accomplished and sophisticated courtiers and, even more importantly, absolutely loyal and devoted to the King.[56] Some of the most eminent among this group of courtiers were elevated to the highest rank of the French noble hierarchy, that of *duc et pair*. Thus Anne de Joyeuse Baron d'Arques saw his Vicomté elevated to the status of a Dukedom (*duché-pairie*) in 1581. At the same the King arranged his marriage with Marguerite de Lorraine, the Queen's half-sister. Henry III henceforth addressed Joyeuse as brother-in-law and Joyeuse almost assumed the role of the King's spiritual son. The King also promoted marriage alliances among the families of his principal courtiers, with the intention of creating a close-knit kinship network headed by his minions which could compensate for the partial breakdown of official administrative and government structures during the Wars of Religion. In practice, however, the resentment and criticism which the *mignons* provoked often outweighed their political usefulness.[57]

Henry III's favourites had often been members of the titled provincial nobility, the 'noblesse seconde', and had acted as leaders of a royalist faction within noble society. Matters were to change in the seventeenth century. Concino Concini, who dominated the French court during the regency of Marie de Medicis (1610–17), was an Italian with few connections in France. Killed on the orders of the young king Louis XIII who hated his mother's favourite, he was replaced by Charles d'Albert Duc de Luynes, who reigned supreme until his death in 1621. He had been very much the King's personal friend, whereas the power of the cardinal ministers of the following decades, Richelieu (1624–42) and Mazarin (1642–1661), was of a different nature. Although Mazarin was accused of being the lover of Anne d'Autriche, the widowed Queen and regent of France, he and Richelieu were primarily statesmen and administrators. Their ascendancy was founded at least in part on their control of French foreign policy, an area in which secrecy became a decisive principle in the seventeenth century. For the developing political culture of the absolute monarchy, foreign relations were an essential part of the sphere of *arcana imperii*, the innermost sanctum of policy reserved for the monarch himself and his most trusted counsellor who, by definition, could only be an exceptional individual clearly separated from the other courtiers and officeholders. But at the same time, the difference between these new principal ministers and the older type of courtier favourites was less pronounced than it may seem. Although many historians are reluctant to see first ministers like Richelieu as favourites in the classical sense, for contemporaries, in particular those who resented the monopoly of power held by an individual, the parallel was obvious. Both Richelieu and Mazarin established a wide-ranging network of clients within the civil administration and the armed forces, while at the same building up a vast personal fortune. Despite their status as clergymen and the fact that the former hailed from a family of small provincial gentry and the other was a foreigner, they became noble magnates in their own right. This was an insurance policy against a possible fall from favour but also, as in Spain, an attempt to supplement the often less than totally efficient royal bureaucracy (staffed by men who had inherited or bought their offices) with a more personal power structure. Thus while opposing the more traditional noble magnates, they became members of the same social world, although their dependence on royal favour was much greater.[58]

Space does not permit us to treat the role of favourites at other courts here. At the smaller German courts non-noble officeholders or the ruler's personal secretaries frequently managed to control politics and patronage. There was often a pronounced tension between a bureaucratic central administration dealing with routine matters and the far less bureaucratic personal rule of the prince, and it was this tension which gave the ruler's personal secretary a chance to rise to the position of favourite.[59]

The power of the favourite who monopolised royal patronage and controlled access to the ruler was often resented by the nobility. The positions of First Gentleman of the Bedchamber and Master of the Horse, which both gave their holders almost unlimited access to the monarch, combined with the ability to deny it to others, were classical strongholds of the courtier-favourite. Unrest and rebellion among the nobility were sometimes a reaction to this lack of political equilibrium at court. But at the same time favourites like Joyeuse in France or Buckingham in England represented a new type of nobleman. First and foremost a courtier and largely dependent on royal favour, he was capable of exploiting the power and resources of the state for his own interests and those of his family.

Versailles and the French nobility under Louis XIV

The favourite's dependence on the monarch was particularly pronounced, but in some ways it was the common fate of all courtiers. It is therefore no surprise that the image of the court as a luxury prison of the aristocracy has survived so long. This image is often based on the quintessential Baroque court: Versailles, a court entirely focused on the person of the monarch whose majesty, authority and power were celebrated by every statue in the vast formal gardens and every fresco and painting in the endless series of apartments and galleries of this vast palace.[60] The courtiers surrounding the King were, it seemed, reduced to a state of political impotence; they were mere drones around an all-powerful monarch. By manipulating the rules of precedence and the etiquette of court life, the King, as the traditional account has it, diverted the political energies of his courtiers into inane status conflicts involving such questions as who was to hold the candlestick when the King went to bed.[61] The Duc de Saint-Simon, who lived for decades in Versailles without holding any office and knew all the details of court life, in his famous memoirs depicted Louis XIV as a man of enormous vanity who pretended to be permanently accessible to all his subjects but hardly ever listened to their complaints or advice and did not even know the pedigree of the most important French aristocratic families. In Saint-Simon's eyes this was a truly unpardonable sin.[62] There had always been disappointed and embittered courtiers such as Saint-Simon; what was remarkable about this French peer was not only his talent as writer, but also the fact that he stayed on at court instead of retiring to his country estates as so many noblemen who had failed to gain the monarch's favour at court had done in the past. Clearly, for the high aristocracy, life in the provinces without the attractions and amenities and the sociability which both the court and the capital provided was no longer a real option during Louis XIV's reign.

However, one should not forget that Saint-Simon's account of life at court – for all its literary brilliance and richness of social detail – remains a jaundiced and somewhat one-sided interpretation of the court's role in early modern politics, as far as Versailles itself is concerned, and even more so if courts in other countries are taken into account. Although there were always notable exceptions, it is certainly true that the style in which most of Europe's rulers governed in the later seventeenth century was designed to create the impression that the prince was all powerful and enjoyed unlimited prerogatives. Undoubtedly the trappings of court culture and the elaborate etiquette which governed the life of the courtiers were essential to create this impression. In many ways the so-called absolute monarchies of this period were theatre states in which the dramatic effect of ceremonial actions was at least as important as the reality of power. This fact immensely enhanced the importance of the court as the principal and, increasingly, the sole stage on which monarchs played their role, but it also limited their political function.[63]

The court was a place where favours were sought by and granted to noblemen and noblewomen. It often worked well enough as an instrument to satisfy the personal ambitions of the prince's most important subjects if the ruler was sufficiently astute as a patronage manager, and it could serve to defuse conflicts which were created by the ever present quest for place and profit. However, it worked much less well as a place for solving genuine political conflicts in which questions of principle or ideological issues were at stake. Such questions and issues, as a rule, could not be articulated openly at court because courtiers were not meant to discuss their master's policies, let alone to criticise him. Moreover the political culture of the court left little or no room for direct negotiations between monarch and subject because it was so much dominated by issues of status and hierarchy. As Peter Campbell has put it for early eighteenth-century France: 'negotiations would detract from the royal claims to absolute sovereignty and ... in a society where status was of vital importance if the crown stooped to open bargaining it effectively enhanced the prestige of the other party – for ever'.[64]

Despite such limitations the court was designed to meet the interests of the aristocracy much more than the traditional image of the court as the stronghold of absolutism has allowed, and in the final resort this was as true of Versailles as of other courts. After decades, if not indeed an entire century of political turmoil, Louis XIV certainly managed to achieve a degree of political stability which had eluded his predecessors. The *noblesse d'epée* and the princes of the blood and other noble magnates in particular accepted the King's authority. At the same time they were largely excluded from the central administrative councils and offices which were dominated by members of the *noblesse de robe*. The initially comparatively favourable financial situation after 1660 (corn prices were falling, thus enhancing the real value of the taxes collected by the Crown and reducing the income of the great landowners),[65] gave the King the opportunity to a create a new political balance in which his own power could no longer openly be challenged. The court certainly fulfilled an important function in this new scheme of things. It satisfied the desire of noblemen to have their own claims to status and prestige acknowledged by the King in person.[66] Living at court gave them access to the monarch, although the King's claim that he was always accessible was perhaps more rhetoric than reality. Although courtiers could freely approach the King on certain occasions – when he went to chapel for example – to be granted a formal audience was much more difficult, as the Duc de Saint-Simon pointed out.[67] However, not to be present at court doomed all suits for favours or grants to failure in advance, unless the petitioner held a high command in the army. When the Marquis de Châteaumorand, for example, who had never attended the court or served in the army was murdered by soldiers, Louis XIV remarked acidly: 'I know the house of Châteaumorand, but I do not know the Marquis'.[68]

In fact, the close connection between service in the armed forces and attendance at court is an important key to understanding the court's social and political function during the reign of Louis XIV. As recent research has shown, a disproportionately high number of colonels and other high-ranking officers in the French army after 1660 had previously served in the elite units which formed the *maison militaire du roi* or in other guard units immediately attached to the King. The very fact that these units were part of the royal household, and that the court's permanent move to Versailles had made life at court much more expensive than in the past, ensured that more positions than ever in these regiments and companies were in the hands of men representing the richest and most powerful noble families, although some of them were descended from judges and civilian officeholders, not from the traditional *noblesse d'epée*. These powerful noble families increasingly dominated the French army's officer corps during the reign of Louis XIV and benefited from the enormous expansion of the armed forces after 1660 which created vast new areas of patronage.[69] And members of these same families also dominated the court society at Versailles to such an extent that some historians have depicted the court as a waiting room for those about to die in action in the next campaign.[70] This may be rather too drastic a way of putting it, but as the years when the court was permanently fixed in Versailles after 1682 were also those when Louis waged almost continous war against his enemies, the military element of court life should certainly not be underestimated.

Louis XIV and his successors had ceased to fulfil the role of *roi con-*

netable; they no longer personally led their noblemen into battle, apart from a number of well-staged sieges over which Louis XIV presided in person. The expansion of the royal household and the attempt to transform the court into an all-powerful centre of social and cultural life, complemented by an expansion of the *maison militaire* as the stronghold of the higher echelons of the nobility, must also be seen as an attempt to create new ties of loyalty between the monarch and his vassals. This became necessary because a shared military life, which had been of considerable importance in the sixteenth century and as late as the reign of Henry IV, could no longer provide such ties to the same extent as in the past.

Germany and the imperial court

Whatever the situation in Versailles, the French court was in many ways rather atypical. Court life in central Europe, in the Holy Roman Empire, for example, followed different rules. Germany was not dominated by one court but had a great variety of princely residences. There were about 15 to 20 courts of some importance in the Empire in the mid-seventeenth century, from the great electoral households such as the Bavarian court in Munich or the Wettin court in Dresden, down to the more modest courts of the Landgrave of Hesse-Darmstadt or the Duke of Brunswick-Wolfenbüttel. The courts of ecclesiastical rulers must be added to this figure. The same person might hold more than one benefice; thus the Archbishop of Cologne was, after 1648, often at the same time Prince Bishop of Münster and Paderborn. Nevertheless there were normally still about half a dozen major residences of ecclesiastical rulers in late seventeenth-century Germany.[71]

With such great variety the ambitious German nobleman at least in theory had a real choice if he wanted to pursue a career at court. The less powerful princes, or those who did not get on with the native nobility of their own dominions, deliberately recruited 'foreigners' as courtiers, that is, either German noblemen from outside their own principalities, or non-Germans such as Italians or Frenchmen.[72] Thus Frederick William of Brandenburg, the Great Elector (1640–88) and his son Frederick I, the first King of Prussia (1688–1713), tried to attract high-ranking aristocrats from outside the heartlands of the Prussian dynasty – Brandenburg, Pomerania and Eastern Prussia – to their court.[73] To have a genuine count of the Empire serve as Lord Chamberlain or President of the Privy Council was a sign that one could compete, at least to some extent, with the most glamorous and powerful court in the Holy Roman Empire, the imperial court. At the same time, the presence of aristocrats of high status at court was also a means of creating an extra-territorial network of clients. Later, under Frederick William I and Frederick the Great, this strategy was abandoned. In fact, Frederick William dissolved his father's enormous household establishment after 1713 and restricted expenditure on the royal household to the bare essentials.[74]

Other rulers, however, who were unable or unwilling to create an army as powerful as the Prussian one, persisted in spending enormous sums on their courts in the eighteenth century. In smaller or medium-sized principalities the cost of the princely household could grow to preposterous dimensions and often accounted for as much as 50 per cent of public expenditure, in particular in territories which spent little or no money on a standing army. In larger states and principalities with military ambitions the court consumed a comparatively smaller percentage of revenues, but even here it was quite common for 25 per cent of all public expenditure to be spent on court and household. Only those states which enjoyed the status of a major European power devoted a much smaller proportion of their revenues to the court. The Habsburg monarchy probably spent no more than about 12 per cent in the early eighteenth century and this share decreased during the following decades.[75] Even if they did not succeed in creating links of patronage with noble families outside their principality – the presence of Italian or French noblemen at German courts, for example, hardly ever paid such political dividends – the luxury and glamour of a large and splendid court enhanced their prestige. And in the age of the Baroque, when questions of rank and prestige were of paramount importance, this seemed an end well worth pursuing.

Among the various German courts, that of the emperor held a special position. Not only was the emperor the ruler to whom all German princes owed fealty as liegemen, at least in theory, but for those princes of the Empire who could not hope to play a truly independent role on the European stage – and very few ever managed to realise this ambition – the emperor's support and favour remained essential, at least in moments of crisis when they were confronted by rebellious subjects or unduly litigious or belligerent neighbours. Thus the imperial court was, even after 1648, in a very real sense one of the political centres of the Empire, at least as important as the seat of the imperial diet, which was permanently in session in Regensburg after 1663. Of course, the ruling members of the major princely dynasties of the Empire had, as a rule, long ago ceased to serve at the imperial court themselves.[76] During the reign of Rudolf II (1576–1612) there were still a number of exceptions to this rule. Duke Heinrich Julius of Brunswick, for example, went to Prague in 1607 to further his legal claims in a number of disputes which were to be decided by the Imperial Aulic Council. During his stay in Prague he became a member of the imperial entourage and the Privy Council and, finally, the president of this body.[77] This was an exceptional career even for the early seventeenth century, but if the heads of princely dynasties were hardly ever permanent members of the imperial household in the seventeenth and eighteenth centuries, younger sons or members of non-ruling cadet branches continued to enter the service of the emperor. Although they did not necessarily hold offices in the imperial household, they nevertheless took commissions in the imperial army and attended the court. But essentially, aristocrats of high status from outside the Habsburg hereditary dominions, serving in the imperial household or in the central administration of the Habsburg monarchy, tended to be of less exalted status; they were, for example, counts of the Empire, not princes. Sometimes, however, their families were raised to princely status in the later seventeenth or eighteenth centuries, often as a reward for their services.[78]

But the imperial court was not only a centre of the Empire. It was also the essential point of contact for the politics of the Habsburg monarchy, the imperial hereditary lands comprising Austria, Bohemia, Moravia, Silesia and – enjoying a special status – the Habsburg-controlled parts of Hungary.[79] More than other parts of Europe, these countries were dominated, as we have seen, by an elite of noble magnates who owned vast latifundia and ruled over substantial numbers of peasant farmers who were often serfs (see above, chapter 2, pp. 44–9). Moreover, at least until the mid-eighteenth century, local and regional government was also controlled by the aristocracy. Urban elites and non-noble officeholders were rarely able to compete with the traditional aristocracy, given that, with few exceptions, towns had never enjoyed the same degree of economic and political autonomy in east-central Europe as they had further to the west. Throughout the seventeenth century the emperor was financially dependent on his aristocracy and their willingness to lend him money; for the Habsburg monarchy a state of financial chaos and near bankrupty was not the exception but the rule for most of the time.[80] Thus between 1648 and the mid-eighteenth century, the imperial court in Vienna was certainly less a stage where an absolute monarch had his acolytes dance to his tune, than a place where nervous creditors kept a watchful eye on their principal debtor whose lack of solvency gave considerable cause for concern.[81]

In Vienna the status most coveted by courtiers was that of a count or, even better, prince of the Empire. Once a family had reached princely status, however, its members sometimes reduced their presence at court. They tended to prefer maintaining their own glamorous households in the provinces where their estates were situated, unless they managed to occupy one of the few top offices at court, such as Lord Great Master of the Household (*Obersthofmeister*) or Lord High Chamberlain (*Oberstkämmerer*).[82] In fact, until the early eighteenth century, princes such as the Liechtensteins, Lobkowitz or Schwarzenbergs had been visibly reluctant to accept a position within the hierarchy of household offices at court which might endanger their claim to take precedence over all other courtiers. Only in 1745, when Maria Theresia threatened to deny the princes the right of access to her apartments at court unless they – at least nominally – held an office in the household, did the princes seek appointment as Gentlemen of the Privy Chamber or Bedchamber.[83]

The basic social and political structures of the Habsburg monarchy gave the imperial court its special character which was clearly visible even in its buildings and outward appearance. Until the eighteenth century and beyond, the emperor's entourage continued to be housed in the old Hofburg, a decidedly unassuming and partly medieval castle straddling the walls of the capital city. Not until the reigns of Joseph I (1705–11) and Charles VI (1711–40) was a major rebuilding programme undertaken. Although Charles extended and cautiously 'modernised' the Hofburg, the Habsburgs had no palace which could compete with Versailles. Schönbrunn, outside Vienna, was not much more than a summer residence, and did not become the principal residence until after 1740.[84]

In fact, the palaces built by great noble magnates on or near their estates and their palatial town houses in Vienna itself, the latter constructed principally after the victory over the Turks in the 1680s, were in many ways more flamboyant and impressive than the rather old-fashioned Hofburg or the emperor's other palaces. No Austrian nobleman needed to fear incurring the ruler's displeasure by building vast and extravagant palaces, whereas Louis XIV had his minister of finance, Fouquet, dismissed and arrested in 1661, not least because he had dared to construct a country house, Vaux-le-Vicomte, which outshone many royal residences.[85] Things were different in Vienna. When the Habsburgs chose to demonstrate their authority on great ceremonial occasions or through works of art or architecture, religion almost always dominated. The piety of the emperor and the entire Casa d'Austria seemed to be their most important claim to eminence ever since Ferdinand II had wholeheartedly espoused the cause of the Counter-Reformation. The *pietas Austriaca* could never be praised enough by poets, musicians and preachers alike.[86]

Outside the purely religious sphere the Habsburgs had a tradition of supporting musical talent. The operas and concerts at court formed the basis of a musical culture which was superior in many ways to that at most other European courts outside Italy. In other respects the imperial court, with its bewildering mix of strict ceremonial rules – essentially based on the Spanish court ceremonial – and the somewhat rustic rudeness displayed by its courtiers on less formal occasions, was by and large a less important cultural centre than Versailles. Its influence on aristocratic culture was probably also more limited, although the court, where Italian was spoken almost as fluently as German and where many important positions were occupied by Italians in the later seventeenth century, fulfilled an important function in familiarising the Habsburg aristocracy with the Baroque culture of southern Europe.[87]

Conclusion

The function and role of the court at our period was ambivalent, as we have seen, and not free of contradictions. On the one hand, monarchs could use the court to educate and groom their nobility, or at least its politically and socially most important sections. The court could act as the breeding ground – literally in the sense that it was also an important marriage market where the monarch often arranged matches for his courtiers[88] – of a new sort of noble elite for which service and loyalty to the prince were the paramount values. Elizabeth I of England (in spite of the inadequate financial means at her disposal) and, a hundred years later, Louis XIV are examples of monarchs who were accomplished actors who for decades daily put on a successful 'show' at court, designed to reinforce the charisma of the monarchy and their own glory as rulers. Both created a cult of their own person – in Elizabeth's case with clearly erotic overtones – which many noblemen eagerly participated in at least initially, until, at the end of their reigns, frustration and boredom became all too visible among their courtiers.[89]

On the other hand, the court was also a place where inherent tensions between competing noble factions, but also between ruler and nobility, surfaced, although the latter could hardly ever be openly articulated. If the monarch failed to keep rivalries bred at court under control, they could easily spill over into other political arenas and poison the atmosphere in assemblies of estates, law courts or administrative councils. There they could create an opposition to those individuals and factions who seemingly enjoyed the king's favour, and such an opposition could permanently paralyse royal or princely government. Both early Stuart England and the later decades of Louis XV's reign in France provide examples of this process.

Of all European courts in our period the Spanish one was probably governed by the strictest rules, ceremony and etiquette. At the same time, the Spanish monarchs after Philip II (d. 1598) were increasingly imprisoned in the golden cage of their own court ceremonial. They ruled but, as we have seen, the business of government was left to first ministers and favourites who were well advised to listen carefully to the wishes of the court aristocracy. Under Charles II (d. 1700), the weakest and last of the Habsburgs who ruled Spain, the aristocracy insisted more than ever that the monarch should receive the outward respect and reverence which the traditional rules of etiquette required. But in reality Charles was hardly more than a cipher in a court dominated by the magnates.[90] This late seventeenth-century example demonstrates sufficiently that the splendour of a well-ordered court centred on the cult of kingship and that of the monarch could present a mere facade concealing the realities of power. We shall return to this problem when looking at the role of the nobility in the process of state formation. However, it needs to be re-emphasised at this point that the political culture of the court did indeed transform noble honour and status by defining both in terms of the honours bestowed by the monarch more than in the past. But even this was a not a one-way process of strengthening the Crown

and reducing noble autonomy, for it created new demands and expectations on the part of the nobility which a monarch ignored at his peril if
he wanted to avoid noble unrest or even rebellion. In many countries
this was a real enough danger between the mid-sixteenth and the mid-
seventeenth centuries.

|5|

Resistance and rebellion

Introduction

In June 1619, during the revolt of the estates of Bohemia against the rule of the Catholic Habsburgs which had begun in May 1618 with the spectacular defenestration of Prague, Bohemian troops took up their positions before the walls of Vienna and threatened to lay siege to the city, the capital of the Habsburg dominions. Archduke Ferdinand of Austria, soon to be deposed as King of Bohemia, but also on the way to being elected ruler of the Holy Roman Empire, was forced to discuss their grievances with the angry representatives of the Lower Austrian Protestant nobility who were about to join forces with the Bohemian rebels. According to some reports, one of the Austrian noblemen, Andreas Thonradel, buttonholed Ferdinand during the audience in the Hofburg and shouted at him: 'Give in, Nandle, or you are done for!'[1] This story may indeed be apocryphal, but the later sixteenth and early seventeenth centuries frequently saw rulers involved in severe conflicts with their nobility, although few such conflicts ended in confrontations as close and as direct as the encounter between Ferdinand II and his liegemen in the Hofburg.

   In a number of European countries, and especially France, the century between 1560 and 1660 was a period of almost continuous noble unrest. Although not all major revolts and civil wars during this period were primarily noble rebellions in origin,[2] most of them, with the partial exception of the more traditional peasants' revolts, were at least to some extent caused by noblemen's resistance to royal or princely authority or led by noble magnates. This applies to the French Wars of Religion as much as to the English Civil War of the 1640s (at least in its initial stages) and the earlier rebellions in Scotland and Ireland, as well as to the Bohemian revolt in 1618–19, and the various provincial rebellions in the Spanish monarchy, in particular in Aragon in 1591 and in Portugal in 1640. Even the Dutch revolt, whose real

stronghold was in the cities of the Habsburg Netherlands with their tradition of urban autonomy, was led by a noble magnate, William Prince of
Orange-Nassau, and would hardly have been successful without the support
of substantial sections of the noble elite in the rebellious provinces.

Prima facie, the religious conflicts of the age provide the easiest explana-
tion for the series of noble revolts between 1560 and 1660. The outbreak of
the French Wars of Religion (1562), the Dutch Revolt (1568) and the
Northern Rebellion in England (1569) can certainly to some extent be
explained in this way. The Bohemian revolt or the English Civil War, and
even more so the risings against the government of Charles I in Scotland
(1638) or Ireland (1641), in many ways correspond to the same pattern.
However, religious grievances are either entirely absent or much less prominent in the French *Fronde* (1648–53) or the Spanish provincial rebellions
mentioned earlier, and the same holds true for many minor rebellions such
as the Essex revolt in England (1601). Traditionally, historians have also
seen noble rebellions as a response to the growth of the early modern state
and the increasing influence of its officeholders, often university-trained
men of non-noble birth, which tended to reduce the power of the nobility.
Although there is certainly some truth in this, one should not assume that
kings and princes systematically tried to undermine noble power or that, on
the other hand, noblemen were normally interested in being ruled by a weak
rather than a strong prince. Both assumptions are questionable. Few early
modern monarchs were opposed to noble power as such. In fact, most
remained very conscious of the fact that kingship or princely rule was only
the pinnacle of a social and political hierarchy unsustainable without a
powerful hereditary nobility. On the other hand, at least in the great monarchies of western Europe – the political culture of east-central Europe and
Scandinavia with their traditions of elective kingship was clearly different in
this respect – most noblemen and gentlemen (the great noble magnates
sometimes less so) saw royal or princely authority as the most important
safeguard of their own status and privileges and accepted that honour and
loyal service to the Crown were closely linked. Thus rebellion could, in fact,
be a response to weak rather than strong royal or princely government.[3]

Situations in which a regent or a council of regency took the monarch's
place or when access to the ruler was dominated entirely by one faction or
individual to the detriment of other noblemen, certainly created the classical
preconditions for a rebellion. Those who were cut off from royal or princely
favour feared that they would lose all credit with their own clients if they
were unable to make their influence felt at court and to defend local interests against outsiders. Opposition and open rebellion thus often seemed the
most obvious political option for restoring the prestige and political credibility of those who were out of favour with the sovereign. Under such circumstances taking up arms could well be a calculated risk, a move by which
the rebels tried to demonstrate their own political indispensability.
Rebellions could be a protest against evil counsellors and bad government.

They were supposed to demonstrate to the ruler that he would be well advised to seek the support of the very men and families who, for the time being, were refusing to obey his orders. Such armed protests could and did get out of hand and might end in protracted civil war or the defeat and execution of the rebels. But in some countries armed confrontations between noblemen and the official representatives of royal authority were still seen as part of a traditional political culture in which a limited amount of more or less ritualised violent conflict was acceptable, as least until the early decades of the seventeenth century. This is a point worth bearing in mind when analysing early modern noble revolt.

Religion and revolt

The most obvious cause of noble revolt in the later sixteenth and early seventeenth centuries was religion. As we have seen (above, pp. 61–7) by no means all noblemen were enthusiastic supporters of the emerging confessional Churches and denominations with their demands for strict religious observance and absolute loyalty. Many, at least initially, were lukewarm or refused to subscribe wholeheartedly to any one particular creed. But like those who refused to obey the ruling prince in religious matters because they feared for the salvation of their souls, they resented any religious settlement imposed from above which left them no personal choice. William of Orange (1533–87), the leader of the Dutch Revolt, is a good example of a nobleman who, without much personal religious commitment, became the leader of a revolt which was a fight for Protestantism as much as for political freedom – although for William the latter aspect was always more important than the former. William hailed from a German noble family, the Counts of Nassau. In the 1540s he inherited vast family estates in the Netherlands as well as the tiny sovereign principality of Orange in southern France. Potentially one of the richest noblemen in the Spanish Netherlands, he was royal governor of several provinces and one of the highest ranking courtiers in Brussels. However, having also inherited vast debts he was forced to marry rich and his choice fell on Anna of Saxony, the niece of the prince elector of this important German principality and daughter of Maurice of Saxony who had defeated Charles V in 1552. His marriage in 1561 to this Lutheran princess, although conctracted for financial not religious reasons, almost immediately made William *persona non grata* at the strictly Catholic Brussels court. Like other noblemen, he was opposed to the constitutional and administrative innovations introduced by Philip II (1556–98) in the Netherlands. When open revolt flared up against the Spanish government in the late 1560s, Orange, who would have been considered as potentially disloyal by the Spaniards anyhow, was the natural leader of the opposition – especially as other noblemen had been imprisoned or executed by the government. He was all the better qualified to lead this revolt as he was not only a count of the Holy Roman Empire, which was outside Spanish jurisdiction, but also, as ruler of the principality of Orange, a sovereign prince, and could thus legitimately wage war against his enemies. Until the very end of his life – he was murdered by a Spanish assassin – Orange fought for religious liberty which, in his opinion, should include toleration for loyal Catholics as much as for the inherited privileges of the Dutch provinces. Although later celebrated as a hero by Dutch Calvinists, his political actions were motivated much more by secular than religious concerns: the conviction that the Spaniards would reduce noblemen like him to the status of mere subjects, his pride as a prince and as a count of the Empire and loyalties based on kinship and personal friendship which transcended the confessional divide.[4]

The Dutch Revolt demonstrates how inextricably religious and constitutional questions were linked in the later sixteenth and early seventeenth centuries. A ruler who against the wishes of his nobility and other privileged subjects could enforce religious conformity could, a fortiori, also ignore ancient liberties and privileges and neglect the advice of his estates. A man such as the Duke of Alba (1507–1582), who tried to suppress Protestantism in the Netherlands, was seen not merely as an enemy of the reformed religion but of the traditional balance of power between prince and estates as well. The excesses which fanatical Catholics committed against Huguenots in France in the early 1570s during the St Bartholomew's Day Massacre and the following years were seen not just by Protestant noblemen but also by many moderate Catholics as an attack on the nobility as such (see below, pp. 109–10).

Constitutional and religious questions were also closely entwined elsewhere in Europe in the late sixteenth and seventeenth centuries. When the Catholic Sigismund Vasa was crowned King of Sweden in 1594, he had to concede an accession charta which granted the estates extensive rights. Such concessions were seen, *inter alia,* as a necessary safeguard for the Lutheran Church. Initially the nobility had, in fact, tried to restore the constitutional arrangements of the fifteenth century, which would have given them a monopoly of all higher offices and would have emasculated royal authority permanently. However, Sigismund Vasa, who was also King of Poland, was deposed in February 1600 and his kinsman and successor, Duke Charles of Södermanland, saw to it that royal authority was maintained. Yet the political influence of the nobility and the Lutheran Church remained much greater than in many other countries.[5]

Religious commitment could certainly lead noblemen energetically to defend constitutional arrangements which seemed to provide a safeguard for the established religion. If the survival of parliament was so important to many members of the English peerage and gentry in the seventeenth century, this was to a considerable extent because parliament seemed to be the only institution capable of preventing the granting of full-scale toleration to Catholics or, even worse, the re-Catholicisation of the country. For religious minorities, on the other hand, such as the English Catholics themselves after 1558, an alliance with foreign powers, in this case Spain, was an ever-present temptation. Nevertheless England was spared the turmoil of a religious war in the sixteenth century. The only major revolt by Catholic noblemen, the Northern Rebellion of 1569–70, was soon suppressed. The revolt was led, although somewhat reluctantly, by the Earls of Northumberland and Westmorland, the greatest magnates in the north of England, and had been fuelled by religious as well as political grievances against the Protestant regime of the Tudor Queen, Elizabeth I. The earls faced the alternative of either losing all credit with their clients and friends if they submitted unconditionally to Elizabeth, or of being imprisoned by the Queen who suspected them of treason and had already sent Westmorland's brother-in-law, the Duke of Norfolk, to the Tower. They knew that open revolt had little chance of success, but saw no honourable way out of the political dilemma they faced. They demanded that Mary Queen of Scots, then a refugee in England, be officially recognised as heir to the English Crown and be allowed to marry a Catholic. However, the rebellion was half-hearted from the start and its defeat marked the end of the special role of the northern counties as a stronghold of aristocratic influence. Elizabeth made sure that the power of the great northern magnate families, the Percies, Nevilles and Dacres, already in decline before the revolt, was finally broken. The days of the traditional regional revolt led by aristocratic magnates who mobilised their tenants, clients and kinsmen were numbered in England even before 1569.[6]

Although the English peerage and gentry were more than capable of using the weapons of litigation, passive resistance to taxation and parliamentary obstruction against unpopular royal policies, armed rebellions seemed to be a matter of the past by the early seventeenth century, as the failure of the Essex Revolt of 1601 (see below, pp. 113–14) had demonstrated. It was significant that Charles I (1625–49), who favoured a highly ritualised version of Protestantism which to many strict Protestants seemed to be merely popery in disguise, did not meet any armed resistance in England until the other two Stuart kingdoms, first Scotland in 1638–9 and later Ireland in 1641 (see below, pp. 121–2) rose in revolt against his rule. In Scotland, Charles I and his Scottish bishops had tried to change the structure and liturgy of the Calvinist Scottish Kirk to bring it into line not just with the Church of England but also with the King's own very personal ideals of a hierarchical Church celebrating its mission in sacramental acts of worship appealing to the faithful by their sacred beauty. There was little room left for the rousing hell-fire sermons which had formed such an important part of the traditional Calvinist church service. Moreover, Scottish noblemen who had acquired former ecclesiastical estates feared for the security of their property, since in an Act of Revocation issued in 1625 Charles had declared his intention to review the transfer of ecclesiastical lands which had taken place over the past 80 years.

The National Covenant formed in 1638 was a sort of sacred bond uniting all Scots, though led by noblemen and the Calvinist clergy. It rejected the religious and constitutional innovations which Charles had imposed on his native country since the beginning of his reign. The pristine Calvinist Church settlement of the early 1580s was to be restored in every detail and the absentee king was to be subjected to the tightest controls by the rejuvenated Scots Parliament and the General Assembly of the Kirk. Thus the Covenanters pursued a constitutional as well as a religious agenda, but undoubtedly religion and the right of resistance invoked in the name of the true faith provided the unifying elements for a movement which otherwise would have been too heterogeneous to be effective.[7]

In England the opposition to Charles I lacked such a unifying religious ideal. Although those who disliked the politics of the Personal Rule (1629–40), when Charles I had ruled without parliament, were united in their distaste for 'popery', some were quite prepared to accept the existing Church settlement provided the power of the bishops was reduced and control of parliament over Church matters strengthened. Others, however, preferred some sort of Presbyterianism and others again wanted to dissolve the national Church altogether and grant religious toleration to a variety of Protestant sects. Yet although the English Civil War of the 1640s was not a religious war in the strict sense of the word, Charles I's eagerness to recruit Catholic support for his cause both in England, abroad and, worse still, in Ireland, led many moderate gentlemen who would otherwise have sided with the King to fight for Parliament.[8] Royalist peers and gentlemen, on the other hand, found to their dismay that the 'common sort' often had a mind of their own and in a number of counties refused to follow the lead of their betters in the fight for King and established Church (or the particular variety of churchmanship the King favoured).[9]

Forty years later, in the 1680s, the threat posed by popery was in many ways much more tangible than in the early seventeenth century. James II (1685–88) was indeed an ardent Catholic. After attempts to exclude him from the succession to the Crown had failed in the 1670s, his position seemed fairly secure when he finally became King in 1685. However, his policy of favouring his co-religionists – often men of little social standing – in all appointments, as officers in the army, as Justices of the Peace and in many positions of influence in Ireland, where such issues were particularly explosive, soon undermined the support of moderate, conservative Protestants which he had initially enjoyed. The Glorious Revolution was as much an attempt to defend the existing social order in England, Scotland and Ireland in the interests of aristocracy and gentry alike against the ambitions of Catholic or generally non-Anglican outsiders and social upstarts, as it was an attempt to defend the religion by law established.[10]

In spite of the prominent part religion played both in the British civil wars of the period 1638–51 and in the Glorious Revolution, England, unlike France, was spared the horrors of a full-scale religious war (although conflicts in Ireland and Scotland were a different matter). France was engulfed by a series of ferocious civil wars after 1562, which were not to end until Henry IV managed to reach a comparatively stable settlement in 1598. Recent research has re-emphasised the genuinely religious character of the conflict which tore France apart.[11] It therefore needs to be stressed that the active participation of the nobility, or at least of certain sections of the nobility, in the war cannot be seen as its primary cause, but it certainly gave the confrontation its special character. Admittedly, as historians have emphasised recently, in most French regions, the majority of noblemen seem to have preferred to stay neutral or give their support to the King rather than to the religious extremists of either side. In any case, only a minority of noblemen saw active military service on a more permanent basis during the second half of the sixteenth century, perhaps not more than 15 per cent. For France as a whole, therefore, the active supporters of the Catholic League in the 1580s and 1590s would represent less than 3 per cent of the entire French nobility. This was slightly less than half as many as fought for the King, although the League certainly enjoyed greater support in some key provinces such as Brittany or Burgundy, for example.[12] Although other noblemen participated in local raids and armed confrontations, these figures put the phenomenon of noble violence and noble rebellion during the Wars of Religion into perspective.

However, as those who actively engaged in the war were often the wealthiest and most powerful, this active minority could and did play an important political and military role. In fact, without denying the importance of religious divisions in causing the outbreak of violence in the 1560s, neither the Huguenots nor their Catholic opponents would have been able to deploy any significant degree of military power if influential noblemen had not been prepared to lead and support the religious parties. Their willingness to do so was certainly motivated to some extent by genuine religious conviction, but political ambition and the grievances they nursed against the Crown or rival noble factions also played an important part.

The premature death of Francis II in 1560 marked the beginning of a political crisis. His successor, Charles IX, born in 1550, was a minor and the regency was in the hands of a woman born outside France, Catherine de Medici, the King's mother. Royal authority was thus crucially weakened at a time when increasing religious tensions created an explosive atmosphere. Influential members of the French nobility under the leadership of the Condé line of the Bourbon dynasty, a distant cadet branch of the royal family, resented the influence the Duke of Guise and his relations had obtained at court. Among noblemen, the decision to support the cause of the reformed faith was at least to some extent an expression of a more widespread discontent. Many feared that the increasing influence of university-trained officeholders of non-noble origin would threaten their privileges and status, which the Crown was trying to control more thoroughly than in the past anyhow. Among the supporters of the Protestant cause in Normandy, for example, noblemen who felt their position threatened by the royal *recherches de la noblesse*, which required them to provide documentary evidence of their status, seem to have been over-represented.[13]

While the Crown pursued a policy which created potential conflicts with noble interests, it showed at the same time dangerous signs of political weakness. It had already become obvious in the late 1540s that it was no longer fully capable of containing tensions between noble factions.[14] The Crown tried to secure the loyalty of local elites by generously distributing favours, but again, the ensuing delegation of royal authority to local magnates had dangerous consequences. 'This decentralisation of power, allied to existing discontent with the Crown, undermined monarchical authority and contributed to political instability', as Stuart Carroll has put it.[15] Tensions between the various factions of the court nobility, already visible in the 1540s, mounted in the 1560s. With the ascendancy of the Guises, a single family seemed to have obtained a monopoly of influence at court after 1560. Finally, whereas the wars Francis I and Henry II had pursued abroad had provided an outlet for noble violence, the absence of such foreign campaigns after 1559 concentrated the warlike energies of the more enterprising members of the noble estate on domestic conflicts. In fact, it has been argued that the appeal to religious loyalties by some noble magnates, for example the governors of the French provinces, was an attempt to curb noble violence. By defining noble honour with reference not only to royal service but to a religious cause, the more individualistic notion of honour favoured by many noblemen could be subordinated to higher principles, and duels, for example, could thus be curbed.[16] Obviously, however, in a country divided between two religious denominations, a high price had to be paid for this redefinition of noble honour, which defused existing tensions by creating new ones. The same was true for the attempt of noble magnates to reinforce the increasingly brittle ties of clientage between themselves and lesser noblemen by appealing to religious loyalties.[17] On the other hand, one has to bear in mind that the traditional noble ties of solidarity between members of the same kinship networks were often strong enough to survive even when brothers or cousins fought on different sides. In fact, some contemporary observers thought that noble families deliberately placed their sons on different sides as a sort of insurance policy against the vagaries of war. In this way, at least one brother was always sure to be on the winning side.[18]

During the initial stages of the Wars of Religion a vague but widespread noble discontent and tensions between rival noble factions had fuelled the conflict, but noble grievances became more pronounced as the war went on and the Crown tried to reassert its authority. The harsh measures which Philip II of Spain took against noblemen who dared to oppose his authority in the nearby Netherlands in the late 1560s (an example which many feared would soon be followed in France), and, more dramatically, the mass slaughter of Protestant noblemen during and immediately after the St Bartholomew's Day Massacre in 1572, created widespread anxiety. Not only Protestants but also moderate Catholics feared a conspiracy against the entire French nobility. Anti-royalist propaganda often stressed not so much the religious aspect of the conflict but the alleged desire of the Queen Mother, Catherine de Medici, and her son Charles IX to abolish the ancient liberties of the French nobility. Protestants as well as moderate Catholics who opposed this tendency and wished to preserve the kingdom's ancient constitution appealed to the Estates General and invoked a fundamental right of resistance to rulers who acted as tyrants by, for example, murdering their own subjects.[19] For a moment, the ideal of a mixed monarchy where the power of the king and the rights of the estates were balanced enjoyed a certain popularity among the French nobility, and not only among Protestants. The Crown was confronted with a united opposition consisting of the great majority of French noblemen during the period 1574–76. Soon, however, religious and political divisions resurfaced and the Protestants realised that they could not obtain a majority in the Estates General.[20]

Moreover, with the increasing likelihood from the early 1580s that neither Henry III (1574–89) nor the other surviving members of the royal dynasty would produce a Catholic heir to the throne, the succession of Henry of Bourbon, King of Navarre, first prince of the blood and a Protestant, became a distinct possibility. Whereas the Protestants were now gradually reconciled to the more traditional forms of strong royal government, the more extreme Catholics took an increasingly critical position towards the monarchy. A Catholic confederation, the League, had already been formed in 1576 when Henry III seemed to be pursuing a policy that was too tolerant towards the Protestants, but the objectives of the second League, created in 1584 under the leadership of the Guises, were more radical. Essentially, it rejected the traditional law of succession; only a sincere Catholic, the supporters of the League argued, could become king of France. Henry III was increasingly seen as a tyrant because he co-operated with the King of Navarre, a heretic, tried to deny the Catholic high nobility its rightful influence in the royal council, and had given power and rewards to his personal favourites, the *mignons* (see above, pp. 90–1), and to foreigners, in particular Italians. The League took an ever more violent anti-royalist position, especially after Henry III had the two leading members of the Guise family, Henri de Lorraine Duc de Guise, and his brother Louis, a cardinal, killed in 1588 by his personal guard, known as the Forty-Five, a group of noblemen from the Gascogne. When the King himself was murdered by a monk a year later, theologians associated with the League presented the assassination as the rightful execution of a tyrant.[21]

In the struggle against Henry III and, after his death, against his successor, Henry IV, noble resistance to a heretical ruler reached its climax, but also its limits. On the one hand, the Guises pursued the traditional policy of a major noble dynasty. They, or at least the main branch of their house, the Dukes of Lorraine, were clearly toying with the idea of claiming the French Crown for themselves, supported by Spain but, if needs be, also in alliance with German Protestant princes. As they, like the Valois and the Bourbons, were descended from Charlemagne, such a claim was not entirely implausible.[22] But on the other hand, they allied themselves with radical religious and social movements in the towns of northern France, and in Paris in particular. These movements demonstrated an extremely hostile attitude not only towards the well-established royalist members of the *noblesse de robe* but also towards all noblemen who were Protestants or just refused to support the religious extremism of the League.[23] In a contemporary pamphlet, the *Dialogue between the Courtier and the Townsman*, the supporter of the League accused the French nobility of fighting for a relapsed heretic, Henry IV, who only pretended to be a Catholic. But this is not really surprising, for 'who has fought against God's authority and his commandments from the beginning of the world, and has oppressed the people as a tyrant, if not Nimrod and his noble followers', just like the new Nimrod, Henry IV. In vain does the courtier reply, that, as a nobleman, he was bound by his oath of allegiance to support the King, as long as he appeared to be Catholic, and if he went to mass, one had no right to question his sincerity. ('Je le vois aller à la messe, et consequemment je croys qu'il est catholique.') Should a nobleman act against his oath of allegiance he would be forever dishonoured ('à jamais infames').[24]

The radical rejection of a specifically noble ethos which refused to accept religious orthodoxy as the only moral and political standard, apparent in this dialogue, was not shared by all supporters of the League. In fact, noble members of the League emphasised that the king and the princes were essentially only members of the noble estate, elevated by their fellow noblemen to their positions of pre-eminence. 'Ce sont les Gentilshommes qui ont élu et créé les Rois: et non les Rois la Noblesse' ('it is the noblemen who have elected and created the kings, and not the kings the nobility').[25] Catholic authors now toyed with the idea of an elective kingship, as in Poland or Germany, which had already appealed to the Protestants in the 1570s. Equally, the autonomy of the French provinces, in particular those which had only become part of the royal demesne at the end of the Middle Ages, such as Burgundy or Brittany, was strenuously defended against all attempts at centralisation.[26] These ideas may have found support among a wider circle of noblemen, even those who did not belong to the traditional clientèle of the Guise, but many members of the nobility rejected the radical overtones of the League's propaganda campaign. Increasingly, pamphlets emanating from the circle of clergymen and intellectuals who led the urban League argued that only those who wholeheartedly supported the Roman Church and cut all ties of loyalty binding them to heretics or less fervent Catholics could really claim noble status. Virtue and religious zeal were the real foundations of social prestige, not lineage.[27]

This was no mere theory. Peasant revolts in the countryside, which some saw as an attempt to turn France into a sort of Switzerland writ large,[28] and the reign of terror exercised in the capital by the 'Sixteen', the governing

body of the Parisian League, dominated by small advocates and officeholders, threatened to undermine the entire social order. Or at least many noblemen perceived these events in this light. The majority of the nobility were
therefore happy enough to come to terms with Henry IV once he had converted to Catholicism in 1594. Only the peripheral provinces such as
Brittany, Picardy and Bourgogne, where the position of the Guises had been
strongest, held out longer. But in the end even the Guises made their peace
with the new King.[29]

During the Wars of Religion important sections of the nobility had openly
opposed the monarchy, if not permanently then at least for long periods. In
the end, however, the idea of a mixed monarchy based on contractual obligations appealed as little to the majority of the French nobility as did the religious fanaticism, with its dangerous overtones of social revolution espoused
by the extremists on both sides of the confessional spectrum. Given that the
Estates General remained a very unwieldy political instrument, the magnates as much as the middling ranks of the nobility, which the Crown had
tried to strengthen during the wars in an attempt to counter the power of the
Grands in the provinces, preferred to come to an informal arrangement with
the Crown. This was based on ties of personal loyalty and the sovereign's
traditional obligation to reward his servants, and lacked clear constitutional
safeguards. The question of whether this informal arrangement constituted
a victory for absolutism will be addressed in the next chapter.

Whereas in France it took the Crown almost forty years to reach a lasting
and halfway stable religious settlement which put an end to religious strife,
open religious revolt in the Habsburg dominions in the early seventeenth
century was a much more short-lived affair. The long-standing political and
religious tensions in Bohemia and the other dominions of the Habsburg
monarchy, which went back to the early sixteenth century when the
Habsburgs had come to power and to some extent even further, to 1417,
when the Hussites had risen against the Roman Church, culminated in open
rebellion in 1618. In May the leaders of the Bohemian estates had tried to
kill the regents who governed the kingdom for the absent Emperor Mathias
by throwing them out of the windows of the royal castle in Prague, the
Hradshin. The famous defenestration was an answer to the Emperor's
counter-reformation policy. When Mathias died in March 1619, the estates
deposed his successor designate, the ultra-Catholic Archduke Ferdinand
who had been crowned as Mathias's future successor in 1617.[30] At this
point there seemed to be a real chance to transform Bohemia and its neighbouring principalities into an aristocratic republic with an elected monarch,
perhaps more as a symbolic than a real head. Poland's constitutional development during the seventeenth century shows that this was more than a
mere utopia in eastern and east-central Europe. The Bohemians found support not only in Moravia but also in the ancient centre of the Habsburg
monarchy, in the Duchies of Lower and, even more so, Upper Austria as
well as in Hungary and beyond the borders of the monarchy, in

Transylvania. Archduke Ferdinand was ill-prepared to confront his rebellious subjects. Nevertheless, the Bohemian revolt was crushed within little more than a year. The support which Ferdinand received from his allies, Spain and Bavaria, was certainly of the utmost importance in helping him to achieve a swift victory. But the opposition to Ferdinand was never quite as strong and unified as it seemed. One of its inherent weaknesses was its inability to rally truly popular support, especially outside the towns. In the final resort, the interests of the nobility and the peasantry were difficult to reconcile. Many noblemen feared that a prolonged civil war would destroy the traditional political and social order, and were reluctant to take such a risk in resisting Ferdinand to the last ditch.

Imperial troops defeated the Bohemian army in the battle of the White Mountain near Prague on 8 November 1620. After the battle, the Catholic troops soon subdued the whole of Bohemia and Moravia, which was subjected to a savage campaign of repression that was to last for several years. The leaders of the Bohemian estates who had not been able to escape were executed. Protestantism was suppressed during the 1620s. Moreover, entire sections of the old-established elite were expropriated and their possessions distributed among Ferdinand's supporters or sold off to them at bargain prices. The nobility of Bohemia and the neighbouring principalities underwent a profound change as we have already noted (above, chapter 2, pp. 44–50) For the next two centuries the Austrian duchies, as well as Moravia and Bohemia, were to be dominated by a Catholic aristocracy of noble magnates with close links to the imperial court which shaped their mentality and culture.[31] Like the French Wars of Religion, the Bohemian rebellion demonstrated to what lengths noble unrest could go if combined with religious grievances. But it also underlined that without wider support among the elites of powerful cities and independent urban centres, which were absent from many regions of east-central Europe, or from the rural population, noble revolt was difficult to sustain against a dynasty which could draw on international connections and outside support.

Frondes and *Frondeurs*: the courtier turned rebel

In the summer of 1642, when English peers and gentlemen had to decide whether to fight for the King or for Parliament in the impending civil war, a surprisingly large number of those who had been among Charles I's highest ranking courtiers, men who held high office in the household or had done so in the past, sided with Parliament. This was true of Charles's Groom of the Stool (the official head of the Royal Bedchamber), the Earl of Holland, his Lord Chamberlain, the Earl of Pembroke, and his Lord Admiral, Northumberland. Even the Marquess of Hamilton, who had been the King's personal friend in the 1630s, proved unreliable, as did the Earl Marshal, the Earl of Arundel, who had advised the King on the purchase of works of art in the past and had commanded the English forces in the fight against the Covenanters in 1639.[32] Quite clearly these courtiers disagreed with official policy, or felt that to follow the King would be their personal ruin. Although this almost wholesale transformation of a group of courtiers into rebels or, at best, neutral bystanders is unusual in this period, there are more than enough examples of courtiers who, disappointed in their personal ambition or slighted in their pride and sense of honour, decided to join those who openly or secretly opposed official policy. Sometimes they did so in the hope of 'being bought off' by grants and offices; in other cases they had already fallen from favour so that going into exile or taking up arms seemed to be the only alternatives left. The history of the French monarchy between 1560 and 1660 offers many examples of such careers. In the early 1630s even the King's brother, the Duke of Orleans (at that time heir presumptive to the throne), and his mother joined rebellions against the King's first minister, Richelieu, and were forced to flee abroad.[33]

Up to the eve of the Civil War, the history of the English nobility seems in many ways less turbulent than that of its French counterpart in the same period, as we have already seen. Nevertheless, England provides an outstanding example of the courtier turned rebel in the guise of Robert Devereux, second Earl of Essex (1566–1601). Elizabeth I was for a long time remarkably successful in containing the corrosive side-effects of aristocratic ambition and rivalry. Although more than usually parsimonious in her distribution of grants, honours and titles, she knew well how to appeal to the chivalric traditions of the nobility and gentry which were consciously revived in the great tournaments staged at court and in the art and literature of the period.[34] In the 1570s and 1580s the political culture of Elizabethan England seemed to combine aristocratic honour and loyal service to the Protestant monarchy as its guiding principles without any apparent tensions. The Queen even managed to turn the potential weakness of her position as an unmarried female ruler into a strength by creating an image of herself as a heroic virgin queen, at once erotically alluring and chaste. However, this seemingly so successful symbiosis between aristocratic values and the ethos of the Protestant state became increasingly strained in the 1590s. Thirty years of obeying an astute but often moody ruler and the fact that Elizabeth was now clearly no longer a charming young woman had diminished enthusiasm for serving her. Moreover, contests over place and profit at court had become much more bitter in the last decade of Elizabeth's reign. One faction, the kinsmen and clients of William Cecil, Lord Burghley (d. 1598) and his son Robert had come to dominate the court.[35] Those who did not belong to this network found it increasingly difficult to obtain grants and favours from the Queen.

Younger courtiers who were dissatisfied with the 'regnum Cecilianum' and the Queen's all too cautious and seemingly inconsistent policies found their spokesman in a man who had once himself been one of the Queen's personal favourites, Robert Devereux, second Earl of Essex. He had begun his career at court in the 1580s with the help of his stepfather, the Earl of Leicester, the favourite of Elizabeth's early years. In the midst of military conflict with Spain, Essex became the patron of military virtue and tried to create a network of clients among the officers who served in Elizabeth's armies. Appointed Earl Marshal in 1597, he became the presiding officer of the Court of Arms (which dealt with disputes over titles, coats of arms and questions of social status) and thus officially the guardian of aristocratic honour. For Essex, serving the Crown in war took pride of place over any services which mere councillors or judges might render the queen. Essex wanted to redefine the English nobility and gentry as a primarily military elite, an ideal shared by a number of younger noblemen and gentlemen who felt that the armed forces needed to undergo a thorough reform if England were to vanquish Spain and be able to defend herself against her continental rivals.[36] For a long time the Queen's attitude towards Essex was ambivalent. Flattered by Essex's chivalrous admiration, she was also keenly aware of the fact that England's lack of financial resources and her haphazard military organisation made the activities of noblemen like Essex indispensable. The Earl spent a fortune on equipping his own military retinue and at times almost single-handedly kept the Queen's army going financially as well. At the same time, the way in which Essex used his military success to create a following among military men, dubbing knights on his campaigns without the Queen's prior consent, for example, was seen as objectionable and even as dangerous.

Yet Essex felt that his services, and those of his followers, were not sufficiently recognised and rewarded. True to older traditions of aristocratic patronage which were still very much alive in the remoter regions of the realm where Essex's local influence was greatest, especially in Wales, he felt that he would lose credit with his supporters and followers if he failed to get them the offices or grants which they expected. He therefore found it difficult to accept the mechanisms of court politics which made occasional setbacks in the quest for influence inevitable. Although officially the Crown remained the font of all honour for him, he did not hesitate to point out that the Queen had a duty to reward the truly virtuous. If she failed to do so she implicitly forfeited her claim to obedience and loyalty.[37]

Essex lost the Queen's favour after an unsuccessful campaign in Ireland against the Earl of Tyrone, the leader of a major rebellion against Elizabeth I. Faced with the prospect of a life in the political wilderness and the loss of his offices and the pensions and other sources of income he had been granted in earlier years, he finally attempted to stage a coup against the Queen in 1601. However, the disgraced favourite discovered that hardly anybody was prepared to join him in his open defiance of the monarch. Arrested by the Queen, he and a number of his followers were put on trial. Confronting his judges, Essex maintained that he had tried to reform the commonwealth and that his status as Earl Marshal 'and therefore as chief officer of the community of honour, the guardian of its values' gave him a warrant to undertake such a reform even against the will of the monarch.[38] However, when condemned to death, he abandoned his pride and his defence of aristocratic honour as the highest political ideal and admitted before his execution that he had grievously sinned and committed treason. This volte-face has been interpreted as a proof that the traditional community of honour had collapsed and that it had become impossible to use the language of honour as 'an idiom of dissent' because the Crown had integrated honour too firmly 'into the structure of the monarchical state'.[39]

This is a judgement which needs to be qualified. Many of the noblemen and gentlemen who fought in the English Civil War in the 1640s did so because they believed that their honour forced them to take sides. Such notions were important not only among the royalists, but among the supporters of Parliament as well. Significantly Essex's son, the third Earl (1591–1646), became the commander of the parliamentary forces in 1642. The third Earl had his own personal reasons for feeling that his honour had been slighted by the Stuarts. James I had arranged a divorce between Essex's wife Frances Howard and her husband, on the grounds of impotence, so that Frances could marry his favourite, the Earl of Somerset. But Essex was not alone in thinking that the Stuarts had failed to defend the aristocratic community of honour and its values.[40] The rise of all-powerful favourites such as the Duke of Buckingham (assassinated 1628) threatened the traditional hierarchy of status. And the often inconsistent foreign policy of the early Stuarts failed, it seemed to many, to uphold the notions of military virtue and honour which were still of considerable importance to peerage and gentry alike.[41] Nevertheless, opposition to official royal policy now found other ways of expressing itself. In 1601, when the second Earl of Essex had attempted his coup, religious arguments had played hardly any part in legitimising this extreme step. In fact, among his supporters there had been some Catholics or crypto-Catholics. But in the mid-seventeenth century the defence of the Protestant faith, the rule of law, and even republican ideals became much more prominent in justifying resistance to royal policy, and this holds good for aristocratic as much as for non-elite opposition.[42] On the other hand, the Stuarts were also much more reluctant than Elizabeth had been to encourage the cult of chivalry and military virtue which had shown itself to have dangerously ambivalent political implications at the end of Elizabeth's reign. James I had seen enough of noble violence in Scotland and was understandably reluctant to foster similar attitudes among his English courtiers. Moreover, with England avoiding military conflict between 1604 and the late 1630s – apart from the years 1625–29 – the courtier, collector and connoisseur of works of art seemed a more appropriate aristocratic role model than the warrior.[43] In many ways James I and his son Charles I were remarkably successful in imposing their own notion of peace and order on England and its elite. Although Ireland and Scotland also became more peaceful in this period, the potential for unrest and armed conflict remained much greater than in England. While England had its fair share of duels fought between gentlemen in the early seventeenth century, the local violence involving noblemen and gentlemen which was so widespread in some parts of France, at least until the 1660s, was largely absent in England.[44] There the ideal of the nobility and gentry as a primarily military elite – an ideal clearly cherished by the second Earl of Essex and his supporters – was slowly but irrevocably abandoned in the seventeenth century.[45] This solved some of the problems which had come to the surface in 1601, such as the conflict between a nobleman's pride and a monarch's ability or desire to reward his virtue and military achievements. But it also ultimately diminished the Crown's role as font of all honour which was so important in fostering a close alliance between Crown and nobility in France and other countries in the second half of the seventeenth century and beyond.

Such an alliance, however, had not yet been achieved in France by the late 1640s. In fact, this period was to witness the last major noble rebellion before Louis XIV laid the foundations for a system of government after 1660 which, although it may have been far less absolute than it claimed to be (see below, pp. 135–9), certainly ensured a high degree of domestic peace and stability for more than a hundred years.[46] In its initial stages the *Fronde* (1648–53) was primarily a rebellion led by the *noblesse de robe*, that is, royal officeholders, in particular the judges of the highest courts, the *parlements*, who feared that the ever increasing financial needs of the virtually bankrupt French state would undermine their own fiscal and social privileges. However, it was soon joined by discontented sections of the *noblesse d'epée* and a number of noble magnates and princes of the blood. The leaders of the *Fronde* were thus often disappointed courtiers and in this respect not all that different from the second Earl of Essex.

The *Fronde* was the final manifestation of an almost continuous series of noble revolts and conspiracies going back to the years of insecurity after the death of Henry IV (1610).[47] Henry IV had only managed to end the Wars of Religion in the 1590s by making considerable concessions to a number of noble magnates who had held out against him until the end. Their opposition had been bought off by enormous financial payments or by granting them important offices, for example as governors of provinces.[48] This set a dangerous precedent; it showed that rebellion could pay off after all. In fact, the objective of many of the minor and not so minor revolts after 1610 was to prove to the monarch or his or her favourite that the leaders of these rebellions were so influential that the Crown would be well advised to seek their co-operation. Cardinal Richelieu, who governed France as the King's first minister between 1624 and 1642, refused to play this game and did not accept such rebellions as a legitimate means of exerting political pressure. But this only exacerbated the resentment against him. It even led to attempts to assassinate the Cardinal, who was widely seen as a tyrant who ignored all legally established rules of government.[49]

Most of the rebellions during this period were led by noble magnates or, in fact, by the princes of the blood such as Gaston, Duc d'Orleans

(1608–60), brother to Louis XIII and, until 1638, the heir apparent, or Louis de Bourbon, Comte de Soissons (1604–41), who managed to win a victory against the King's army in 1641 with Spanish support but died soon afterwards with a bullet in his head, possibly killed by Richelieu's assassins, or Louis II, Prince de Condé (1621–86), who became the real leader of the *Fronde* in its later stages. The end of the Wars of Religion, which had reasserted the principle of the purely hereditary succession against all ideas of a partially elective kingship, had implicitly exalted the status of the princes of the blood. After all, Henry IV had himself been only a very distant relative of the last Valois king, Henry III (d. 1588). But on the other hand, it had left the political status of the princes largely undefined, and Henry IV, who had often shown generosity towards the noble leaders of the League who had initially opposed him, had deliberately curtailed the power of the princes of the blood whom he saw as dangerous rivals. Sometimes they were even openly humiliated, like Henry II, Prince de Condé, whose legitimacy was called into question by the King, and whose fiancée was almost turned into a royal mistress.[50]

The princes, on the other hand, were reluctant to accept a merely ornamental position without any real influence, all the more so when the King was either a minor or had submitted to the tutelage of a favourite of far lesser status than the *Grands*. Finally, and this is a point emphasised by Arlette Jouanna, in seventeenth-century France no nobleman of whatever status could hope to maintain his place in the noble hierarchy if he failed to receive visible marks of honour from the King in the form of offices, titles or material rewards. Thus whether they liked it or not, even the greatest noblemen, the princes of the blood, had to join the race for royal favours. Because of their exalted status, however, they found it difficult to accept defeats and setbacks in this race, as this could be seen as a stain on their honour,[51] and revolt could then seem the only means of restoring it. This also applied to some extent to other magnates who were not members of the royal dynasty. Thus the Vicomte de Turenne, one of the most successful military commanders of the French army, decided to join the *Fronde* not least because the status of his family, the de la Tour d'Auvergne, as 'princes étrangers' was at risk. After the regent had guaranteed this status in early 1651, Turenne soon rejoined the royalist side.[52]

The prince de Condé's discontent had similar causes. Louis de Bourbon, Prince de Condé was the hero of the war against Spain, having won the battles of Rocroi and Lens (1643 and 1648), and in the past he had always supported the cause of a strong royal government. In fact, his family had been closely allied with Richelieu and during the initial phases of the *Fronde* he had sided with Mazarin against the *parlement* in Paris and besieged the capital held by the rebels.[53] However, he was not prepared to accept Mazarin's dominant position. Not opposed to the concept of a strong, or even an absolute monarchy as such, in the last resort he wanted the position of first minister in such a monarchy for himself, not for a foreign clergyman, a mere parvenu. Moreover, Condé resented Mazarin's attempts to gain a position within the French aristocracy for himself and his family which would have made him the equal of the most powerful noble magnates. Richelieu had in many ways pursued a similar strategy, which was to some extent typical of early seventeenth-century royal favourites who did not by birth belong to the highest echelons of the nobility. Public criticism of Mazarin's influence and open rebellion threatened to undermine his position. This resulted in him trying to render his power unassailable by amassing a vast personal fortune and by establishing ties of kinship with important noble dynasties through a careful marriage policy. As a magnate in his own right Mazarin could hope to counter the attacks against him, even if he were temporarily to lose the regent's support.[54]

But the ascendancy of Mazarin's family as a magnate dynasty threatened Condé's position as the first of the *Grands*. He therefore tried to counter Mazarin's family strategy, even at a time when he was still officially allied with him, and managed to prevent some of the most important marriage alliances which Mazarin had planned for his nephews and nieces among the French aristocracy (in particular the marriage of his niece Laura Manzini with the Duc de Mercoeur in 1649, the Guise Governor of the Bretagne) while extending successfully his own network of relations and clients. At the same time he tried to protect the noble *Frondeurs* over whom Mazarin had won a temporary victory, with Condé's help, against the Cardinal's revenge. As a result, relations between Condé and Mazarin deteriorated in the autumn of 1649 and the Cardinal had Condé and the Prince of Conti, as well as the Duke of Longueville, arrested in January 1650.[55] Under pressure from the nobility in the provinces and the Paris *parlement*, Condé and the two other prisoners were set free in February 1651, but the rupture with the Cardinal was permanent and Condé now took up arms against his enemy. His revolt ensured that the kingdom remained in a state of turmoil until the end of 1652 when Mazarin and the Queen regained control of Paris and of most of the French provinces.[56]

However, the position both of Condé and the other magnates remained ambivalent. The *Grands*, like Condé, may have resented the influence of men like Mazarin and tried to find a place in the established structure of government commensurate with their honour and status or the exalted notions they had of both. But they did not want to destroy this structure any more than the judges and officeholders who had played a prominent part in the first phase of the Fronde.[57] The lesser nobility as opposed to the magnates may have dreamed of a mixed monarchy in which the sovereign shared his power with the nobility as an estate. But, in the final resort, the majority of these noblemen saw their own relationship with the king as one of personal loyalty and service and not as based on mutual contractual obligations. There was therefore no room for a clear constitutional division of power between Crown and the Estates General as representatives of the whole body of the realm.[58]

Noble revolt in the *Fronde* hardly amounted to a principled and consistent 'political liberalism' as some historians have argued with regard to the earlier opposition to Richelieu.[59] It would be more appropriate to say that the Crown, which for decades had simultaneously bestowed new favours and privileges and often quite arbitrarily revoked or called into question old ones, had failed to create a stable hierarchy of honour. In such a context otherwise limited conflicts over fiscal exemptions or social status could easily get out of hand and lead to a general breakdown of royal authority. In the end, however, the monarchical state was able to restore order against its disunited and often half-hearted opponents, although noble unrest in the provinces continued well into the late 1650s.[60] Not until the end of the war with Spain in 1659 and the beginning of Louis XIV's personal government in 1661, could political stability be taken for granted.

Provincial elites and noble rebellion

Noble rebellion in the late sixteenth and seventeenth centuries had many faces. It could be inspired by traditional notions of noble liberty or by the ideal of a mixed monarchy in which the ruler shared power with his nobility, even perhaps of an aristocratic republic, as for example in Poland, Hungary or, until 1620, Bohemia. But it could also be driven by a much more limited attempt by noble magnates to maintain their credit among their clients, who resented the policies of a centralising state or the pressure of ever increasing fiscal demands, and expected their patron to take effective action against such grievances, if need be by taking up arms against the ruler or his officeholders. Older traditions of feuding and aristocratic violence which, in particular in border regions, had often been encouraged by the very monarchs and princes who later tried to stamp out feuding (see above, pp. 71–2), also played a role in fuelling rebellions, as did the provincial or national loyalties which led noblemen to oppose the demands of the rulers of the major composite monarchies of this period.

Such tensions between centre and localities or regional communities became particularly acute in many European countries during the Thirty Years War which, in one way or another, engulfed most of the continent. The growing burdens, both fiscal and military, which the state imposed on local communities posed a serious problem for the local elites. They could act as the state's agents and try to mobilise local resources for their rulers' military and political objectives in distant provinces or abroad. The Castilian or the Sicilian aristocracy did, by and large, follow this line in the seventeenth century, thereby vastly extending their privileges but also incurring enormous debts (see below, pp. 144–6). Other local or regional elites were more cautious and tried to mediate between local interests and the centralising agencies. This largely held true for the English gentry in the 1620s and 1630s when the country, although it was at war only for a few years

(1625–30), was put on an almost permanent war footing. The unpopularity of official policy, especially in religious matters, certainly did not facilitate this task. In fact, members of the county gentry faced a double risk. If they went along too far with official demands they could easily lose credit with the local community. Given that wealthy tenant farmers and well-to-do urban citizens expected to be wooed rather than simply commanded by their betters, gentlemen or peers who lost touch with local sentiment could soon become isolated in their counties and lose their influence. On the other hand, local officeholders such as Justices of the Peace or Deputy Lieutenants who dragged their feet when asked to comply with unpopular royal orders might be replaced by others who had no such scruples, possibly outsiders – Catholics for example – who compensated for their lack of local standing by their eagerness to implement royal orders.[61] In fact, tensions between rival personalities and factions within the county community greatly exacerbated the political conflicts caused by war and growing fiscal demands in early Stuart England. Given the struggle between factions within the gentry, the temptation to denigrate one's opponent as a rebel or – at the other extreme – to tar him with the brush of abject servility towards greedy and possibly Popish courtiers was often too great to be resisted.[62] Such propaganda did not in itself make the Civil War inevitable and most historians nowadays would hesitate to see the English Civil War as a revolt of the provinces *tout court*. Nevertheless, 20 years of local in-fighting helped to undermine stability and consensus and prepare the gentry and peerage for war.[63]

In France the Crown could rely on much stronger bureaucratic structures in the early seventeenth century, which made the co-operation of local elites in raising taxes prima facie less imperative. Nevertheless the 1630s and 1640s were to show that the enormous fiscal pressure and financial manipulations, such as the sale of ever more offices and ever greater shares of royal revenue, both caused by France's participation in the Thirty Years War, taxed the loyalty of large sections of the *noblesse de robe* and the provincial nobility to their limits. The popular revolts which shook France in the 1630s, such as the rising of the *Nu-Pieds* in Normandy (1639), would hardly have been as serious as they actually were without the secret connivance of large sections of the provincial governing classes.[64] Equally the drastic fall in revenues raised in the 1640s was also due to some extent to the silent resistance of the elites to official financial policy. A *seigneur* whose peasants had been bled white by royal tax farmers and fiscal agents could hardly expect them to pay their full rent. It was therefore in his own interest to minimise the amount of royal taxation under such circumstances.[65] However, in the end, as we have seen, a strong monarchy remained an ideal which had the support of most noblemen in France. What they rejected was the arbitrary emergency policies which Richelieu and Mazarin had pursued during the war.

Noble revolt was often more radical, and also more successful, when fuelled by strong regional or national sentiments. Such was the case in

Scotland in 1638, an example we have already mentioned (above, pp. 105–6). Here the attempts James VI (I) had made to create a genuinely British aristocracy had been largely abandoned by his son Charles I. The few Scottish noblemen among his entourage were often deracinated officeholders who no longer wielded much power in their native country. The resentment of those who were cut off from contacts with the court, because it was just too costly for them to live in England, was all the greater and fuelled the Scottish revolution of the late 1630s.[66] The situation was similar in Portugal in 1640s, when the Portuguese rejected the Union with Castile (established in 1580) and chose to go their own way under a native dynasty, and in Hungary in 1703–11, when large sections of the Magyar nobility rose against the Habsburgs under the leadership of Ferenc Rákóczi, son of the last independent prince of Transylvania and in many ways another example of the courtier turned rebel, as he had been brought up at court, in Vienna, as a Catholic.[67] Unpopular absentee monarchs provided an easy target for criticism, and a nobility left without a clear political role because of the absence of a royal court could find a new identity as the leader of a national movement; moreover, sometimes a populous but poor provincial nobility which (like the Scottish lairds or the Hungarian gentry), was unable to compete with the richer and more narrowly defined metropolitan elite, tried to assert its own claims to status and prestige.[68] However, in Catalonia, which rose against Castilian rule in 1640, matters were more complicated. The regional nobility, though mostly with few links to the court in Madrid, was reluctant to give its wholehearted support to a revolt which might endanger its own extensive privileges and rights of jurisdiction.[69] In Ireland, on the other hand, in the early seventeenth century, the Catholic elite, the so-called Old English (descendants of the medieval Anglo-Norman and English settlers), were torn between loyalty towards the Stuarts as their rulers and resentment against the Protestant Church settlement and the plans of English politicians and courtiers for future confiscations and plantations. Their position in Ireland had been undermined for decades by new settlers and officeholders who tried to denigrate the old elite as popish traitors infected by Gaelic customs and cultural traditions incompatible with English notions of civility. Although most of the Old English were reluctant to abandon their co-operation with the Crown entirely, their Catholic faith gave them a specific political identity which undoubtedly facilitated the decision to join the Irish rebellion of 1641, in the hope of gaining security for their Church and their property. The real leaders of the revolt, however, in particular in Ulster, were mostly indebted or impoverished Gaelic landowners. Even they initially protested their loyalty to the King and his Catholic wife – but then, many early modern rebels liked to pretend that they were fighting only against the monarch's evil councillors, not against the king himself.[70] In Ireland, as in Bohemia in 1618 or in the Netherlands in the 1560s, the conflict between royal authority and local elites had been exacerbated by a religious divide. However, this was in itself to some extent the result of earlier tensions between local interests and the policies of the absent monarch and his agents, which were often pursued with scant regard for traditional political and constitutional arrangements.[71]

The large number of revolutions and rebellions in the years around 1640 (Catalonia, Portugal, Scotland, Ireland, England and, later, France and Naples as well) has led some historians to see these conflicts as part of a wider-ranging crisis of the seventeenth century, fuelled not least by increasing alienation between the court and those social elites which did not directly participate in the life of the court and therefore had no access to the sources of power.[72] This interpretation certainly commands less support now than it did a few years ago. In fact, what looks at first glance like a European-wide structural crisis of society turns out in many ways to be no more than the effects of protracted warfare on the political and social order. This is particularly obvious in France and Spain.[73] Nevertheless, the early seventeenth century was a period when the political outlook of most noblemen, even to some extent that of the greatest among them, the magnates, was still shaped by the problems and values of provincial or regional society. At the same time, however, they were confronted by problems caused by international conflicts on an unprecedented scale. Scottish noblemen discovered that their own Kirk would not be secure without the victory of Calvinist Protestantism in England and Ireland, if not, in fact, on the Continent itself,[74] and Catalan *hidalgos* realised that wars between Spain and its many enemies, waged for decades in distant Flanders or northern Italy, were now being fought in their own backyards. Revolt was to some extent a reaction to such bewildering new problems with which most provincial elites were ill equipped to deal.

Nevertheless, in most countries there were limits to the radicalism of noble rebellion. Once revolt threatened the traditional social hierarchy, as during the final stages of the French Wars of Religion or near the end of the English Civil War, noblemen understandably became reluctant to support a political movement which undermined the foundations of their own status and power. The radicalism of religious resistance theories, in particular, was seen by many noblemen as a threat to the social order on which their own power was based and to the traditional ties of allegiance which transcended confessional and political frontlines. Such fears, however, may have been weaker in societies where noble power was paramount and where neither rival elites nor peasant unrest threatened aristocratic ascendancy. Seventeenth-century Scotland and Poland are both examples of such a situation.[75]

Conclusion

In many parts of Europe a strong monarchy once again became attractive in the later seventeenth century, even to those who, in the past, had acted as champions of noble autonomy but who now wanted order and stability to be restored. But then, many rebellions were not opposed to monarchical authority as such anyway. What had provoked noblemen to rebel was often the feeling that royal authority had already broken down or was being usurped by a rival faction that had made the monarch their prisoner and impaired his (or her) ability to act as an arbiter between competing claims for favour and support. Thus rebellion could be as much an attempt to restore the independence of a strong monarchy as a struggle for noble liberty against a centralising state. The frondeur and the favourite were both possible role models for the nobleman in this period, as we have seen, and the difference between the two was often far smaller than might be imagined. Thus Thomas Wentworth, Earl of Strafford (1593–1641), for example, who was impeached by the House of Commons and executed in London in 1641 as an advocate of arbitrary government, had started out as a champion of traditional liberties and a defender of the local community against allegedly illegal taxation. It would be simplistic to see his 'change of sides' merely as an example of political opportunism. Rather Wentworth, like other early seventeenth-century noblemen, played many parts during his life, depending on the stage on which he was acting: 'honest patriot' and defender of the liberties of the subject, conscientious and autocratic officeholder, potential favourite and leading minister relentlessly in search of personal advancement and profit, and, finally, his last role as the allegedly 'evil counsellor' sacrificed to atone for his master's misguided policies. He chose or accepted these different roles because political circumstances and social conventions prompted or sometimes, in fact, forced him to do so, always guided by a strong, and perhaps in his case particularly obsessive, sense of his own honour and status.[76]

If his political career ended in violent death and failure, this was due not only to the political hothouse climate of the early 1640s, with its stark religious and confessional antagonism which he had failed to anticipate, but also to the fact that in the course of his career he had too often used his power to humiliate others while defending not just royal policy but his own honour. Early Stuart England failed to provide a political and social equilibrium, which would have given those who were out of favour at court an assurance that their social status and honour as such were not in jeopardy. In this respect England was by no means an exception in the late sixteenth and early seventeenth centuries which, for many countries, was a period of deep political instability. An accumulation of royal minorities (for example in France in the 1560s and again after 1610, and in Scotland during the youth of James VI, after 1567), dynastic succession disputes (both in France and in Sweden in the 1590s, for example) and conflicts within the ruling dynasty (e.g. the Austrian Habsburgs during the last years of Rudolph II's reign before 1612) undermined royal or princely authority. Moreover, in an age of acute religious conflict, radical resistance theories flourished and monarchy lost its aura of sacredness. Tyrannicide become more than a distant theoretical possibility. It was a realistic political option or, depending on one's point of view, threat, as the murder of two kings of France within less than 25 years (1589 and 1610) and the attempts to assassinate Elizabeth I and James I of England demonstrated clearly enough. Finally, the assemblies of estates, which in the past had often been institutions capable of defusing political tensions and integrating potentially disruptive forces of opposition into a political process based on negotiation instead of armed conflict, could no longer cope with mounting religious and financial problems.[77] Their meetings now often led to confrontation rather than consensus. General political instability and noble unrest could reinforce each other in a vicious circle, as they did in France and Scotland in the late sixteenth century, in Bohemia before 1618 and, to some extent, in the Stuart monarchy in the late 1630s and early 1640s.

The return of political stability after 1660 in many European countries and the renewed strength of royal or princely authority in this period will be examined in the next chapter in greater detail. Suffice it to say at this point that to a considerable extent both were the result of the establishment of a new balance between the noble quest for honour and the exigencies of public service. In the late sixteenth and early seventeenth centuries the monarchical state had often appealed to noble ambition and the noble sense of prestige in the hope of making royal or princely service attractive, but at the same time it had failed to satisfy the need for offices and rewards as a token of an officially acknowledged status and pre-eminence it had created in the first place. Those who failed to obtain the marks of royal favour which they sought had to fear for their social status and their honour, not just for their influence on politics. Their fear of humiliation could easily lead them to endorse open rebellion. In the later seventeenth century, however, a new accommodation between noble prestige and the demands of the state was achieved. Royal patronage managed to defuse the tensions between traditional notions of noble honour and the honours which the monarchical state granted to its servants.

| 6 |

Noble power and state formation

Towards a new symbiosis?

Introduction

According to an older school of thought, the early modern state was the sworn enemy of noble power in all its forms. Only after the 'overmighty subjects', the noble magnates, had been subdued and their network of clients and dependants destroyed, could the authority of the state be established, so that the prince's will reigned supreme everywhere, at court as much as in the remotest village of his realm. More recent research, however, has become much more sceptical with regard to the notion of royal and princely absolutism. The preceding chapter has demonstrated that even the causes of open conflict between noblemen and the state were often far more complicated than an interpretation which assumes a permanent structural tension between the interests of the Crown and the nobility suggests.[1]

Kings and princes did indeed at times undermine noble power, replacing the rule of local magnates with bureaucratic administrative institutions. But more often than not a new symbiosis between aristocracy and state developed during the second half of the seventeenth century – according to the received wisdom, the classical age of absolutism. The state lent new legitimacy to the prerogatives and privileges of noblemen and the latter often acted as the representatives of the state at the local level, enforcing and implementing royal policies, but also benefiting from the new role which the expansion of the state gave them.[2] The fiercely independent noble warlord, who opposed royal policy by force of arms whenever this seemed expedient, did indeed become a figure encountered less and less frequently in the great European monarchies in the course of the seventeenth century. The centralisation of military power in the hands of the state and the growing fiscal resources rulers had at their disposal certainly helped to put an end to such radical expressions of noble liberty, but cultural changes were equally important. As we have seen, under the influence of Church, court and town alike, noble ideals of conduct became less violent and less heroically independent. To succeed at court or to shine among one's equals in society had become a higher mark of distinction than to permanently demonstrate one's ability to exercise power over inferiors or to use physical force against one's enemies.

The accommodation with the princely state favoured by such developments certainly had its price. In the seventeenth century noble power was based at least as much on the offices noblemen held, their influence at court and the benefits they derived from the ever growing fiscal resources of the state in the form of pensions, 'alienated' taxes and interest payments they received as the state's creditors, as on traditional feudal rights of jurisdiction and the possession of landed estates. While certain groups within the nobility were advantaged by the process of state formation, others lost out and were politically and socially marginalised, as the fate of the Protestants and the lower nobility in general in the Habsburg monarchy or the Old English in Ireland demonstrates (see above, pp. 111–12, 121):

Warfare and noble power

It has often been argued that the driving force behind the process of state formation in the early modern period was the need to fight wars.[3] The increasing costs of early modern warfare led to growing fiscal demands on the population; the need to maintain large armies drove rulers to override legal constraints and to resort to emergency measures which gradually eroded traditional privileges and liberties. In this process of military centralisation and growing fiscal exactions, the nobility seems at first glance to have been on the losing side. Whereas at the beginning of the sixteenth century noble magnates and, on a lesser scale, even many less powerful noblemen had been able to wage war on their own against cities or other noblemen, this capacity was increasingly diminished. In the end, standing armies exclusively controlled by the prince replaced the forces which military entrepreneurs had raised or which noblemen had recruited for the Crown as part of their feudal or semi-feudal obligations.[4]

Before the turn of the seventeenth century most European states were a long way from achieving anything like a state monopoly of military power. The financial resources which kings and princes could mobilise to wage war were, in most cases, inadequate for protracted conflicts. Although the traditional feudal hosts – still raised occasionally in an emergency for purposes of local defence and sometimes even for large-scale warfare – had lost most of their military usefulness, at least in the latter case,[5] rulers still had to rely to a considerable extent on noblemen to recruit and pay armies. The simplest form this reliance on noble power could take was an appeal to noblemen at times of crisis to raise troops privately among their tenants and retainers. Until the late sixteenth century, England, for example, relied on such a system to complement the county militias which had been formed under Elizabeth I to defend the country. As late as 1588, during the attack of the Armada, three-quarters of Elizabeth I's own guard of about 20,000 men were drawn from the private retinues of peers and great landowners, while only 5,000 were recruited from the county militia. Even after 1603, during the reign of James I, prelates and peers could muster about 20,000 footsoldiers and 4,000 horse as armed retainers.[6]

However, such armed retainers could more easily be used for local defence than to wage war abroad, and this holds good for England as much as for Spain or France. For such purposes the easiest solution in the late sixteenth and early seventeenth centuries was to entrust the task of warfare to military entrepreneurs. These were men who recruited and equipped soldiers for a campaign or a series of campaigns. The companies, regiments or sometimes even entire armies, which they recruited at their own expense, were in many ways their property, but they could expect their costs to be reimbursed in some way or other. If it proved impossible to provide them with wages and supplies for their soldiers, the simplest method was to let them raise contributions and requisition provisions in an area allocated to their regiment or company. Raising contributions often implied looting or holding to ransom towns and villages occupied during the war. Rewards in the form of confiscated estates which the rulers gave their officers to compensate them for unpaid debts were another possible source of financial profit.[7]

Not all military entrepreneurs were members of the landed nobility. Some were soldiers of fortune who had risen through the ranks, while others were the sons of rich urban patricians or of bankers already involved in financing warfare. Among the most prominent one could single out were the Spínola, a Genoese business dynasty which provided Spain with one of its most gifted military commanders in the Netherlands, Ambrogio Spínola (1569–1630), who earned and lost a fortune in the service of the Spanish Crown in the early seventeenth century. Most military entrepreneurs, however, were less closely connected to the world of finance or business, although such connections were certainly valuable in raising the credit necessary to levy troops. However, the local power base provided by landed estates and rights of jurisdictions, and the network of tenants and clients noblemen maintained, were equally useful. Both facilitated the arduous task of recruiting soldiers and officers.[8] In Italy, many leading military entrepreneurs belonged to the cadet branches of princely houses such as the Medici, the Della Rovere, the Este and Gonzaga.[9] The same holds good for some prominent commanders in the Thirty Years War, which was in many ways the heyday of the military entrepreneur. Soldiers and commanders from all over Europe – from Italy, the Spanish Netherlands, Ireland and Scotland and from east-central Europe as well as, of course, from Germany itself – served in it.

The greatest and most famous – or infamous – among the military entrepreneurs of the war was Albrecht von Wallenstein, a Bohemian nobleman
who had benefited from the confiscation of Protestant property after 1620.
He commanded and, to all intents and purposes, owned an army of almost
100,000 men at the height of his power. Although officially he was only the
Emperor's *generalissimus*, he pursued political objectives of his own in the
later stages of his career. He paid a high price for this dangerous course of
action as he was murdered on the Emperor's orders in 1634.[10]

Wallenstein was an exceptional figure in more ways than one, if only
because of the scale of his military enterprise. But other military commanders harboured similar ambitions and hoped to establish themselves at least
as major landowners, if not, indeed, as powerful sovereign princes. Thus
Bernhard von Weimar (1604–39), born the eleventh son of Duke Johann of
Saxe-Weimar, inherited only a tiny principality and was largely left to shift
for himself. Serving the elector palatine during the early years of the war, he
later became an officer in Christian of Denmark's army. After Christian's
defeat he took up service as a general in Gustavus Adolfus's expeditionary
corps in 1631, and as one of the most important Swedish commanders, he
was rewarded for his services by the Swedish Crown with the territories of
the Bishoprics of Würzburg and Bamberg – transformed into a new Duchy
of Franconia in 1633.

Defeated at Nördlingen in 1634, he offered the services of the remaining
troops under his command to Louis XIII of France. Bernhard managed to
elicit a promise from the French that they would confer the Habsburg
Landgraviate of Upper Alsatia on him as a principality.[11] After Bernhard's
death in June 1639, the Golden Age of the large-scale military contractor
and entrepreneur, who recruited and commanded whole armies, was over in
central Europe. However, generals and officers continued to treat war as a
business in a more limited way. Colonels and captains could still expect to
make a profit from the charges they held beyond the official remuneration
they received even in forces as tightly controlled by the Crown as the
Prussian army of the eighteenth century.[12]

The entrepreneurial system had not been accepted to the same extent in
all European countries. Spain, for example, had not only been the greatest
military power in Europe in the second half of the sixteenth century, but it
had also successfully avoided the pitfalls of the entrepreneurial system during this period. The Spanish *tercios*, the famous native infantry units of the
Spanish army, were recruited during the reign of Philip II by captains
appointed and paid by the Crown. The commanders were essentially royal
officeholders and the companies and regiments were not their property.
However, the worsening crisis of public finances after about 1580 and the
fact that it was becoming increasingly difficult to find genuine volunteers
in Castile brought about important changes in military organisation. These
changes have been seen as part of a wide-ranging process of de-centralisa-
tion and even 'refeudalisation'. From the 1580s onwards, noblemen were

entrusted with the task of recruiting large military contingents among their tenants and vassals, especially but not exclusively for purposes of local or regional defence. Often the most powerful local magnate almost automatically became the military commander in the province which he dominated. Thus the successive dukes of Medina Sidonia controlled the defence of south-western Spain in the last two decades of the sixteenth century and the early seventeenth century. They were in charge of practically every recruiting drive that took place in Andalusia between 1580 and 1641. The seventh duke, Don Alonso Pérez de Guzmán (1549–1615), played an important role in the military campaign of 1580 which gave Philip II control of Portugal and was almost single-handedly responsible for fitting out in Lisbon the Armada which he was to command in 1588. He acted as Philip II's Captain General of Andalusia and was responsible for getting the annual Atlantic fleets ready and safely back to port in his capacity as Captain General of the Ocean Sea. Moreover he ran a flourishing private port at San Lucar and had extensive interests in the salt industry and the tuna fisheries. His enormous personal wealth made his services almost indispensable for the Crown.[13] His successors continued this tradition, combining almost unlimited local power with loyal service to the Crown until Gaspar Pérez de Guzmán, the ninth duke, was involved in a political conspiracy in 1641. At this stage Medina Sidonia had 42 pieces of artillery in his castle of Santiago, a considerably larger arsenal than that held by his ancestors 60 years earlier.[14]

Spanish noblemen were largely expected to pay out of their own pockets for warfare waged by the troops they had recruited, but they could expect to be generously rewarded. As the Crown increasingly had to rely on those with sufficient wealth and local power to organise the defence of the Empire, it alienated rights of jurisdiction and taxation on a massive scale. I.A.A. Thompson has pointed out that about a third of the population of Castile paid direct taxes (the *alcabala*) not to the Crown but to various noble lords in 1637, and that between 1625 and 1668, when the war with Portugal ended, at least 169 new lordships with extensive rights of jurisdiction were created by the Crown and sold to noblemen.[15]

Recent research has questioned the idea of a 'refeudalisation' of the Spanish monarchy after 1580, a problem we shall come back to later (see below, pp. 145–6). However, it remains true for Castile as much as for other parts of the Spanish Empire, such as southern Italy, for example, that warfare did not favour the forces of centralisation let alone of 'absolutism'. Rather it forced the Crown increasingly to rely on those who were able to organise the war effort on their own at a local level. More often than not these were, apart from the magistrates, mayors and *corregidores* of major towns (who were themselves usually noblemen of at least *hidalgo* status), great aristocrats. The specific nature of the war in Spain, which after 1640 was increasingly defensive in character and was now being waged not only in Italy and the Netherlands but also on the Iberian peninsula, in Catalonia as much as in Portugal, may have contributed to these developments as much as the fact that the Crown's financial resources were becoming ever more inadequate.[16] But Spain demonstrates clearly that it would be wrong to identify military developments in the seventeenth century exclusively with a tendency to concentrate all military power in the hands of the Crown while reducing the capacity of the nobility to mobilise troops.

In contrast to Spain, France is often seen as a country where the growth of royal authority was closely connected with the establishment of a standing army in the seventeenth century. The chronology of the development of a royal monopoly of military power in France indeed differs from that in Spain. In France the armed forces, which in times of war had contained a high proportion of foreign mercenaries, especially among the infantry, had been comparatively tightly controlled by the King in the first half of the sixteenth century, but had then fallen apart in the Wars of Religion.[17] The chaos of these wars left a lasting political trauma, and Henry IV and his successors were determined to avoid anything which might lead to a renewed outbreak of noble violence on a comparable scale. During Henry's reign the Crown pursued a programme of dismantling fortifications within the kingdom which could not be controlled by royal troops. This policy was continued under Richelieu when, in the 1620s, all domestic castles and fortified places which the Crown could not safely garrison were ordered to be razed. Only fortifications protecting the borders were to remain.[18] Even earlier, at the beginning of the century, Henry IV and his minister, Sully, as Grand Master of the Artillery, had built up a powerful royal artillery comprising more than 300 guns; no noble magnate could even remotely match this arsenal.[19]

Admittedly, royal mistrust of noble military entrepreneurs had its drawbacks as well. In the war against Spain (1628/35–1659), France tried to finance warfare at least to some extent through taxation, in an attempt to avoid a full-blown system of military entrepreneurship, because the King and his ministers suspected that nobles might join provincial revolts led by aristocratic magnates if given enough leeway. Although aristocratic patronage was rampant in the army and commands had, as a rule, to be purchased, the king remained legally in control and regiments did not become the full property of their colonels. However, officers were expected to finance their companies or regiments to a large extent out of their own pockets, with no chance, at least officially, to recoup their losses by raising contributions, and no guarantee that the regiments they had recruited would not be dissolved or merged with other troops ('reformed') at the first opportunity. The result was that the morale of French officers was not particularly high, corruption was widespread and the fighting capacity of the French army, theoretically under closer royal control than the mercenary armies of other powers, was inferior to that of its opponents. Moreover, most noblemen considered a commission in the army not so much as the first step of a long-term military career but only as a transient phase in their lives: 'For the great majority of the French elite who served as officers, military activity was a *rite de passage*, a crucial element in defining their subsequent social status' which depended on acquiring an aura of military valour. But officers, in the words of David Parrott, 'had never separated themselves from the preoccupations of a civil society into which they soon expected to return.' Hence they tended to leave their regiments, with or without permission, at the first opportunity. Absenteeism among officers was a permanent and almost insurmountable problem in the French army. [20]

At the same time royal control was far from perfect. Charges as colonel could even be sold to women, who, of course, did not serve themselves but entrusted the position in question to a deputy. As late as 1650 the French secretary of war, Le Tellier, could say that the King's army was a virtual republic in which the lieutenant generals considered their brigades as 'so many cantons'.[21]

After the war and the end of the *Fronde*, more thoroughgoing reforms were undertaken. Gradually, strongholds of aristocratic power such as the position of the *colonel général de l'infanterie* were either abolished or stripped of their prescriptive rights, so that appointments to charges within the army now rested exclusively with the king. However, they still had to be purchased, in particular those of colonel and captain, the commanders of regiments and companies respectively. Purchase seemed to be necessary to ensure that officers had the necessary financial means to maintain their units. As the French military system remained semi-entrepreneurial, commanders of regiments and companies were required to invest substantial sums in their units, and it has been argued that 'maintenance became an undeclared but unavoidable tax on the nobility'.[22] Nevertheless, the number of noblemen who volunteered to pay this tax was considerable. In some French provinces up to 90 per cent of the families belonging to the titled nobility and 64 per cent of untitled families had at least one member serving as an officer in the army during the reign of Louis XIV, though the national average may have been slightly lower, at about 50 per cent.[23] In fact, one of the real achievements of Louis XIV's policy was to persuade the rank and file of the provincial nobility, but also many sons of the *robe*, to serve as officers in the armed forces. Prospects for promotion were limited for those who did not belong to a titled family or at least had very substantial financial means to further their careers. Yet the honour and prestige attached to military service made it attractive in spite of the many drawbacks associated with it. Military service could bolster claims to social status which either relative poverty (as in the case of many provincial members of the *noblesse d'epée*) or a less than illustrious line of bourgeois ancestors (as in the case of many *robins*) threatened to undermine. Moreover, with the comparative decline of provincial culture a peaceful life in the provinces just seemed too boring for many lesser noblemen to endure.[24]

While nobles continued to pay a high price both in blood and money for social advancement, as well as the honour and glory they sought on the field of battle, the control which the secretary of state for war – a civilian and a member of the *noblesse de robe* – and his officials exercised over the army increased considerably in all matters regarding military finance and logistics. This in itself made it less desirable for great noblemen to act as colonel-in-chief for more than one or two regiments. With the end of fraudulent practices, which had been so widespread before 1660, and of similar cost-cutting devices, this form of military patronage just became too costly to be pursued on as large a scale as in the past.[25]

While Louis XIV was able to impose some bureaucratic controls on his commanders in logistical matters, the higher echelons of the army officer corps remained decidedly aristocratic in composition, or became even more so than in the past.[26] To pursue a military career leading to a position as colonel or general it was now essential to have held a prior position in the elite units of the army – the guard companies belonging to the *Maison du Roi,* or the guard regiments stationed at court in peacetime. And these positions were generally reserved for young men of the great titled families who had the necessary financial means to purchase a charge in these regiments. A *captain-lieutenance* in the prestigious *Gensdarmerie de France* – a guards unit attached to the royal household – could cost up to 130,000 livres in the 1690s, whereas entire cavalry regiments which did not enjoy the special status of the household and guard units could be bought for 25,000 livres, and newly formed infantry regiments often for even less, perhaps as little as 10,000 livres.[27]

Despite the strong position the aristocracy enjoyed in the army, a royal monopoly of military power had been established in France at the end of the seventeenth century. In many ways the French army may have remained semi-feudal in structure; nevertheless, it was undoubtedly much more the king's army than it had been a hundred years before, quite apart from the fact that an army which had numbered less than 20,000 men in peacetime in the early seventeenth century achieved a permanent peacetime strength of 130,000–150,000 men after 1680, and a wartime strength of up to 350,000 men in *c.*1693. The maximum size for French armies in the sixteenth century may have been 80,000.[28] Such rapid growth necessarily brought about a change not just in quantity but also in quality, not least regarding the political implications of military power both abroad and in potential domestic conflicts.

Important as structural improvements in such areas as finance and taxation and the techniques of warfare were in promoting this change, Louis XIV would hardly have been as successful as he was in the role of 'Legislateur des ses armées' (the lawgiver of his armies, according to Voltaire) had the French nobility not willingly supported him in it. And this support was, as Guy Rowlands has argued, at least to some extent due to the fact that noble culture had changed and now placed greater emphasis on self-discipline and self-restraint and less on the flamboyant heroism and the highly individualistic pursuit of honour and glory so popular in the first half of the seventeenth century.[29]

Military developments in France after 1660, the greatest military power in Europe at this period, were eagerly imitated by other European countries. Even England maintained a substantial standing army in the early eighteenth century.[30] Warfare all over Europe became professionalised and the nobility took a leading role in this process almost everywhere. In Prussia the officer corps was in some ways almost identical to the country's nobility in the eighteenth century,[31] although foreign noblemen either from other German states or from abroad could still successfully pursue a career in the Hohenzollern army. Nevertheless this foreign element in the officer corps was much less prominent than it had been in the late seventeenth century,[32] and clearly also less numerous than in the armed forces of the Habsburg monarchy, which retained the multinational character they had acquired in the Thirty Years War. Noblemen from Austria and Bohemia were often too rich and too much addicted to life at court or on their vast estates to find an army career attractive, quite apart from the fact that there were simply not enough of them to provide the Emperor with officers for all his regiments.[33] Many officers in the imperial army, therefore, were foreigners from all over Europe, and, in the lower ranks at least, often commoners as well. In contrast to eighteenth-century Prussia however, in Austria commoners had a fair chance of being ennobled in reward for their services, although their social position in a state which continued to be dominated by great noble magnates remained a somewhat awkward and isolated one. Often they were not even admitted to the regional assemblies of estates, which denied them the crucial *ius incolatus*, that is, the full rights of a local denizen.[34]

A high road to absolutism? Nobility and state in France

Important as the trend towards the monopolisation of military power in the hands of the sovereign state was, it was only one aspect of state formation in the sixteenth and seventeenth centuries. State formation is often identified with the success of absolutism, and France is seen as the classical paradigm of an absolute monarchy in which the Crown undermined the power of the ancient nobility and transformed it into a privileged but idle caste of courtiers who left the serious business of politics to officeholders, at best members of the *noblesse de robe*. It has already been emphasised that this interpretation considerably oversimplifies matters. Neither the mechanisms of noble rebellion nor those of life and politics at court really correspond to this traditional interpretation (see above, pp. 92–5 and pp. 110–19) without major qualification. Nevertheless, there is no denying that there were phases in the development of the French monarchy when the Crown took harsh measures against nobles who opposed royal policies, and when noble resentment against royal policy was voiced more loudly than usual. This holds true not only for the Wars of Religion and the *Fronde* (above, pp. 105–11 and 116–19) but also for the years when the Cardinal de Richelieu dominated French politics (1624–42). Undoubtedly Richelieu regarded as politically dangerous the powerful position which the *Grands*, the princes of the blood, but also the *ducs et pairs* in general, held as provincial governors, military commanders and leaders of widespread aristocratic patronage networks and affinities. As he repeatedly emphasised, he wanted to diminish the pride of these unruly magnates and he did not hesitate to punish and humiliate those who proved to be disloyal. Thus Henri de Montmorency, the last of his line, governor of Languedoc and head of one of the most ancient and powerful noble families in France, who had joined forces with the King's brother, the Duke of Orleans, to overthrow Richelieu and had been defeated by the royal army in the battle of Castelnaudary in September 1632, was convicted of treason and executed in the courtyard of the town hall of Toulouse shortly after the battle. Other enemies of the Cardinal fared no better unless they managed to escape abroad – where they could join the King's brother and his mother, who both preferred a life in exile after they had been outmanoeuvred and defeated by Richelieu.[35]

But as recent research has demonstrated, Richelieu's attitude towards the French noble magnates was less hostile than is commonly assumed. In spite of all his claims that the greatness of the state and the King's authority and glory were his only objectives, he not only amassed a vast fortune, one of the greatest in France, but also collected offices, governorships and benefices, placed his clients and creatures in key positions in the civil and military administration and, by carefully arranging marriage alliances for his nieces and nephews, created a powerful kinship network – just like any other noble magnate of his time.[36] Although Richelieu was often ruthless when pursuing a vendetta against a particular noble faction or dynasty, such as the various branches of the Guise family, which he saw as particularly unreliable and dangerous, he had no problem in allying himself with other magnates and their families, such as the Prince de Condé or – for a time – the Dukes of Epernon or Longueville.

Moreover, the Cardinal largely respected the claims of the ancient titled nobility and, in particular, the peers to monopolise the highest positions of command in the French army. If his relations with provincial governors acting as military commanders of troops in their provinces and with other noblemen commanding French armies nevertheless visibly deteriorated after 1635, this was at least to some extent because he expected too much from the high nobility. Governors and commanders were required to work military miracles with too few troops and inadequate financial resources, and at the same time the Crown denied them the liberty of action and the material rewards which the military entrepreneurs fighting for other states or the Spanish magnates could claim (see above, pp. 130–1).[37]

From this perspective it could be argued that the emergency measures to which Richelieu increasingly resorted during the war and the establishment of novel administrative structures, such as the new authority granted to special royal commissioners, appointed more systematically than in the past to deal with fiscal and judicial problems – the *intendants* – was not really an answer to the threat posed by the excessive power of the aristocratic governors. Rather, the fact that the governors, who were in any case now often absent from their home provinces commanding armies elsewhere, were no longer able to mobilise the fiscal and military resources required by the war effort led the Crown to look for new administrative methods.[38]

The tensions which had marked relations between Crown and nobility during Richelieu's government were temporarily and partially defused by the military victories of the 1640s, which brought glory and honour to Crown and nobility alike. But the collapse of the royal finances in 1648 revived earlier resentment against royal policy and the emergency measures which had become so widespread since the early 1630s. Even after the *Fronde* the provincial French nobility – probably more so than the magnates – continued to be in a state of unrest in the late 1650s (cf. above, pp. 119), and it was left to Louis XIV to overcome aristocratic opposition and re-establish royal authority.

After a century of noble unrest and internal turmoil, Louis XIV achieved a new political equilibrium which ensured that the king's claim to reign supreme was no longer openly challenged. However, as has already been emphasised, the conflicts and rebellions of the preceding century had often been motivated not so much by a principled desire to defend noble liberty and autonomy, as by a feeling that the Crown had failed to uphold noble honour and prestige while overtaxing the nobility's capacity to serve the king. Thus Louis XIV's achievement was less spectacular than it might seem at first sight. Louis XIV knew not only how to govern, but also how to act the role of king on the magnificent self-created stage provided by his court. As Louis conceived this role, the king was not only the highest judge, the Church's advocate and commander-in-chief of the armed forces, but also, and even more importantly, the first nobleman of his realm. The King deliberately cultivated the image of the perfect nobleman with impeccable taste, clothing style, self-discipline and manners. It has been suggested that he modelled himself on Turenne, France's foremost military commander during the first half of his reign and a truly perfect gentleman who had acted as a sort of fatherly tutor to the young King.[39] While those who failed to serve in the army or appear at court could expect little favour and were excluded from access to any real power, the King was careful not to slight or humiliate them. Old aristocratic families generally received the respect due to them, even if they were not part of the inner circle in Versailles.[40]

Such matters of political style apart, developments beyond his direct control undoubtedly favoured the King's policy. The fall in grain prices after 1660 diminished the income noblemen could derive from agriculture and the rents their tenants paid. In the frontier provinces, and elsewhere as well, to some extent, noblemen had already suffered the disastrous effects of the war against Spain (1635–59), the *Fronde* and the 'tax of violence' which undisciplined royal troops tended to impose on the civilian population in the form of plunder, rape and atrocities wherever they were quartered. The nobility was therefore hit even more severely by the agricultural depression of the 1660s and 1670s.[41] Royal pensions and the other material rewards which the King offered those who served him at court or in the armed forces were therefore all the more welcome. On the other hand, after the end of war with Spain in 1659 royal finances gradually recovered and royal debts could be reduced.[42]

At least as long as Colbert controlled public finances, that is, until his death in 1683, the Crown was in a comparatively strong position fiscally and could generously subsidise the life of the court nobility and its office-holders.[43] But even more important than such financial considerations may have been the fact that Louis XIV gave his nobility that feeling that he appreciated their services and that he recognised the Crown's responsibility to uphold the honour and prestige of the nobility as an estate.[44] This held true both for the *noblesse d'epée* and the *noblesse de robe*. The former found employment and had the chance of a successful career in the ever expanding army. In fact, the highest positions in the army were generally, reserved for the high aristocracy, as we have seen (above, pp. 132).[45] Although noblemen from *robe* families who had risen to eminence as lawyers and judges or as financiers also tried to place their sons – especially their younger sons – in the army, nobles who did not belong to the ancient *noblesse d'epée* were often confined to the lower ranks of the officer corps. Admittedly, the almost permanent warfare of the years 1689–1714, with its enormous demand on manpower, created favourable career opportunities even for officers from less well-established families, as the army was expanding fast and many senior officers were killed in action or badly wounded. In peacetime, however, they lacked the court connections necessary for a succesful career, and as *robe* families rarely demonstrated the same sense of dynastic solidarity (extending far beyond the core family to distant cousins and nephews) as the older nobility, they had no network of relatives in the army on which to rely.[46]

In politics, the *noblesse de robe*, in particular, the judges of the Parisian and the provincial *parlements*, saw their direct influence curtailed under Louis XIV. Thus in 1673 the Parisian *parlement* lost its right to remonstrate against royal orders and letters patent before they were registered. However, recent research no longer sees legislation as the essential hallmark of the absolute monarchy. In fact, in France as elsewhere, the King was reluctant to meddle – outside narrowly defined areas of public and criminal law – with existing legal customs and arrangements.[47] Furthermore, while their political weight was diminished, the administrative and judicial role of the parliaments was enhanced. Although the King did not directly attack the established rights of jurisdiction held by noble seigneurs, their courts increasingly lost out in the competition with the royal courts which were

more attractive for litigants, as they were more efficient and found it far easier to enforce their judgements. With the drift of the upper echelons of the
nobility to Versailles, to Paris and into army garrisons outside their own
provinces (see below, pp. 38), the *noblesse de robe*, which dominated the
provincial parliaments and the other legal and administrative councils, now
became the real representative of royal authority in the regions – next to the
intendants who were in social terms themselves members of the *noblesse de
robe*.[48]

The *robins* and other members of the local elites in general took pride in
acting as the King's agents, a function which not only gave their claims to
social precedence a new legitimacy but was often also financially rewarding.
Noblemen, clergy and officeholders serving the Crown could often – officially or unofficially – divert a reasonable percentage of public income into
their own pockets.[49] Moreover, many members of the *noblesse de robe* and
the higher echelons of the *noblesse d'epée* had a vested interest in the stability of the state and the success of royal policy. Although both pretended to
despise the unpopular financiers who raised credit for the King and acted as
tax farmers, many had business dealings with this financial elite. In fact, a
high percentage of the money which the financiers lent to the King had first
been borrowed by them from wealthy officeholders or aristocrats. Other
financiers were hardly more than mere men of straw for their aristocratic
patrons. The extent to which the seemingly absolute monarchy was dependent on its financiers and the aristocracy considerably qualifies the idea of
absolutism. Or, as Daniel Dessert has put it: 'La mise au pas des élites, à
partir de 1661, n'est qu'une tentative pour limiter indirectement la pouvoir
réel d'une oligarchie, en apparence vaincue politiquement et en réalité
victorieuse financièrement.' ('Putting the elites in their place after 1661 is no
more than an attempt to limit indirectly the real power of an oligarchy,
which was seemingly defeated politically but in reality triumphed in the field
of public finance.')[50]

The Crown's dependence on its aristocratic creditors explains to some
extent why Louis XIV was cautious enough to refrain from any major
attack on noble privileges. Only in the last decades of his reign did he make
a half-hearted attempt to raise new revenues by taxing not just the mass of
the population but also the elites. However, the *capitation* introduced during the Nine Years War in 1695 – a sort of poll tax on a crude sliding scale
in proportion to the status and wealth of the taxpayers – and the *dixième*
introduced in 1710, a 10 per cent tax on income, which temporarily put a
somewhat heavier fiscal burden on the rich, were comparatively cautious
measures. Yet they undoubtedly contributed to the deterioration of relations between the King and the elites in the period leading up to his death.[51]

Even before the last desperate years of Louis' reign the nobility had to
redefine its role in the new monarchy, and this applies particularly to the
noblesse d'epée. After 1660 France fought her wars almost exclusively on
foreign soil, as the kingdom was now protected in the north and north-west

by an almost impenetrable ring of modern fortresses which made it extremely difficult for foreign armies to invade the country. This gave added protection to noble landed property, but such developments and other changes in warfare also greatly diminished the value of the local power noblemen wielded. They were no longer needed to defend frontier provinces or raise soldiers among their own tenants in an emergency. In fact, those nobles who pursued a military career often did so outside their home provinces, as military organisation was now much more centralised.

To the extent that they were more frequently absent, they also sought marriage partners, friends and patrons outside their own provinces.[52] This holds good at least for the wealthier and more ambitious titled noblemen, the class which has been called the *noblesse seconde* and which had consti-tuted the real regional elite in the late sixteenth and early seventeenth cen-turies – in contrast to the *ducs et pairs* who had always pursued their interests on the national stage.[53] The division between the nobility of court and capital on the one hand and the provincial nobilities on the other thus became much more pronounced than in the past, although it was never absolute and insurmountable. In many ways it was defined more by a dif-ferent way of life than by a clear separation between two distinct social groups, as most families in Versailles or Paris had relations or cadet branches in the provinces, or married off some of their daughters to provin-cial noblemen.[54] Nevertheless, those who lacked the wealth and status to live at court or in the capital – the simple gentlemen and *hobereaux* – were now increasingly left to their own devices in the provinces. They had little political influence, and even their social standing was markedly lower than that of the provincial *noblesse de robe*, who now often acted as the real rep-resentatives of the state in the regions. Thus late seventeenth-century France witnessed a process of centralisation which had important cultural dimen-sions. The provincial elites tried to imitate the court culture of Versailles in their own capitals and increasingly looked to Paris and the court as the places which set the standards of good taste.[55] To stress this process of cen-tralisation is not to deny that magnates could still exert considerable influ-ence on provincial politics. But they now normally did so from Versailles or Paris, as absentees, only occasionally visiting the province where they tried to maintain a network of clients. Such absentee government could succeed, but it required a great deal of effort and hard work.[56]

In spite of the general decline of Marxist approaches to history, some recent Marxist or post-Marxist interpretations of the *ancien régime* have revived the idea that so-called absolute monarchy was really a form of class rule. They suggest that it was government not necessarily by, but in the interests of, the privileged elites, who siphoned off a considerable share of the public revenues and benefited from the offices and positions of power they held.[57] The *ancien régime* was undoubtedly based on an accommoda-tion between the Crown and the social elites, or rather, certain sections of these elites. Research on government in the French provinces has demonstrated that it was often a comparatively small number of families which benefited directly from co-operation with the Crown. In Brittany between 60 and 100 great noble houses enjoyed an income of more than 30,000 *livres* p.a. Members of these families held the more important seigneurial jurisdictions, the most significant military posts and dominated the estates which granted the taxes. They benefited substantially from royal largesse in the form of pensions and other grants and were, moreover, able to protect their own tenants against fiscal exactions, whereas simple country gentlemen found it much more difficult to adapt to the growth of the state, visible, for example, in the rising level of taxation.[58]

However, in stressing the alliance between the king and the higher echelons of the nobility – which in Fance included the more powerful families of the *noblesse de robe* – one should not forget that in France as in other countries this elite had achieved its social position in the service of the state and was itself increasingly shaped and defined by the state (see above, pp. 10–14, 17–18). This is obviously true for the *noblesse de robe*, the group of hereditary officeholders, but it is no less true for the *noblesse d'epée,* or at least its upper echelons. The families of most *ducs et pairs*, as well as those who belonged to the titled *noblesse seconde*, had risen to their exalted place in the social hierarchy after the mid-sixteenth century, although they had often achieved their status of nobility much earlier, in the Middle Ages. But it was the opportunities offered by the Wars of Religion and careers at court and in the army which had made the fortune of many families prominent in the late seventeenth century. The Duke of Saint-Simon's father, for example, had obtained his peerage at the court of Louis XIII as one of the King's personal friends and favourites. This did not prevent his son from severely criticising Louis XIV for humiliating the ancient nobility and showing too much favour to parvenus and mere *roturiers*.[59] In France, as in other countries, the process of state formation created new elites and transformed or replaced old ones. But at the same time it created new vested interests which in the eighteenth century would – fatally – prevent any real reform of the administrative and fiscal structure created under Louis XIII and XIV.

New political alignments in the later seventeenth century

Like France, Brandenburg-Prussia is traditionally considered one of the strongholds of absolutism where a once independent elite was transformed into an obedient service nobility. However, as in the case of France, this account oversimplifies the complicated relationship between dynasty and nobility. In the sixteenth century the Hohenzollern had indeed found it difficult to impose their will on the country against the interests of the established families. The local *Amtleute* (bailiffs) had little authority outside the princely demesne which the Hohenzollern ruled as landlords. Moreover many of the local *Ämter* (districts) had been pawned to powerful nobles who supported the electors financially by granting them credit.[60] When the elector wanted to intervene in legal or political conflicts outside his demesne lands or the towns, he normally appointed a commission of local noblemen who were to seek a compromise solution. Only in extreme cases did the princely law courts decide these matters on their own, without prior consultation with the interested parties and their implicit consent.[61]

It was, however, a highly select circle of particularly powerful noblemen who acted as the ruler's partner in politics. The nobility of the Mark Brandenburg consisted of about 260 families in the early seventeenth century, some with several sub-branches (comprising about 3,600 individuals or slightly less than 1 per cent of the overall population),[62] but both in political and economic terms, a small elite of about 15 families totally overshadowed the rest of the nobility. Members of these families held the most important positions, both in the central and the local administration, and also acted as leaders of the nobility in the assembly of estates (*Landtag*). Some of these families, such as the Schulenburg, Alvensleben and von Arnim enjoyed a degree of political and economic power which put them virtually on a par with some counts of the Empire (*Reichsgrafen*); some of the richest Junker families were even able to modernise their medieval castles before the Thirty Years War so that they could withstand a serious artillery siege.[63]

However, the Thirty Years War, which ruined many noblemen as much as their peasant farmers, deeply transformed the framework of politics and ended the rule of the select noble elite which had lorded it over the country before 1618. After 1648 the nobility tried to stabilise its shaky economic and financial position by further extending the system of *Gutsherrschaft* (the economic, social and jurisdictional structures which enabled a nobleman, as lord of the manor, to control not only the economic activities but the entire lives of his tenants) and *Erbuntertänigkeit* (literally hereditary 'serfdom', although serfdom is really too strong a word in this context) which had already formed the basis of their wealth before the war. In the early 1650s the nobility persuaded the elector to confirm legal arrangements which legitimised the existing system of *Gutsherrschaft* and facilitated further encroachments on the rights of peasants. In exchange for these privileges they were largely prepared to leave high politics to the elector and his councillors, and abandoned any claim to intervene in these matters.[64]

The situation of many noblemen was quite desperate, as the devastations of the war, the extreme lack of manpower – Brandenburg had lost more than 50 per cent of its pre-war population between 1618 and 1648 – and agricultural depression all worked to their disadvantage. It is therefore no surprise that a ruler determined to increase his power, such as Frederick William, the 'Great Elector' of Brandenburg (1640–88), exploited this situation successfully to bolster his authority. The wealthy families who had dominated the Brandenburg estates in the sixteenth century and managed to maintain their economic status despite the demographic and agricultural crisis after 1648, often preferred to stay away from the elector's court. Their members sought employment outside Brandenburg or were content to supervise their estates instead of serving as officers in the Hohenzollern army or accepting positions as officeholders.[65] Most noble landowners in the Kurmark could not, however, afford the luxury of such independent behaviour and were eager enough to enter the elector's service in the civil administration or, preferably, the army.

In spite of the trend towards 'absolutism', the Prince Elector and his successors who, from 1701, reigned as kings over their dominions, found it difficult to implement their policies in the localities without the nobility's co-operation. In the eighteenth century the king's representative in the local administrative district, the *Landrat*, was as a rule a local nobleman, often appointed with the advice and consent of the local estates (the *Ritterschaft*). In fact, outside the towns, there was hardly any local bureaucracy on which the ruler could rely to enforce his political decisions. Without the support of the local nobility, the countryside was virtually ungovernable without military coercion, at best a weapon of last resort. The nobility remained capable of defending their position against encroachments by the electoral bureaucracy, although the fiscal pressure exerted by the latter slowly eroded the landlord's position as the sole or principal source of authority for the rural population.[66]

Outside the principality of Brandenburg – the heartland of the emerging Prussian state – the prince electors of the late seventeenth century and the Prussian kings of the eighteenth century found it even more difficult to enforce their will. In Eastern Prussia, where Polish political influence remained strong until the mid-seventeenth century – officially the King of Poland enjoyed rights of suzerainty over Prussia until 1660 – the elector of Brandenburg in his capacity as Duke of Prussia had to make a great effort to subdue the recalcitrant estates in the later seventeenth century. The liberty which noblemen enjoyed in Poland remained an ideal which many Prussian subjects continued to admire until the eighteenth century, although the decline of the Polish republic into chaos and political impotence undoubtedly diminished the attractions of the Polish constitution. Recent research has demonstrated that the estates retained considerable influence at the local level, although they retreated from the sphere of high politics after about 1700. Even here, however, their influence slowly revived at the end of the eighteenth century after an earlier resurgence during the Russian occupation of East Prussia during the Seven Years War.[67]

The nobility of Brandenburg-Prussia has often been depicted as a class of landowners who ruthlessly exploited their own peasant farmers while at the same time selling out politically to a dynasty bent on enforcing its will at all costs, transforming its dominions into an absolutist military state.[68] This image, however, is in many ways a misrepresentation.[69] What does remain true is that in most Prussian provinces a comparatively poor nobility benefited from the chances for employment offered by an expanding army and, to a lesser extent, civil bureaucracy. Yet it was a long time, probably not until the mid-eighteenth century, before the nobility had fully adjusted to the new political developments. At the same time, official policy now deliberately defended noble privileges, which before 1740 had often been called into question by the Crown.

Both France and Brandenburg-Prussia, in different ways, offer an example of a strengthening of the authority of the monarchical state achieved, after a period of conflict between ruler and nobility, in the last resort with the co-operation of large sections of the nobility itself. In Austria this co-operation is even more clearly visible. The noble elite which dominated the Habsburg monarchy in the later seventeenth century had been remodelled and transformed by the Counter-Reformation and the measures the Habsburgs took against rebellious noblemen in Bohemia and Austria in the 1620s. Yet the small group of noble magnates who combined enormous power in the localities, based on landed wealth and extensive seigneural rights, with influence at court and in the regional administration of the provinces (which continued to be controlled largely by the Estates) were more partners than mere subjects of the emperor (see above, pp. 44–9).

The tendency towards absolutism seems to be more dominant in Scandinavia, and in Denmark in particular. Until the 1660s, Denmark had been an elective monarchy. Domestic policy was to a large extent dominated by a small group of old-established noble families, perhaps not more than 1,500 individuals (counting only adult male noblemen) in about 1660.[70] As the king owned extensive demesne lands and derived valuable revenues from the customs levied at the entrances to the Baltic Sea, he did not need to rely on taxation to finance his policy. Most monarchs had therefore accepted the traditional noble privileges, in particular, freedom from taxation, without too much ado, so long as they were free to pursue their own dynastic and foreign policies. This they were able to do for a long time, being rich enough to finance such policies out of their own pockets.

However, a series of wars in which Denmark found it increasingly difficult to hold its own, in particular, the military confrontation with Sweden in the 1650s, brought this constitutional structure tumbling down. Clearly some sort of reform, in particular, fiscal reform, was needed if Denmark was to survive as a state against the Swedish onslaught. With the support of the urban elites and the powerful clergy, Frederik III abrogated the Old Danish constitution in 1660–4, transformed Denmark into a hereditary monarchy and dissolved the old aristocratic Council of the Realm whose members had seen themselves as virtual co-regents. The army backed the revolution from above which the King had staged. Although members of the old nobility held important positions of command in the army, they had to share commissions as officers with foreign nobles and men from new families. Moreover, even representatives of the old-established families had come to accept new ideas and new social norms while serving as professional soldiers. These ideas and norms prepared them for the new autocratic monarchy created in the 1660s.[71]

The new constitution was confirmed by the *Lex Regia* of 1664, which proclaimed absolute royal power as the guiding principle of politics. However, as historians have pointed out, the constitutional revolution and the reforms of the 1660s were more 'a redefinition of nobility than an attack upon it'. Noble status was now, as in other countries, increasingly defined in terms of service in the army and the civil administration, and commoners who held certain high-ranking offices in the administration were automatically ennobled from the late seventeenth century onwards.[72]

As in Denmark, warfare transformed the traditional political balance in Sweden in the seventeenth century. Sweden, in contrast to Denmark, had been a hereditary monarchy since the 1540s. The numerically quite small nobility had to share its power in the assembly of estates, the *Riksdag*, not only with the clergy and the representatives of the towns, but also with delegates elected by the peasantry. Despite the fact that noble magnates dominated the *Riksrad*, the Privy Council which the monarch was obliged to consult on all matters of importance, the nobility's hold on power was therefore less secure than in Denmark. However, Sweden became a major military power in the early seventeenth century, fighting against Poland, Denmark and, during the Thirty Years War, the Emperor. The military expansion of the country was a process in which the nobility actively participated and from which it, or at least certain noble families, clearly benefited, in the form of rich spoils of war (some Swedish castles and country houses are even today furnished with booty from the Thirty Years War) and generous donations of land which officers and influential magnates received from the Crown for their services.

Nevertheless, when Sweden suffered a number of military setbacks in the 1670s this policy was reversed. Unlike his predecessors, Charles XI (1660–97) was determined to reduce the political power of the noble magnates. He could count on the support not just of the clergy, the peasants and the urban elites, but also to some extent on that of many simple country gentlemen who had failed to benefit from the generous donations and grants the noble magnates had received. Moreover, the enormous expansion of the nobility as an estate had created a class of newly ennobled military officers and officeholders who owed their social position almost exclusively to the King's favour. For these men it was essential that the state managed to solve the financial crisis which had been precipitated by the demands of warfare. Otherwise the Crown would not be able to pay their salaries and the other sums it owed to its servants, and would be forced to abolish the fiscal privileges noblemen enjoyed. The King therefore found support for his radical reforms among the newly created service nobility.[73] In the face of resistance from the old-established magnates, the higher nobility who had once dominated Swedish politics, he was therefore able to enact a number of statutes in 1680–2 which declared the earlier, very extensive, alienations of Crown

estates and demesnes void. The King now took back a considerable percentage of the land which noblemen had acquired from the Crown in one
way or another over the past decades, as a reward for their services or in lieu
of cash payments. Although few noble families were actually ruined, many
suffered severe financial losses.[74]

Such a radical measure is unparalleled elsewhere in Europe. But as the
Swedish nobility in the past had largely supported an active, warlike foreign policy, it found it difficult to resist the reforms which were now
undertaken to create the financial and administrative foundations required
to defend the empire which this policy had created. Moreover, as has
already been pointed out, many noblemen drew salaries or pensions from
the state, and they were likely to lose these if the Crown's financial solvency could not be restored.[75] As in Denmark, the change towards a more
authoritarian style of government under Charles IX had social as well as
political implications. The King continued the policy of generously
ennobling new men – foreigners and his own subjects alike – who served
as officers or in an administrative or legal capacity. In 1600 the Swedish
nobility had been a small class of hereditary landowners; one hundred
years later it was a much larger elite, essentially a service nobility. Its members may also have owned land, but they had acquired their status in war
or through their skills as legal or administrative experts.[76] However, once
this new nobility was securely established in the early eighteenth century, it
pursued an ideal of aristocratic liberty which was, in many ways, inspired
by the values which the old nobility had subscribed to in the past. When
Sweden's last great warrior king, Charles XII, had fallen in battle (1718)
and Sweden had abandoned any ambition to play a major role in
European politics, the country was transformed into a sort aristocratic
republic, governed by and for the nobility.[77]

Both in Denmark and in Sweden the constitutional changes of the later
seventeenth century were closely connected with the challenge posed by
warfare and the conflict with neighbouring states. Whereas in both
Scandinavian countries this led to a more authoritarian style of government
and greater administrative centralisation, in Castile and the Spanish Empire
in general the effect of warfare on administration and government was
much more ambivalent, as we have already seen (above, pp. 128–9).
Admittedly, recent research has questioned the idea that the financial crisis
of the state and permanent warfare led to a genuine breakdown of the
Castilian state and a wholesale decentralisation of royal power. The legal
structures which ensured that the exercise of rights of lordship could be controlled by royal law courts remained basically intact – an important point of
great significance for the relationship between state and nobility (cf. below,
pp. 148–9).[78] The great aristocratic magnates who took over so many functions – recruiting soldiers, raising taxes, rights of jurisdiction – exercised
directly by the Crown in the past were essentially not feudal lords, but members of a political elite which had risen in the service of the state and owed

its power to its influence on the administrative, legal and military machinery of the monarchy. Moreover, some recent accounts have emphasised that the so-called 'refeudalisation' 'did not mean any decrease in the institutional power of the state'.[79] I.A.A. Thompson, one of the principal exponents of the idea of refeudalisation, now himself prefers to speak of 're-señorialisation' instead of refeudalisation.[80]

Nevertheless, the undeniable tendency to strengthen local lordships was reinforced by the fact that during the period when the population of Spain and of Castile in particular was being subjected to an ever increasing tax burden, between c.1580 and 1660–70, it seemed attractive to many men and women to leave their native cities and settle in a village or small town under a nobleman's control. Here a different fiscal regime obtained, as noble magnates were often able to achieve freedom from direct royal taxation in exchange for payment of a – limited – lump sum. They could therefore afford to tax their own vassals at a lower rate than the king. Hence it is not surprising that in the early seventeenth century 'seigniorial territories were seen as taxhavens for the oppressed'. Whereas the population of royal cities declined, the size of the rural population living under seigniorial jurisdiction remained more or less stable and sometimes even increased.[81] Admittedly peasant communities under the rule of a noble lord seem to have sometimes entered into direct negotiations with the Crown over tax demands, thereby bypassing their own lord. In the 1680s and 1690s there were even cases in the Kingdom of Valencia where peasant communities offered to ensure the payment of higher taxes at the expense of their own seigneur.[82]

Such cases, however, remained by and large exceptional. In general, the fiscal crisis and the shortcomings of the bureaucratic institutions forced the king to rely on noblemen with court connections to enforce his decisions at the local level, or as I.A.A. Thompson has put it:

> Royal authority was simply not transferable, on a regular basis, to the local level without the informal machinery of affinity and clientage which linked the court aristocracy and the higher bureaucracy with the local elites. It was with the *poderosos*, therefore, that power in the country rested.[83]

If this held true for the heartland of the Spanish monarchy, Castile, it applied even more to the peripheral provinces such as Naples and Sicily. In our period, next to Castile, they bore the brunt of the fiscal pressure warfare had generated, although, or perhaps because, these provinces were by and large not directly affected by military operations. In Naples sources of public revenue were sold to private contractors and noble magnates on a truly gigantic scale to raise short-term loans. In the words of one historian, 'this amounted to nothing less than the wholesale privatisation of state resources, the abrogation of the authority of the state, and the rejection of that policy of state-building which fifteenth-century kings had so laboriously crafted.'[84]

Matters were similar in Sicily, where everything that could be sold by the Crown was effectively put on the market in the reign of Philip IV (1621–65). Those who bought castles, rights of taxation and entire lordships with *merum et mixtum imperium* (full jurisdiction) included financiers, often from Northern Italy and in particular Genoa, officeholders and bureaucrats, as well as members of the older aristocracy. In fact, the new elite of state contractors, tax farmers and lawyers holding state offices seems to have merged easily enough with the old elite of rural barons. Although the latter clearly benefited politically from the sell-off of public rights and revenues, they did not necessarily prosper economically. Often they were heavily in debt themselves. Serving the state may have brought political dividends but not necessarily financial ones, at least in the short term. In fact, although the Crown to all intents and purposes sold out to the nobility, it was neverthe-less capable to some extent of defining the terms of trade for this bargain. By generously granting new titles and dignities to old and new families alike, it created a new social hierarchy. In Spanish Italy as well as in Spain itself social status depended largely on the access an individual or a family had to the sources of political power, that is, in Italy, the vice-regal courts in Palermo or Naples or the governor's court in Milan, and in Spain, the court in Madrid and the conciliar bodies representing the king in the capital and provinces. But only those who enjoyed noble status, granted or confirmed by titles or a knighthood in the Spanish military orders (cf. above, pp. 16, 25), could fully participate in the race for place and profit because the most important charges in the administration and the army were reserved for nobles.[85]

In many European countries the nobility was transformed by the process of state formation which offered new opportunities for old-established fam-ilies and social newcomers alike, and created an elite defined increasingly by the criterion of 'Herrschaftsnähe' (proximity to power).[86] Nevertheless, there were exceptions to this rule. Apart from countries such as Poland or the Northern Netherlands, which lacked strong monarchical power, England is the most striking of these exceptions. In England, neither peerage nor gentry enjoyed any extensive legal privileges, and as the number of lucra-tive offices in the gift of the Crown and the size of the army were limited, even in the later seventeenth century, the Crown had comparatively little to offer the social elite.[87] It is certainly true that unsalaried local offices such as the positions of Lord-Lieutenant, Deputy-Lieutenant and Justice of the Peace remained prestigious and were important to confirm the social status of a family. Although the king could in theory freely choose those who held such offices, he was nevertheless well advised not to bypass individuals or fami-lies who dominated a county. If he chose to appoint outsiders, Catholics, for example, or persons of insufficient social standing, as Charles I did in the later 1620s in some counties, and James II on a much larger scale after 1685, the system could easily become unworkable. Under James II, the decision to bypass the old elites led to administrative collapse and revolution.[88]

In other countries the higher ranks of the nobility largely owed their position to their influence at court, to high commands in the army, prestigious royal offices which gave those who held them ample opportunities for patronage and to dispense favours, or to the fact that they acted as the Crown's creditors. In England, however, parliament remained the essential focus for defining the identity of the social elite, as we have already seen (above, pp, 27–8). For the peers, their seat in the House of Lords was the most important of their otherwise rather limited legal privileges, but even for the upper echelons of the gentry, the ability to influence parliamentary elections, or, even better, to obtain a seat in the House of Commons themselves, was an essential mark not just of political influence but of social distinction.[89] It is therefore not surprising that the English elite tenaciously defended the rights of parliament both before and after the Civil War; not only its interests but its social identity would have been threatened and undermined by the demise of parliament.

Some members of the elite went further and dreamt of a republican constitution. After the Restoration they remained true to the memory of the 'Good Old Cause', the republican principles of the 1650s. Their ideal was an aristocratic republic of which an idealised Venice or ancient Rome could offer an example. This group of high-ranking republicans, which included Anthony Ashley Cooper, Earl of Shaftesbury, John Locke's patron, found their philosophical spokesman in Algernon Sidney, a younger son of the second Earl of Leicester and great-nephew of Sir Philip Sidney, the Elizabethan hero and poet, and their martyrs in William Lord Russell (1639–83, executed for high treason), Arthur Capel, Earl of Essex (1631–83, committed suicide in the Tower) and in Sidney himself (1622–83, executed for high treason).[90]

The Revolution settlement of 1688–89 protected both gentry and peerage against any attempts an authoritarian state might make to intervene on a regular basis in county politics and disturb the monopoly of power the country's 'natural rulers' held. However, as has already been emphasised (above, pp. 52–53), in the last resort the members of the peerage benefited more than simple country gentlemen from the constitutional arrangements of 1688, although the House of Lords as a political institution gradually declined in importance over the next century. But the eighteenth century was very much an aristocratic century. With the decline of political tensions after 1720, the electoral patronage exercised by the great landowners came into its own. In many constituencies it was now predominant, and ensured that the House of Commons became an assembly representing aristocratic interests.[91]

Conclusion

England is often seen as the great exception among the European monarchies, where, it seems, absolutism triumphed over older ideas of noble autonomy and liberty in the later seventeenth century. The 1650s and 1660s certainly marked a political sea-change in a number of European countries. After decades of domestic unrest and turmoil, as in France, for example, strong royal or princely government was established or re-established. A nobility which faced serious economic problems, due not least to falling agricultural prices, was often only too glad to co-operate with a state which protected noblemen against their creditors, reinforced their power as landlords or seigneurs as well as their patriarchal authority as fathers, and offered them gainful and prestigious employment in the army or administration. However, the new political equilibrium which was established in the seventeenth century between Crown and nobility was often based more on a compromise than on a straightforward victory of the state over aristocratic interests. In the Spanish monarchy, but to some extent under the rule of the Austrian Habsburgs as well, noble lordship at the local level was perhaps stronger in around 1700 than it had been a century before. It was, however, now embedded more firmly than ever in a legal framework which subjected it to the control of the law courts.[92] Thus the ability to use litigation as a means to further one's own interests became an essential precondition for defending or extending seigneural rights and noble power in general, and this was also true for a country such as France, where political and cultural centralisation was more marked than in Austria or Spain. The 'essence of local government' and, one may add, of local politics and noble faction fighting in the provinces, was 'the pursuit of large numbers of cases in the courts'.[93]

Noble power survived and did, in fact, prosper in the seventeenth century. But for noblemen to be successful under the new dispensation they had to be prepared to play the new games, to act as brokers between the court and regional and local interests, and, even more importantly, to use or manipulate the legal structure for their own ends. These days state formation is increasingly seen as a process which was not just imposed from above, but which was also driven by social forces and local interests, using the state apparatus to achieve their own objectives. This is nowhere more apparent than in the field of litigation. Litigation served to link local communities to a national political culture and, in the words of the British historian Steve Hindle, 'embedded the state deeper into the social order.'[94] The traditional perspective still influential and enshrined in the catchword 'juridification' ('Verrechtlichung'), popular with German historians in particular, implies that the increase in litigation represents the triumph of peace and order and a centralising state asserting its monopoly of the legitimate use of force and violence against recalcitrant subjects and unruly noblemen.[95] This, however, is at best a half-truth. In fact, litigation in the later sixteenth and early seventeenth centuries was a deeply divisive process. Injured or allegedly injured noblemen used the law courts to humiliate and dishonour their opponents and assert their own honour and status within the local or regional community. As Hindle emphasises, 'the legitimacy of the state was reinforced by the frequency with which its institutions were employed for the resolution of social conflicts.' But social harmony was rarely the result and even less frequently the objective of such a resort to the state and its resources of authority and physical force.[96]

We are now more likely to accept that the early modern state was not so much 'consciously built or centralised' as that state formation was a process fuelled by the interests of social groups which benefited from the resources the state put at their disposal.[97] Among these interests, those of the nobility loomed large, in particular, in countries such as Spain or France. Noblemen in the seventeenth century had to accept the new rules of the game entailed in the process of state formation. But they were still at liberty to play this new game pursuing their own objectives, trying to gain power, wealth and status, rather than those of a ruler whose authority was theoretically subject to no constraints but who, in reality, could govern successfully only if he were seen to uphold the traditional social order and defend the honour of those who served him as military commanders, high-ranking officeholders and courtiers – his nobility.

Conclusion

The later sixteenth and seventeenth centuries were a period of profound change for the noble elites of most European countries, as we have seen. Noblemen were confronted by radical challenges. Traditional, warlike noble virtues were in danger of being made obsolete by changes in warfare. Faced with new cultural standards imposed by the confessional Churches and humanists alike, the nobility was found deficient in education and manners, and the slow but – in most countries – seemingly irreversible concentration of power in the hands of the state, which successfully centralised fiscal and military resources, potentially undermined the authority of noblemen in local communities. However, as we have seen, noble elites often displayed a remarkable resilience. The process of state formation put new resources at the disposal of the nobility, which successfully employed them for its own ends. Moreover, new social groups, such as university-trained officeholders, military career officers of non-noble origin and, in some cases, even financiers and tax farmers were integrated into the nobility when their rise to power and social eminence could not be prevented. Often these very newcomers were most eager to demonstrate that they were part of the traditional elite by adhering to its values and ideals even more strictly than families which had been firmly established for centuries. Men whose fathers had been newly ennobled lawyers and judges, or royal favourites who had charmed or danced their way into the prince's favour and thereby acquired new titles and benefited from the royal bounty, complained incessantly about the rise of social parvenus, as did the Duke of Saint-Simon, for example. Or they demonstrated the same sense of aristocratic freedom and liberty which the great feudal lords of the past had nurtured. Many newcomers were eager to have their own sons fight as soldiers in the monarch's service, to return victorious from the battlefield or to die a glamorous death to the everlasting glory of their family.[1]

At the same time Baroque court culture, whose apogee was in the second half of the seventeenth century, was deeply aristocratic in character, with its obsessive concentration on rank and precedence and its emphasis on all those seemingly effortless social graces noblemen and noblewomen were most likely to acquire at an early age through breeding and the imitation of their elders. It decidedly dampened the social aspirations of those who dared to think that mere book learning, hard work and intelligence – or even military valour – combined with the necessary number of fencing, dancing and riding lessons, was enough to gain a place at the top of the social hierarchy.

It could, of course, be argued that this appearance of continuity and of a nobility triumphant in the face of adversity is actually deceptive. What did the titled patronage brokers of the classical Baroque court who were dependent on enormous royal pensions, the newly ennobled civil servants, the disciplined professional soldiers who were content to serve in standing armies controlled ultimately by a distant bureaucracy, or even the aristocratic magnates who astutely managed and manipulated parliamentary politics in early eighteenth-century England have in common with their predecessors? Did they really belong to the same estate or class as the great feudal magnates of the late Middle Ages, with their hosts of armed followers and retainers? In what way could they be related to those fiercely independent local squires and petty warlords who had been so prominent in the remoter regions of many European kingdoms, in the sixteenth century and even later, from the Auvergne to Catalonia and the Anglo-Scottish borders, and who had often derived a substantial part of their income from running profitable protection rackets? The social structures which defined the status, authority and ethos of the new nobilities were, it seems, quite different from those which had defined the identity of the nobility a hundred years earlier. However, despite the profound social, political and cultural transformation of the nobility in most European countries in this period, there were decisive elements of continuity.

In particular, noblemen and -women continued to define their position in society by reference to a specific code of honour which was intended to set them apart from the rest of society. In fact, the ideals which determined noble self-perception and self-fashioning were and remained to a considerable extent dependent on a set of contrasting images which embodied everything that was vulgar and ignoble and therefore to be rejected.[2] These anti-types were in many ways not very different around 1700 from what they had been in the early sixteenth century. The money-minded retailer, merchant or manufacturer who was visibly involved in the less salubrious aspects of trade and commercial production (quietly investing capital in profitable long-distance trade might be a different matter), the lowly 'mechanic' craftsman, the devious lawyer who caught the honest country squire in the trap of his legal trickery and pettifoggery, the pedantic scholar who paraded his encyclopaedic knowledge in every sentence he wrote or spoke or, in a more complicated way, the vulgar peasant who lacked manners and graces, were in many ways still the most influential anti-types for noblemen in the late seventeenth century, as they had already been 150 or

200 years earlier. Noblemen and -women needed these negative social stereotypes – to which others could perhaps be added, such as the over-zealous clergyman of lowly origin or, even worse, the Puritan lay preacher who failed to show due respect to his social betters – to define their own identity by contrast.

However, important changes occurred during the period, in particular in the relationship of the nobility with peasant society and peasant culture. There had certainly always been tensions and clashes of interest between noblemen and peasants, as has just been emphasised, and in many ways the simple peasant was an anti-type to the gentleman. In fact, nobles were often tempted to poke fun at the vulgar who, in their opinion, lacked virtue and honour, or even to humiliate or intimidate them when they seemed to develop ideas above their station. Nonetheless noble culture and peasant culture still had a great deal in common in the early sixteenth century, at least in northern Europe, though probably less so in the Mediterranean countries where noble families had always been more likely to live in towns and cities.[3]

But north of the Alps, for both peasant and noble culture in the early sixteenth century, oral traditions were still in many ways more important than written records or the accomplishments of literacy in general. Both were to some extent defined by the deep cultural divide between the village and the town.[4] Although the local squire and his family played a very specific part in village life which set them apart from the rest of the population, they still participated actively in local festivals and rituals, even those which a later age was to condemn for their lack of restraint, thinly disguised paganism, and tendency to favour all kinds of excess from drunkenness to sexual licence. Nobles employed the sons and daughters of the local peasants as their retainers and servants who lived in the same house, often, for example, sharing meals in the great hall of the castle with their masters and mistresses. Moreover, local noblemen were expected, at least on certain occasions, such as Christmas, to show generous hospitality to all those in need of help by keeping open house.[5] Thus the manor house or castle and the farm house were still very much part of the same social and cultural environment. However, to the extent that well-to-do nobles adjusted to the new values of urbanity and literary culture, they suscribed to a new ideal of high culture which set them apart more radically than in the past from their own tenants and peasants and to some extent from the simple country squire as well.[6] They no longer participated in public festivals together with the mass of the population, and:

> from the very end of the seventeenth century there was a marked acceleration in the rate at which the privileged and affluent withdrew from traditional beliefs and leisure activities, as those became associated not only with ungodliness (as was previously the case) but also, and more damningly, with social inferiority.[7]

Of course all this holds true primarily for those who were rich enough to leave their native counties and provinces, to acquire the necessary luxury items, such as art collections and libraries, and wealthy enough to have at least their sons if not their daughters educated in appropriate style, preferably not only at home but also abroad. For the simple country squire who could barely afford to employ two or three servants, let alone build a vast Palladian country house or Baroque palace in town, matters were different. He was often unable to adapt to the new political and cultural trends with their tendency towards centralisation and urbanisation respectively. Lacking the necessary means to spend the season at court, in the capital or the nearest major city, left high and dry by the disappearance of important aristocratic households in the regions, which had been both a source of patronage and important centres of noble culture, he was likely to be on the losing side both in political and social terms.[8] The best he could hope for was profitable employment in the army or the civil administration, provided he could meet the necessary educational requirements, or perhaps, in the case of Spain, France or England, in the colonies. Simple country gentlemen may have coped best with the changes of the seventeenth century in areas where they did not have to compete with a powerful class of noble magnates or a rich urban elite. This was the case, for example, in north-eastern Germany, where the local *Junker* successfully held their own and later, in the eighteenth century, benefited from rising prices of agricultural products, as they had already done in the sixteenth century. The outlook for the Castilian *hidalgos* or the French *hobereaux* was decidedly less bright, and the same could be said of many small noblemen in Bohemia, Moravia and Austria, who had, moreover, made the mistake of choosing the wrong confessional allegiance before 1620. But then, the decline and fall of families had always been part of the social history of the nobility, in the late Middle Ages as much as in the seventeenth century. As detailed studies have shown, it was often the older families with their many different branches and cadet lines (who often supported each other in the quest for place and profit as they shared a strong sense of belonging to the same house or dynasty) who ultimately had a better chance of survival than younger ones, which lacked such an extensive kinship network.[9]

It is, indeed, true that noble self-perception and noble culture underwent profound changes in our period, changes which were perhaps of greater long-term significance than the visible shift in the political balance of power between nobilities and kings or sovereign princes. The emphasis on physical and military prowess was toned down, and other virtues, such as the art of conversation, or the ability to recognise, judge and contextualize valuable works of art, for example, were given a more prominent place than in the past. In fact 'taste became a matter of breeding' and 'social pre-eminence was based on cultural superiority'.[10] Moreover, noblemen had reluctantly to accept that the informal educational practices of an earlier age, such as bringing up young men in the household of a prominent magnate, had to be abandoned in favour of a more formalised education at an academy or university. Even the hunt, which had not been just a pastime but, as a recent French study has put it, an 'école sans école', an informal apprenticeship for the young where they learnt the ways and manners expected of a member of noble society, was reduced in importance and depreciated. In the eighteenth century it became almost a mere leisure activity to the extent that institutions such as noble academies, learned societies, or, in fact, metropolitan salons served as places where noblemen, but also potentially commoners, could acquire the 'savoir faire' and the 'savoir vivre' which were necessary for a career at court or to achieve social success.[11]

It is equally true that at the end of the seventeenth century the authority and status of noblemen was defined more in terms of privileges granted by the state and less in terms of autonomous power than in the past. As the Cardinal de Bernis remarked in the eighteenth century, in the past a great lord was a man who owned vast estates and held important offices, but who nevertheless lived in the country among his dependants, both his vassals and his clients ('créatures'), who were not ashamed to show him respect and deference. For it was in the power of the great noblemen ('grands seigneurs') to make or unmake the good fortune and prosperity of a gentleman thanks to the credit they had with the king. Now, however, the lords who lived at court had neither any real 'credit' of their own, nor a local network of clients among the lesser noblemen who were loyal to them. They just had their titles and dignities.[12]

The Cardinal may have overemphasised the decline of noble power, but a price certainly had to be paid, even by the most powerful and richest noble families, for their success in adapting to social and political change. In fact, the French Restoration writer Chateaubriand, who looked back to the Ancien Régime from the vantage point of a society which had been deeply transformed by revolution, saw three ages in the history of aristocracy: 'the age of natural superiority, the age of privileges and the age of vanities. Originating in the first age, aristocracy degenerates in the second and comes to an end in the last.'[13] From such a point of view, the late sixteenth and seventeeth centuries, which was certainly, especially in its later stages, an 'age of privileges', may indeed appear as a period of degeneration for the nobility. But what to a writer of the Restoration, who could already see the first seeds of the Revolution in the all too close alliance concluded between monarchy and nobility at this period, may have been a sign of degeneration was to contemporaries more likely to mean a revival and rejuvenation of noble power.

Select bibliography

Preference is given in this short bibliography to works in English and French.

J. Aalbers and M. Prak (eds.) *De Bloem der Natie. Adel en patriciaat en de Nordelijke Nederlanden* (Amsterdam, 1987).

J.S.A. Adamson, 'Chivalry and Political Culture in Caroline England' in K. Sharpe and P. Lake (eds.), *Culture and Politics in Early Stuart England* (Basingstoke, 1994), pp. 161–98.

J.S.A. Adamson (ed.), *The Princely Courts of Europe: Ritual, Politics and Culture under the Ancien Régime 1500–1750* (London, 1999).

J.S. Amelang, *Honored Citizens of Barcelona: Patrician Culture and Class Relations, 1490–1714* (Princeton, New Jersey, 1986).

F. Angiolini, 'Les noblesses italiennes à l'époque moderne: approches et interprétations', *RHMC* 45 (1998), pp. 66–88.

R.G. Asch (ed.), *Der europäische Adel im Ancien Régime: Von der Krise der ständischen Monarchien bis zur Revolution (1600–1789)* (Cologne, 2001).

R.G. Asch and A.M. Birke (eds.), *Politics, Patronage and the Nobility, The Court at the Beginning of the Modern Age (c.1450–1650)* (Oxford, 1991).

R.G. Asch and H. Duchhardt (eds.), *Der Absolutismus – ein Mythos? Strukturwandel monarchischer Herrschaft in West- und Mitteleuropa (ca.1550–1700)* (Cologne, 1996).

I. Atienza Hernández, *Aristocracia, poder y riqueza en la España moderna. La casa de Osuna, siglos xv–xix* (Madrid, 1987).

B. Bastl, *Tugend, Liebe, Ehre. Die adelige Frau in der Frühen Neuzeit* (Vienna, Cologne and Weimar, 2000).

G. Batho, 'Landlords in England, 1500–1640, B: Noblemen, Gentlemen and Yeomen' in C. Clay (ed.), *Rural Society: Landowners, Peasants and Labourers, 1500–1750 (Chapters from the Agrarian History of England and Wales*, vol. II, Cambridge, 1990), pp. 41–71.

J.V. Beckett, *The Aristocracy in England, 1660–1914* (Oxford, 1986).

K. Béguin, *Les Princes de Condé. Rebelles, courtisans et mécènes dans la France du grand siècle* (Paris, 1999).

W. Beik, *Absolutism and Society in Seventeenth-Century France: State Power and Provincial Aristocracy in Languedoc* (Cambridge, 1985).

J.A. Bergin, *The Making of the French Episcopate, 1598–1661* (New Haven, CT, 1996).

G. Bernard (ed.), *The Tudor Nobility* (Manchester, 1992).

F. Billacois, *Le duel dans la société française des XVIe–XVIIe siècles: essai de psychologie historique* (Paris, 1986). (English edn.: *The Duel: its Rise and Fall in Early Modern France*, New Haven, CT, 1990).

M. Bogucka, *The Lost World of the Sarmatians: Custom as the Regulator of Polish Social Life in Early Modern Times* (Warsaw, 1996).

D. Bohanan, *Crown and Nobility in Early Modern France* (Basingstoke, 2001).

L. Bourquin, *Noblesse Seconde et Pouvoir en Champagne aux XVIe et XVIIe siècles* (Paris, 1994).

J. Boutier, *Construction et anatomie d'une noblesse urbaine. Florence à l'epoque moderne* (2 parts, Paris, 1988).

P. Brioist, H. Drévillon, and P. Serna, *Croiser le fer. Violence et culture de l'épée dans la France moderne (XVIe–XVIIIe siècle)* (Seyssel, 2002).

K.M. Brown, *Noble Society in Scotland: Wealth, Family and Culture from Reformation to Revolution* (Edinburgh, 2000).

O. Brunner, *Adeliges Landleben und Europäischer Geist* (Salzburg, 1959).

A. Bryson, *From Courtesy to Civility: Changing Codes of Conduct in Early Modern England* (Oxford, 1998).

P. Burke, *The Fortunes of the Courtier: The European Reception of Castiglione's Cortegiano* (Cambridge, 1995).

M.L. Bush, *The European Nobility*, vol. I: *Noble Privilege* (Manchester, 1983).

M.L. Bush, *The European Nobility*, vol II: *Rich Noble–Poor Noble* (Manchester, 1988).

V. Bůžek and P. Mat'a, 'Wandlungen des Adels in Böhmen und Mähren im Zeitalter des "Absolutismus" (1620–1740)' in Asch, *Adel*, pp. 287–322.

S. Carroll, *Noble Power during the French Wars of Religion* (Cambridge, 1998).

J. Casey, *Early Modern Spain: A Social History* (London, 1999).

E. Chaney, *The Evolution of the Grand Tour* (London 1998).

G. Chaussinand-Nogaret et al. (eds.), *Histoire des élites en France du XVIe au XXe siècle* (Paris, 1991).

S. Clark, *State and Status: The Rise of the State and Aristocratic Power in Western Europe* (Cardiff, 1995).

J.T. Cliffe, *The Yorkshire Gentry: From the Reformation to the Civil War* (1969).

T. Cogswell, *Home Divisions: Aristocracy, the State and Provincial Conflict* (Manchester, 1998).

J.B. Collins, *Classes, Estates and Order in Early Modern Brittany* (Cambridge, 1994).

J.B. Collins, *The State in Early Modern France* (Cambridge, 1995).

N. Conrads, *Ritterakademien der Frühen Neuzeit. Bildung als Standesprivileg im 16. und 17. Jahrhundert* (Göttingen, 1982).

J.-M. Constant, *La vie quotidienne de la noblesse française aux XVIe–XVIIe siècles* (Paris, 1985).

J.-M. Constant, *La Ligue* (Paris, 1996).

J.P. Cooper, 'Patterns of Inheritance and Settlement by Great Landowners from the fifteenth to the eighteenth centuries' in J. Goody, J. Thirsk and E.P. Thompson (eds.), *Family and Inheritance. Rural society in Western Europe 1200–1800* (Cambridge, 1976), pp. 192–327.

J.P. Cooper, 'Ideas of Gentility in Early Modern England' in *idem, Land, Men and Beliefs. Studies in Early-Modern History*, ed. G.E. Aylmer and J.S. Morrill (London, 1983), pp. 43–77.

J. Cornette, 'Les nobles et la foi, du siècle des réformes au siècle de l'état absolu' in *Société, Culture vie Religieuse aux XVIe et XVIIe siècles* (*Association des Historiens Modernistes, Bulletin* 20, Paris, 1995), pp. 139–96.

R. Cust, 'Honour and Politics in Early Stuart England: The Case of Beaumont *v.* Hastings', *PP* 149 (1995), pp. 57–94.

R. Descimon, 'Chercher de nouvelles voies pour interpréter les phénomènes nobiliaires dans la France moderne. La noblesse "essence" ou rapport social?' *RHMC* 46 (1999), pp. 5–21.

J. Dewald, *Pont-St.-Pierre 1398–1789: Lordship, Community and Capitalism in Early Modern France* (Berkeley, CA, 1987).

J. Dewald, *Aristocratic Experience and the Origins of Early Modern Culture: France 1570–1715* (Berkeley, CA, 1993).

J. Dewald, *The European Nobility, 1400–1800* (Cambridge, 1996).

A. Domínguez-Ortiz, *Las clases privilegiadas en la España del antiguo régimen* (Madrid, 1973).

C. Donati, *L'idea di nobiltà in Italia, secoli XIV–XVIII* (Rome and Bari, 1995).

C. Duhamelle, *L'héritage collectif: La noblesse d'èglise rhénane, 17e et 18e siècles* (Paris, 1998).

N. Elias, *Die höfische Gesellschaft* (Darmstadt, 1969). (Engl. transl. *The Court Society*, Oxford, 1983).

J.H. Elliott, *The Revolt of the Catalans* (Cambridge, 1963).

J.H. Elliott, 'A Provincial Aristocracy: The Catalan Ruling Class in the Sixteenth and Seventeenth Centuries' in *idem, Spain and its World, 1500–1700* (New Haven, CT, 1989), pp. 71–91.

J.H. Elliott and L.W.B. Brockliss (eds.), *The World of the Favourite* (New Haven, CT and London, 1999).

R. Endres, *Adel in der Frühen Neuzeit* (Munich, 1993).

R.J.W. Evans, *The Making of the Habsburg Monarchy* (Oxford, 1979).

R.J.W. Evans and T.V. Thomas (eds.), *Crown, Church and Estates: Central European Politics in the Sixteenth and Seventeenth Centuries* (Basingstoke, 1991).

F.L. Ford, *Robe and Sword: The Regrouping of French Aristocracy after Louis XIV* (Cambridge, MA, 1953).

D. García Hernán, *La nobleza en la España moderna* (Madrid, 1992).

M. Girouard, *Life in the English Country House* (New Haven, CT, 1978).

F. Göse, 'Zum Verhältnis von landadliger Sozialisation zu adliger Militärkarriere. Das Beispiel Preußen und Österreich im ausgehenden 17. und 18. Jahrhundert', in *MIÖG* 109 (2000), pp. 118–53.

W.W. Hagen, 'Seventeenth-Century Crisis in Brandenburg: The Thirty Years' War, the Destabilization of Serfdom, and the Rise of Absolutism', *American Historical Review* 94 (1989), pp. 302–35.

P.-M. Hahn, *Struktur und Funktion des brandenburgischen Adels im 16. Jahrhundert* (Berlin, 1979).

P.-M. Hahn, *Fürstliche Territorialhoheit und lokale Adelsgewalt. Die herrschaftliche Durchdringung des ländlichen Raumes zwischen Elbe und Aller (1300–1700)* (Berlin, 1989).

P.E.J. Hammer, *The Polarisation of Elizabethan Politics. The Political Career of Robert Devereux, 2nd Earl of Essex* (Cambridge, 1999).

G. Hanlon, *The Twilight of a Military Tradition: Italian Aristocrats and European Conflicts, 1560–1800* (London, 1998).

R.R. Harding, *Anatomy of a Power Elite: The Provincial Governors of Early Modern France* (New Haven, CT, 1978).

F. Heal and C. Holmes, *The Gentry in England and Wales 1500–1700* (Basingstoke, 1994).

P. Hersche, *Die deutschen Domkapitel im 17. und 18. Jahrundert* (3 vols., Bern, 1984).

A. Höfer and R. Reichardt, 'Honnêteté, Honnêtes gens' in R. Reichardt and E. Schmidt (eds.), *Handbuch politisch-sozialer Grundbegriffe in Frankreich 1680–1820*, vol. VII (Munich, 1986), pp. 7–73.

J. Gallet, *Seigneurs et paysans en France, 1600–1793* (Rennes, 1999).

C. Jago, 'The Influence of Debt on the Relations between Crown and Aristocracy in Seventeenth-Century Castile', *Economic History Review* 26 (1973), pp. 216–36.

C. Jago, 'The "Crisis of the Aristocracy" in Seventeenth-Century Castile', *PP* 84 (1979), pp. 60–90.

M. James, *Society, Politics and Culture. Studies in Early Modern England* (Cambridge, 1986).

P. Janssens, *L'évolution de la noblesse belge depuis la fin du moyen âge* (Brussels, 1998).

A. Jouanna, *Ordre social, mythe et hiérarchies dans la France du XVIe siècle* (Paris, 1977).

A. Jouanna, *Le devoir de révolte. La noblesse française et la gestation de l'État moderne, 1559–1661* (Paris, 1989).

A. Jouanna, J. Boucher, D. Biloghi and G. Le Thiec, *Histoire et dictionnaire des Guerres de Religion* (Paris, 1998).

K. Keller, and J. Matzerath (eds.), *Geschichte des sächsischen Adels* (Cologne, 1997).

S. Kettering, *Patrons, Brokers and Clients in Seventeenth-Century France* (Oxford, 1986).

V.G. Kiernan, *The Duel in European History* (Oxford, 1989).

J.-P. Labatut, *Les ducs et pairs de France au XVIIe siècle* (Paris, 1972).

J.-P. Labatut, *Les noblesses européennes da la fin du XVe siècle à la fin du XVIIIe siècle* (Paris, 1978).

E. Ladewig Petersen, *The Crisis of the Danish Nobility, 1580–1660* (Odense, 1967).

N. Le Roux, *La Faveur du Roi. Mignons et courtisans au temps des derniers Valois (vers 1547–vers 1589)* (Seyssel, 2000).

E. Le Roy Ladurie and J.-F. Fitou, *Saint-Simon, ou le système de la cour* (Paris, 1997).

J.A. Lynn, *Giant of the Grand Siècle. The French Army 1610–1715* (Cambridge, 1997).

K. MacHardy, 'The Rise of Absolutism and Nobel Rebellion in Early Modern Habsburg Austria, 1570–1620', *Comparative Studies in Society and History* 34 (1992), pp. 411–27.

K. MacHardy, 'Cultural Capital, Family Strategies and Noble Identity in Early Modern Habsburg Austria 1579–1620', *PP* 163 (1999), pp. 36–75.

K. MacHardy, *War, Religion and Court Patronage in Habsburg Austria* (Basingstoke, 2002).

M. Magendie, *La politesse mondaine et les théories de l'honnêteté en France de 1600 à 1660* (Paris, 1925).

J. Russell Major, *From Renaissance Monarchy, to Absolute Monarchy: French Kings, Nobles and Estates* (Baltimore, 1994).

R. McCoy, *The Rites of Knighthood. The Literature and Politics of Elizabethan Chivalry* (Berkely, CA, 1989).

E. Melton, 'Population Structure, the Market Economy and the Transformation of *Gutsherrschaft* in East Central Europe, 1650–1800: the Cases of Brandenburg and Bohemia', *GH* 16 (1999), pp. 297–327.

R. Mettam, *Power and Faction in Louis XIV's France* (Oxford, 1988).

J. Meyer, *Noblesses et pouvoirs dans l'Europe d'ancien régime* (Paris, 1973).

J. Meyer, *La noblesse française à l'époque moderne (XVIe–XVIIIe siècles)* (Paris, 1991).

J. Miller (ed.), *Absolutism in Seventeenth-Century Europe* (Basingstoke, 1990).

M. Motley, *Becoming a French Aristocrat: The Education of the Court Nobility, 1580–1715* (Princeton, New Jersey, 1990).

K.B. Neuschel, *Word of Honour: Interpreting Noble Culture in Sixteenth-Century France* (Ithaca, 1989).

H.F.K. Nierop, *The Nobility of Holland: From Knights to Regents, 1500–1650* (Cambridge, 1993).

D. Parker, *Class and State in Ancien Régime France: The Road to Modernity?* (London, 1996).

D. Parrott, 'Richelieu, the *Grands* and the French Army' in J. Bergin and L. Brockliss (eds.), *Richelieu and his Age* (Oxford, 1992), pp. 135–73.

D. Parrott, *Richelieu's Army: War, Government and Society in France, 1624–1642* (Cambridge, 2001).

V. Press, *Adel im Alten Reich* (Tübingen, 1998).

V. Press, 'Adel, Reich und Reformation' in *idem, Das Alte Reich. Ausgewählte Aufsätze* (Berlin, 1997), pp. 329–78.

B. Redford, *Venice and The Grand Tour,* (New Haven, CT, 1996).

F. Redlich, *The German Military Enterpriser and his Workforce: A Study in European Economic and Social History* (2 vols., Wiesbaden, 1964–65).

W. Reinhard (ed.), *Power Elites and State Building* (Oxford, 1996).

C.J. Rogers (ed.), *The Military Revolution Debate* (Boulder, CO, 1995).

J.M. Rosenheim, *The Emergence of A Ruling Order: English Landed Society 1650–1750* (London, 1998).

G. Rowlands, *The Dynastic State and the Army under Louis XIV: Royal Service and Private Interest, 1661–1701* (Cambridge, 2002).

F.-J. Ruggiu, *Les élites et les villes moyennes en France et en Angleterre, XVIIe–XVIIIe siècles* (Paris and Montreal, 1997).

P. Salvadori, *La chasse sous l'Ancien Régime* (Paris, 1996).

E. Schalk, *From Valor to Pedigree: Ideas of Nobility in France in the Sixteenth and Seventeenth Centuries* (Princeton, NJ, 1986).

H.M. Scott (ed.), *The European Nobilities in the Seventeenth and Eighteenth Centuries* (2 vols., London, 1995).

J.M. Smith, *The Culture of Merit: Nobility, Royal Service and Making of Absolute Monarchy in France, 1600–1789* (Ann Arbor, 1996).

A. Spagnoletti, *Stato, aristocrazie e Ordine di Malta nell'Italia moderna* (Rome and Bari, 1988).

A. Spagnoletti, *Prìncipi italiani e Spagna nell' età barocca* (Milan, 1996).

A. Stannek, *Telemachs Brüder. Die höfische Bildungsreise des 17. Jahrhunderts* (Frankfurt/M., 2001).

V.L. Stater, *Noble Government: The Stuart Lord Lieutenancy and the Transformation of English Politics* (Athens, GA, 1994).

L. Stone, *The Crisis of the Aristocracy, 1558–1641* (Oxford, 1965).

L. Stone and J.C. Fawtier Stone, *An Open Elite? England 1540–1880* (Oxford, 1984).

F. Tallett, *War and Society in Early-Modern Europe, 1495–1715* (London, 1992).

I.A.A. Thompson, *War and Government in Habsburg Spain 1560–1620* (London, 1976).

M.A. Visceglia (ed.), *Signori, patrizi, cavalieri nell'età moderna* (Bari, 1992).

M.A. Visceglia (ed.), *Identità nobiliari in età moderna* (*Dimensioni et probleme della ricerca storica*, Rome, 1993).

A. Wall, *Power and Protest in England, 1525–1640* (London, 2000).

E. Wasson, *Born to Rule: British Political Elites* (Stroud, 2000).

T. Winkelbauer, *Fürst und Fürstendiener. Gundaker von Liechtenstein, ein österreichischer Aristokrat des konfessionellen Zeitalters* (Vienna and Munich, 1999).

J.B. Wood, *The Nobility of the Election of Bayeux, 1463–1666* (Princeton, NJ, 1980).

B. Yun Casalilla, *Sobre la transición al capitalismo en Castilla. Economía y sociedad en Tierra de Campos, 1500–1830* (Salamanca, 1987).

B. Yun Casalilla, 'The Castilian Aristocracy in the 17th Century: Crisis, Refeudalisation or Political Offensive?' in I.A.A. Thompson and B. Yun Casalilla (eds.), *The Castilian Crisis of the Seventeenth Century: New Perspectives on the Economic and Social History of Seventeenth-Century Spain* (Cambridge, 1994), pp. 277–300.

H. Zmora, *State and Nobility in Early Modern Germany: The Knightly Feud in Franconia, 1440–1567* (Cambridge, 1997).

H. Zmora, *Monarchy, Aristocracy and the State in Europe, 1300–1800* (London, 2001).

Notes

Introduction

1 R.-P. Fuchs, *Um die Ehre. Westfälische Beleidigungsprozesse vor dem Reichskammergericht (1525–1805)* (Paderborn, 1999), p. 11, quoting, J. Nolden, *De statu nobilitatis* (Gießen, 1623), p. 121: 'Ich bin ein Mann wie ein ander Mann, nur daß mir Gott der Ehren gann,' Maximilian's response to the saying 'When Adam delved, and Eve span, where was then the gentleman?'

2 'Pour acquerir l'honneur et pour nous rendre capables de servir le roy', *Mémoires du Marquis de Beauvais-Nangis*, ed. M. Mommerque and A.H. Taillander (Paris, 1862), pp. 74–80, in particular p. 75.

3 Fuchs, *Um die Ehre*, pp. 326–7 and 201–2.

4 Ibid, p. 139.

5 The classical account of this crisis remains L. Stone, *The Crisis of the Aristocracy, 1558–1641* (Oxford, 1965).

6 For an early attack on this approach see J. Hexter, 'The Myth of the Middle Class in Tudor England' in *idem, Reappraisals in History* (Chicago, 1979), pp. 71–116.

7 See for example H. Zmora, *Monarchy, Aristocracy and the State in Europe, 1300–1800* (London, 2001), p. 91: 'The tortuous process of alignment between monarchy and nobility that had begun in the fourteenth century culminated in the seventeenth with both state and society aristocratized to the core.'

8 J. Dewald, *Aristocratic Experience and the Origins of Early Modern Culture: France 1570–1715* (Berkeley, CA, 1993). Arlette Jouanna's work has been equally important in giving us a new, deeper and more balanced understanding of noble society in the century between the oubreak of the Wars of Religion and the personal rule of Louis XIV; see in particular A. Jouanna, *Le Devoir de révolte. La noblesse française et la gestation de l'État moderne, 1559–1661* (Paris, 1989).

9 A good summary of research can be found in G. Chaussinand-Nogaret, J.-M. Constant, C. Durandin and A. Jouanna (eds.), *Histoire des élites en France du XVIe au XXe siècle* (Paris, 1991).

10 For a survey of research on local history see A. Hughes, 'Local History and the Origins of the Civil War', in R. Cust and A. Hughes (eds.), *Conflict in Early Stuart England* (London, 1989), pp. 224–53. See also T. Cogswell, *Home Divisions: Aristocracy, the State and Provincial Conflict* (Manchester, 1998). For a recent survey of the history of the gentry in our period see F. Heal and C. Holmes, *The Gentry in England and Wales 1500–1700* (Basingstoke, 1994).

11 Examples of this approach, which undoubtedly remains valuable, are a number of recent publications dealing with the counts of the Empire and their political corporations. See in particular G. Schmidt, *Der Wetterauer Grafenverein* (Marburg, 1989), J. Arndt, *Das Niederrheinisch-Westfälische Grafenkollegium und seine Mitglieder, 1651–1806* (Mainz, 1991) and E. Böhme, *Das fränkische Reichsgrafenkollegium im 16. und 17. Jahrhundert* (Stuttgart, 1989). Cf. for recent research on the history of the nobility in Germany R. Endres, *Adel in der Frühen Neuzeit* (Munich, 1993). Research on the early modern nobility in the Holy Roman Empire was greatly stimulated by the publications of Volker Press although his premature death denied him the opportunity to publish the great survey of this topic which he would have been particularly well qualified to write. See now for a number of important articles V. Press, *Adel im Alten Reich* (Tübingen, 1998) and *idem, Das Alte Reich. Ausgewählte Aufsätze* (Berlin, 1997).

12 See, for example, T. Winkelbauer, *Fürst und Fürstendiener. Gundaker von Liechtenstein, ein österreichischer Aristokrat des konfessionellen Zeitalters* (Vienna and Munich, 1999); P.-M. Hahn, *Fürstliche Territorialhoheit und lokale Adelsgewalt. Die herrschaftliche Durchdringung des ländlichen Raumes zwischen Elbe und Aller* (Berlin, 1989) or for noblewomen B. Bastl, *Tugend, Liebe, Ehre. Die adelige Frau in der Frühen Neuzeit* (Vienna, Cologne and Weimar, 2000), and, for a later period and a region which after 1648 became part of France, E. Pelzer, *Der Elsässische Adel. 1648–1790* (Munich, 1990). See also K.J. MacHardy, *War Religion and Court Patronage in Habsburg Austria* (Basingstoke, 2002); unfortunately this work was published too late for me to consult in writing this book.

13 J. Dewald, *The European Nobility, 1400–1800* (Cambridge, 1996), p. xv: 'Especially where the nobility was concerned France was not simply one society among many. It was by far the largest European state, and it provided a series of models that other countries emulated, in matters ranging from politics to culture.' For other surveys which give less weight to France and are more evenly balanced see M.L. Bush, *Rich Noble–Poor Noble* (Manchester, 1988); *idem, Noble Privilege* (Manchester, 1983); S. Clark, *State and Status: The Rise of the State and*

Aristocratic Power in Western Europe (Cardiff, 1995), as well as the excellent collection of essays edited by H.M. Scott, *The European Nobilities in the Seventeenth and Eighteenth Centuries* (2 vols., London, 1995).

14 J.B. Collins, *Classes, Estates and Order in Early Modern Brittany* (Cambridge, 1994), pp. 272-3; cf. R.G. Asch and H. Duchhardt (eds.), *Der Absolutismus – ein Mythos? Strukturwandel monarchischer Herrschaft in West- und Mitteleuropa (ca.1550–1700)* (Cologne, 1996), and N. Henshall, *The Myth of Absolutism* (London, 1992), as well as J. Miller (ed.), *Absolutism in Seventeenth-Century Europe* (Basingstoke, 1990).

15 G. Tomasi di Lampedusa, *Der Leopard* (Munich, 1959), p. 42; cf. O.G. Oexle, 'Aspekte der Geschichte des Adels im Mittelalter und in der Frühen Neuzeit', in H.-U. Wehler (ed.), *Europäischer Adel 1750–1950* (Göttingen, 1990), pp. 19–56, at pp. 21–6.

Status and the quest for exclusiveness: the foundations of noble identity

1   As the Earl of Northampton put it in 1610: 'Honour in all parts of Europe will be ever like itself'. Henry Howard, Earl of Northampton, *A Publication of his Majesty's Edicts and Severe Censure against Private Combat* (London, 1614), p. 8, quoted by J. Adamson, 'Introduction: The Making of the Ancien Régime Court', in *idem* (ed.), *The Princely Courts of Europe* (London, 1999), pp. 7–42, at p. 19.

2   W. Demel, '*European nobility* oder *European nobilities?* Betrachtungen anhand genealogischer Verflechtungen innerhalb des europäischen Hochadels (*ca*.1650–1800)', in W.D. Gruner and M. Völkel (eds.), *Region – Territorium – Nationalstaat – Europa* (Rostock, 1998), pp. 81–104.

3   F. von Klocke, *Justus Möser und die deutsche Ahnenprobe des 18. Jahrhunderts* (Leipzig, 1941), pp. 29 and 39–40.

4   Thus the patricians of Berne and Fribourg adopted the noble 'von' as part of their name in the late eighteenth century. See U. Im Hof, 'Ancien Régime', in H. Helbing (ed.), *Handbuch der Schweizer Geschichte*, vol. II (Zürich, 1977), pp. 673–784, at p. 709, cf. W. Demel, 'Der europäische Adel vor der Revolution: sieben Thesen', in R.G. Asch (ed.), *Der europäische Adel im Ancien Régime: Von der Krise der ständischen Monarchien bis zur Revolution (1600–1789)* (Cologne, 2001), pp. 409–33, at pp. 409–10.

5   Jean Louis Guez de Balzac, 'De la noblesse', in *Les Oeuvres de Monsieur de Balzac* (2 vols., Paris, 1665), II, pp. 503–6, at p. 504.

6   See below, pp. 23–25.

7 C. Ulrichs, *Vom Lehnhof zur Reichsritterschaft. Strukturen des fränkischen Niederadels am Übergang vom späten Mittelalter zur frühen Neuzeit* (Stuttgart, 1997), pp. 135–52.

8 See below, pp. 19–21.

9 S. Clark, *State and Status: The Rise of the State and Aristocratic Power in Western Europe* (Cardiff, 1995), p. 162.

10 J. Morsel, 'Die Erfindung des Adels: Zur Soziogenese des Adels am Ende des Mittelalters – das Beispiel Frankens', in O.G. Oexle and W. Paravicini (eds.), *Nobilitas: Funktion und Repräsentation des Adels in Alteuropa* (Göttingen, 1997), pp. 312–75; cf. H. Zmora, *Monarchy, Aristocracy and the State in Europe, 1300–1800* (London, 2001), pp. 21–36.

11 Cf. below, pp. 25–28.

12 R. Descimon, 'Chercher de nouvelles voies pour interpréter les phénomènes nobiliaires dans la France moderne. La noblesse "essence" ou rapport social?', *RHMC* 46 (1999), pp. 5–21. For the definition of noble status cf. Clark, *Status*, pp. 155–207.

13 Morsel, 'Erfindung', in particular p. 330; cf. Ulrichs, *Lehnhof*, pp. 85–8.

14 K. Bleeck and J. Garber, 'Nobilitas, Standes- und Privilegienlegitimation in deutschen Adelstheorien des 16. und 17. Jahrhunderts', in E. Blühm et al. (eds.), *Staat und Gesellschaft in der Literatur des 17. Jahrhunderts* (*Daphnis* 11; Amsterdam, 1982), pp. 49–114; cf. K. Garber, 'Sozietät und Geistes-Adel: Von Dante zum Jakobiner-Club, Der frühneuzeitliche Diskurs *de vera nobilitate* und seine institutionelle Ausformung in der gelehrten Akademie', in K. Garber and H. Wismann (eds.), *Europäische Sozietätsbewegung und demokratische Tradition* (2 vols., Tübingen, 1996), I, pp. 1–39.

15 A. Jouanna, 'Des "gros et gras" aux "gens d'honneur"', in G. Chaussinand-Nogaret et al. (eds.), *Histoire des élites en France du XVIe au XXe siècle* (Paris, 1991), pp. 17–144, at pp. 40–8. For the informal acquisition of noble status as a normal practice see also M. Cassan, *Les temps des Guerres de Religion. Le cas du Limousin (vers 1530–vers 1630)* (Paris, 1996), pp. 50–5. Cassan stresses that the comparatively weak presence of public administrative institutions (e.g. higher law courts) in the Limousin was responsible for the small influence the Crown had on social mobility into the noble estate.

16 J.-M. Constant, *La Vie quotidienne de la noblesse française aux XVIe–XVIIe siècles* (Paris, 1985), p. 112; cf. B. Guillemain (ed.), *L'annoblissement en France XVE–XVIIIe siècles* (Bordeaux, 1985).

17 In the early seventeenth century a Polish nobleman – rejecting ennoblement by letters patent – wrote 'let the man be *nobilis* only for the King, and peasant for the entire nobility as long as he lives'; see M. Bogucka, *The Lost World of the Sarmatians: Custom as the Regulator of Polish Social Life in Early Modern Times* (Warsaw, 1996), p. 25.

18 For the rise of professionally trained administrators see H. de Ridder-

Symoens, 'Training and Professionalization', in W. Reinhard (ed.), *Power Elites and State Building* (Oxford, 1996), pp. 149–72; W. Reinhard, *Geschichte der Staatsgewalt* (Munich, 1999), pp. 192–6; R. Schnur (ed.), *Die Rolle der Juristen bei der Entstehung des modernen Staates* (Berlin, 1986), and J.-P. Genet and G. Lottes (eds.), *L'état moderne et les élites XIIIe–XVIIIe siècles* (Paris, 1996).

19 Jouanna, '"Gros et Gras"', pp. 70–8.

20 E. Schalk, *From Valor to Pedigree: Ideas of Nobility in France in the Sixteenth and Seventeenth Centuries* (Princeton, NJ, 1986), pp. 65–114, cf. A. Jouanna, *Ordre social, mythe et hiérarchies dans la France du XVIe siècle* (Paris, 1977), pp. 194–7 and 160–72.

21 Historians have calculated that at the end of the century in most French provinces about two-thirds of all noblemen belonged to families which had not yet been part of the nobility 100 years before. These new families were, however, often also the first to decline and disappear again at times of crisis; the older ones, which had often several cadet lines, clearly had a better chance of survival. See Constant, *Vie quotidienne*, pp. 105–6, cf. 107–9, and J.B. Wood, *The Nobility of the Election of Bayeux, 1463–1666* (Princeton, NJ, 1980), pp. 45–53, 121–6, 154–5.

22 C. Donati, *L'idea di nobiltà in Italia, secoli XIV–XVIII* (Rome and Bari, 1995), pp. 278–82.

23 L. Stone, *The Crisis of the Aristocracy, 1558–1641* (Oxford, 1965), pp. 97–119; J. Cannon, *Aristocratic Century: The Peerage of Eighteenth-Century England* (Cambridge, 1984), pp. 13–15.

24 C.R. Mayes, 'The Sale of Peerages in Early Stuart England', *JMH* 29 (1959), pp. 21–37; *idem*, 'The Early Stuarts and the Irish Peerage', *EHR* 73 (1958), pp. 227–51; cf. L. Levy Peck, *Court Patronage and Corruption in Early Stuart England* (Boston, 1990), pp. 194–5, 211–12.

25 H. Schilp, 'Die Neuen Fürsten. Zur Erhebung in den Reichsfürstenstand und zur Aufnahme in den Reichsfürstenrat im 17. und 18. Jahrhundert', in V. Press and D. Willoweit (eds.), *Liechtenstein – Fürstliches Haus und staatliche Ordnung* (Vaduz and Munich, 1987), pp. 249–92, at p. 252; cf. T. Klein, 'Die Erhebungen in den weltlichen Reichsfürstenstand 1550–1806', *Blätter für deutsche Landesgeschichte* 122 (1986), pp. 137–92.

26 J. Arndt, 'Zwischen kollektiver Solidarität und persönlichem Aufstiegsstreben. Die Reichsgrafen im 17. und 18. Jahrhundert', in Asch, *Adel*, pp. 105–28.

27 N. Le Roux, *La Faveur du Roi: mignons et courtisans au temps des derniers Valois (vers 1547–vers 1589)* (Seyssel, 2000), pp. 466–7.

28 J.-P. Labatut, *Les Ducs et pairs de France au XVIIe siècle* (Paris, 1972), pp. 61–9, 80–5.

29 P. Hersche, *Italien im Barockzeitalter (1600–1750)* (Cologne, 1999), pp. 109–11; C.F. Black, *Early Modern Italy: A Social History* (London, 2001), p. 135.

30 A. Spagnoletti, *Principi italiani e Spagna nell' età barocca* (Milan, 1996), pp. 84–128, 205–14.

31 I.A.A. Thompson, 'The Nobility in Spain', in H.M. Scott (ed.), *The European Nobilities in the Seventeenth and Eighteenth Centuries* (2 vols., London, 1995) I, pp. 174–236, at p. 192, cf. 190–1.

32 Clark, *Status*, p. 182.

33 G. Schmidt, 'Adeliges Selbstverständnis und späthumanistische Geschichtsschreibung: Der Stammbaum des Reinhard von Gemmingen', in S. Rhein (ed.), *Die Kraichgauer Ritterschaft in der frühen Neuzeit* (Sigmaringen, 1993), pp. 263–87; B. Bei der Wieden, *Außenwelt und Anschauungen Ludolf von Münchhausens (1570–1640)* (Hanover, 1993), pp. 179–81.

34 F. Heal and C. Holmes, *The Gentry in England and Wales 1500–1700* (Basingstoke, 1994), pp. 34–7.

35 Donati, *Idea*, p. 281; cf. R. Villari, *The Revolt of Naples* (Cambridge, 1993), p. 187: 'The most important task [of genealogists] was apparently contradictory; to reaffirm, ... the validity of genealogical criteria, and at the same time provide a conventional moral justification for the expansion of the aristocracy by showing the ancient heritage of the families that had recently acquired fiefs and titles.' For the role of genealogy cf. A. Burguière, 'L'état monarchique et la famille (XVIe–XVIIIe siècle)', *Annales HSS 57* (2001), pp. 313–35, at pp. 325–7, and the various contributions to *Annales ESC 46*, 4 (1991) on 'La culture généalogique'.

36 Jouanna, '"Gros et gras"', p. 41

37 Wood, *Bayeux*, p. 42.

38 For the *recherches de noblesse* see J. Meyer, *La Noblesse française à l'époque moderne (XVIe–XVIIIe siècles)* (Paris, 1991), pp. 69–74; J.-M. Constant, 'Absolutisme et modernité', in Chaussinand-Nogaret, *Histoire des élites*, pp. 145–216, at pp. 196–200, as well as F.-J. Ruggiu, *Les Élites et les villes moyennes en France et en Angleterre, XVIIe–XVIIIe siècles* (Paris and Montreal, 1997), pp. 68–72.

39 J.-M. Constant, Article 'Recherches de noblesse', in L. Bély (ed.), *Dictionnaire de l'Ancien Régime* (Paris, 1996), p. 1052; *idem*, 'Les structures sociales et mentales de l'annoblissement: analyse comparative d'études récentes XVIe–XVIIe siècles' in Guillemain, *L'annoblissement*, pp. 37–67, at p. 44.

40 See Ruggiu, *Villes*, p. 71, with reference to the 'solidarités locales' as the basis for the security of noble status.

41 P. Janssens, *L'Évolution de la noblesse belge depuis la fin du moyen âge* (Brussels, 1998), pp. 107–76 and pp. 334–9. For similar developments in Savoy see Donati, *Idea*, pp. 177–8, 318.

42 V. Hunecke, *Der venezianische Adel am Ende der Republik, 1646–1797* (Tübingen, 1995), pp. 30–7; J. Boutier, *Construction et anatomie d'une noblesse urbaine. Florence à l'époque moderne* (2 parts, Paris, 1988), II,

pp. 325–7; R.B. Litchfield, *Emergence of a Bureaucracy: The Florentine Patricians, 1530–1790* (Princeton, 1986).

43 Donati, *Idea*, pp. 247–60.

44 F. Angiolini, 'La nobiltà "imperfetta": cavalieri e commende de S. Stefano nell Toscana moderna', in M.A. Viscegla (ed.), *Signori, patrizi, cavalieri nell'età moderna* (Bari, 1992), pp. 146–67; A.M. Rao, 'Antiche storie e autentiche scitture. Prove de nobiltà a Napoli nel Settecento', ibid., pp. 279–308, at pp. 298–9; cf. A. Spagnoletti, *Stato, aristocrazie e Ordine di Malta nell'Italia moderna* (Rome and Bari, 1988).

45 Spagnoletti, *Stato*, pp. 103–38.

46 Boutier, *Anatomie*, vol. II, pp. 340–1; cf. F. Angiolini, *I Cavalieri e il Principe. L'Ordine de Santo Stefano e la società Toscana in età moderna* (Florence, 1996).

47 K.J. MacHardy, 'Der Einfluß von Status, Konfession und Besitz auf das politische Verhalten des niederösterreichischen Ritterstandes, 1580–1620', in G. Klingenstein and H. Lutz (eds.), *Spezialforschung und 'Gesamtgeschichte'* (*Wiener Beiträge zur Geschichte der Neuzeit 8*, Munich, 1982), pp. 56–83, at pp. 58–67; cf. below, chapter 2, pp. 47–8.

48 E. Riedenauer, 'Zur Entstehung und Ausformung des landesfürstlichen Briefadels in Bayern', *Zeitschrift für bayerische Landesgeschichte* 47 (1984), S. 609–73.

49 A. Dylong, *Das Hildesheimer Domkapitel im 18. Jahrhundert* (Hanover, 1997), p. 119.

50 M. Weidner, *Landadel in Münster 1600–1760. Stadtverfassung, Standesbehauptung und Fürstenhof* (2 vols., Münster, 2000), I, pp. 153–5.

51 P. Hersche, *Die deutschen Domkapitel im 17. und 18. Jahrundert* (3 vols., Berne, 1984), II, pp. 115–37.

52 See E. Schubert, 'Adel im ausgehenden 18. Jahrhundert: Nordwestdeutsche Edelleute und süddeutsche Reichsritter im landes-geschichtlichen Vergleich', in J. Canning and H. Wellenreuther (eds.), *Britain and Germany Compared: Nationality, Society and Nobility in the Eighteenth Century* (Göttingen, 2001), pp. 141–230, at pp. 185 ff.

53 A. Flügel, *Bürgerliche Rittergüter. Sozialer Wandel und politische Reform in Kursachsen (1680–1844)* (Göttingen, 2000), pp. 72–84.

54 W. Neugebauer, 'Brandenburg im absolutistischen Staat. Das 17. und 18. Jahrhundert', in I. Materna and W. Ribbe (eds.), *Brandenburgische Geschichte* (Berlin, 1995), pp. 291–394, at p. 381.

55 L. Enders, '"Aus drängender Not": Die Verschuldung des gutsherrlichen Adels der Mark Brandenburg im 17. Jahrhundert', *Jahrbuch für die Geschichte Mittel- und Ostdeutschlands* 43 (1995), pp. 1–21.

56 R. Schiller, '"Edelleute müssen Güther haben, Bürgen müssen die Elle gebrauchen": Friderizianische Adelsschutzpolitik und die Folgen', in W. Neugebauer and R. Pröve (eds.), *Agrarische Verfassung und Politische Struktur. Studien zur Gesellschaftsgeschichte Preußens 1700–1918*

(Berlin, 1998), pp. 257–86. I am grateful for information provided by Wolfgang Neugebauer and Frank Göse.

57 Schubert, 'Adel', pp. 188–9.

58 W. Neugebauer, *Standschaft als Verfassungsproblem. Die historischen Grundlagen ständischer Partizipation in ostmitteleuropäischen Regionen* (Goldbach, 1995), pp. 26–36.

59 G.W. Pedlow, *The Survival of the Hessian Nobility, 1770–1870* (Princeton, NJ, 1988), pp. 18–21, but cf. G. Hollenberg and H. Maulhardt (eds.), *Hessische Landtagsabschiede, 1526–1603* (Marbug, 1994), p. 19, who emphasise that at least until the seventeenth century the *Ritterschaft* remained relatively open to newcomers (I am grateful for this reference to R. v. Friedeburg). There were of course nobles in Hesse who were not members of the Ritterschaft; they enjoyed a lesser social prestige, however.

60 J. Aalbers, 'Geboorte en Geld, Adel in Gelderland, Utrecht en Holland tijdens de eerste helf van de achttiende eeuw', in *idem* and M. Prak (eds.) *De Bloem der Natie. Adel en patriciaat en de Nordelijke Nederlanden* (Amsterdam, 1987), pp. 56–78, at p. 73.

61 Cf. J.C. Streng, 'Le Métier du Noble. De Overijsselse Ridderschap tussen 1622 en 1795', in A.J. Mensema, J. Mooijweer and J.C. Streng (eds.), *De Ridderschap von Oberijssel: Le Métier du Noble* (Zwolle, 2000), pp. 49–110, in particular pp. 51–2, and H.F.K. Nierop, *The Nobility of Holland: From Knights to Regents, 1500–1650* (Cambridge, 1993).

62 R. Frost, 'The Nobility of Poland-Lithuania, 1569–1795', in Scott, *Nobilities*, II, pp. 183–222, at pp. 192–6.

63 E. Opalinski, 'Die Freiheit des Adels. Ideal und Wirklichkeit in Polen-Litauen im 17. Jahrhundert', in Asch, *Adel*, pp. 77–104.

64 Thompson, 'Nobility', pp. 176–85; J. Fayard and M.-C. Gerbert, 'Fermeture de la noblesse et pureté de sang en Castille à travers les procès de hidalguía au XVIème siècle', *Histoire, économie et société* 1 (1982), pp. 51–75; cf. I.A.A. Thompson, '*Hidalgo* and *pechero*: the language of "estates" and "classes" in Early-Modern Castile', in P.J. Corfield (ed.), *Language, History and Class* (Oxford, 1991), pp. 53–78; *Hidalgos et Hidalguía dans l'Espagne des XVIe–XVIIIe siècles, théories, pratiques et représentations* (Collection de La Maison des Pays Ibériques 37, Paris, 1989), and J. Casey, *Early Modern Spain: A Social History* (London, 1999), pp. 140–4.

65 J. Hernández Franco, *Cultura y limpieza de sangre en la España moderna* (Murcia, 1996), pp. 163–72; cf. M. Hernández, *A la sombra de la Corona. Poder local y oligarquía urbana (Madrid, 1606–1808)* (Madrid, 1995), p. 223.

66 E. Postigo Castellanos, *Honor y privilegio en la corona de Castilla. El Consejo de las órdenes y los caballeros de hábito en el siglo XVII* (Almazán, 1988); Spagnoletti, *Principi*, pp. 205–14; during the reign of

Philip IV, 468 Italians received the habit of one of the military orders; the total number of new knights in the Spanish Empire was 5,147 (p. 212).

67 Thompson, 'Nobility', p. 178.

68 As an influential contemporary analysis of England's social structure stated: 'Whosoever ... can live without manual labour, and thereto is able and will bear the port, charge, and countenance of a gentleman, he shall for money have a coat and arms bestowed upon him by heralds ... and thereunto being made so good cheap, be called master, which is the title that men give to esquires and gentlemen, and reputed a gentleman ever after' (William Harrison, *The Description of England*, ed. G. Edelen (Washington and New York, 1994), pp. 113–14). Harrison agreed in this point with Sir Thomas Smith and his *De Re Publica Anglorum*. However, cf. J.P. Cooper, 'Ideas of gentility in early modern England', in *idem, Land, Men and Beliefs. Studies in Early-Modern History*, eds. G.E. Aylmer and J.S. Morrill (London, 1983), pp. 43–77.

69 R. Cust, 'Honour and Politics in Early Stuart England: The Case of Beaumont v. Hastings', *PP* 149 (1995), pp. 57–94; *idem*, 'Catholicism, Antiquarianism and Gentry Honour: The Writings of Sir Thomas Shirley', *Midland History* 23 (1998), pp. 40–70.

70 I owe this argument to an unpublished paper by Richard Cust which he gave in a seminar at the Institute of Historical Research in London in summer 2000.

71 G.D. Squibb, *The High Court of Chivalry* (New York, 1959), in particular pp. 52 ff.

72 A. Fletcher, 'Honour, Reputation and Local Officeholding in Elizabethan and Stuart England', in *idem* and J. Stevenson (eds.), *Order and Disorder in Early Modern England* (Cambridge, 1987), pp. 92–115; for the selection of Justices of the Peace see A. Wall, *Power and Protest in England, 1525–1640* (London, 2000), pp. 45–61, and for the mechanics of local politics in the early seventeenth century T. Cogswell, *Home Divisions: Aristocracy, the State and Provincial Conflict* (Manchester, 1998).

73 Cust, 'Honour and Politics', cf. *idem*, 'Honour, Rhetoric and Political Culture: The Earl of Huntingdon and his Enemies', in Susan D. Amussen and M.A. Kishlansky (eds.), *Political Culture and Cultural Politics in Early Modern England: Essays Presented to David Underdown* (Manchester, 1995), pp. S. 84–111, as well as *idem*, 'Catholicism, Antiquarianism'.

74 L.K.J. Glassey, *Politics and the Appointment of Justices of the Peace 1675–1720* (Oxford, 1979), pp. 32–99, in particular pp. 75–92. For comparative attempts to appoint Lord-Lieutenants according to political criteria, see V.L. Stater, *Noble Government: The Stuart Lord Lieutenancy and the Transformation of English Politics* (Athens, GA, 1994), pp. 165–7.

75 J.M. Rosenheim, *The Emergence of a Ruling Order: English Landed Society 1650–1750* (London, 1998), pp. 115–24.

76 P.J. Corfield, 'The Rivals: Landed and other Gentlemen', in N. Harte and R. Quinault (eds.), *Land and Society in Britain, 1700–1914* (Manchester, 1996), pp. 1–33; for the importance of 'politeness' as a social ideal see P. Langford, 'Polite Manners from Sir Robert Walpole to Sir Robert Peel', *Proceedings of the British Academy* 94 (1996), pp. 103–25.

77 M.W. McCahill, 'Open Elites: Recruitment to the French *Noblesse* and the English Aristocracy in the Eighteenth Century', *Albion* 30 (1998), pp. 599–629, in particular pp. 614 and 627.

78 For this problem see L. Stone and J.C. Fawtier Stone, *An Open Elite? England 1540–1880* (Oxford, 1984).

79 E. Wasson, *Born to Rule: British Political Elites* (Stroud, 2000), p. 15: included are all families with at least three members of the House of Commons, or three tenures in the House of Lords, or three memberships of either House in combination. Precisely because the English governing elite cannot be defined in legal terms (the peerage is too small a group), it is plausible to define the elite for the early modern age as those families represented in Parliament on more than an occasional basis.

80 Wasson, *Born to Rule*, pp. 43–64, cf. 87–92.

81 M. Nassiet, *Noblesse et pauvreté. La petite noblesse en Bretagne, XVE–XVIIIe siècles* (Banalec, 1993), pp. 242–5, 378–80.

82 G. Chaussinand-Nogaret, *La noblesse au XVIIIe siècle. De la féodalité aux Lumières* (Brussels, 1984), pp. 93–117, in particular p. 103: 'Ainsi tout oppose deux noblesses: fortune, formation, culture'.

The changing landscape of noble society

1 R. Frost, 'The Nobility of Poland-Lithuania, 1569–1795', in H.M. Scott (ed.), *The European Nobilities in the Seventeenth and Eighteenth Centuries* (2 vols., London, 1995), II, pp. 183–222, at p. 192. For the density of the noble population in general see M.L. Bush, *Rich Noble–Poor Noble* (Manchester, 1988), pp. 7–10.

2 I.A.A. Thompson, 'The Nobility in Spain', in Scott, *Nobilities*, I, pp. 174–236, at p. 175.

3 P. Schimert, 'The Hungarian Nobility in the Seventeenth and Eighteenth Centuries', in Scott, *Nobilities*, II, pp. 144–82, at pp. 148–66.

4 Bush, *Rich Noble*, p. 114.

5 Schimert, 'Nobility', pp. 154–8.

6 Frost, 'Nobility', pp. 185–6; cf. M. Bogucka, *The Lost World of the Sarmatians: Custom as the Regulator of Polish Social Life in Early Modern Times* (Warsaw, 1996), and J. Lukowski, *Liberty's Folly: The Polish–Lithuanian Commonwealth in the Eighteenth Century, 1697–1795* (London, 1991), pp. 13–21.

7 Bush, *Rich Noble*, p. 8; M. Myška, 'Der Adel der böhmischen Länder, seine wirtschaftliche Basis und Entwicklung', in A. v. Reden-Dohna and R. Melville, (eds.), *Der Adel an der Schwelle des Bürgerlichen Zeitalters* (Stuttgart, 1988), pp. 168–91, at pp. 169–70.

8 K.J.V. Jespersen, 'The Rise and Fall of the Danish Nobility, 1600–1800', in Scott, *Nobilities*, II, pp. 41–79, at pp. 44–5. Jespersen estimates that 543 new families acquired noble status in Denmark between 1660 and 1848, whereas between 1536 and 1660, 151 new families had entered the Danish nobility (p. 64). Cf. P. Ingesman and J.V. Jensen (eds.), *Riget, Magten og æren. Den Danske Adel 1350–1660* (Aarhus, 2001) (English summaries).

9 A.F. Upton, 'The Swedish Nobility, 1600–1772', in Scott, Nobilities, II, pp. 11–40, at p. 28.

10 See below, pp. 51.

11 For Bohemia see J. Čechura, *Adelige Grundherrn als Unternehmer. Zur Struktur südböhmischer Dominien vor 1620* (Munich/Vienna, 2000). For east-central Europe in general see J. Peters (ed.), *Gutsherrschaftsgesellschaften im europäischen Vergleich* (Berlin, 1997); *idem* (ed.), *Gutsherrschaft als soziales Modell* (*HZ*, Supplement 18, Munich, 1995), and *idem* (ed.), *Konflikt und Kontrolle in Gutsherrschaftsgesellschaften* (Göttingen, 1995).

12 J. Gallet, *Seigneurs et paysans en France, 1600–1793* (Rennes, 1999), pp. 78–90, 208–14; *idem*, art. 'Droits féodaux et seigneuriaux', in L. Bély (ed.), *Dictionnaire de l'Ancien Régime* (Paris, 1996), pp. 438–45; J.Q.C. Mackrell, *The Attack on 'Feudalism' in Eighteenth-Century France* (London, 1973); H.L. Root, *Peasants and King in Burgundy: Agrarian Foundations of French Absolutism* (Berkeley, CA, 1987), pp. 155–204.

13 For England see C.G.A. Clay, *Economic Expansion and Social Change: England 1500–1700* (2 vols., Cambridge, 1984), I, pp. 81–91, cf. pp. 37–48.

14 A. Domínguez-Ortiz, *Las clases privilegiadas en la España del Antiguo Régimen* (Madrid, 1973), pp. 27–8, 120–8; cf. J. Casey, *Early Modern Spain: A Social History* (London, 1999), pp. 116–20; D. García Hernán, *La nobleza en la España moderna* (Madrid, 1992), pp. 26–7; H. Kamen, *Spain in the Later Seventeenth Century, 1665–1700* (London, 1980), pp. 158–65.

15 For Catalonia see J.S. Amelang, *Honored Citizens of Barcelona: Patrician Culture and Class Relations, 1490–1714* (Princeton, 1986), in particular pp. 87 and 118 for economic interests and common ideals of high culture as factors which united rural noblemen and patricians. For Sicily and Palermo see F. Benigno, 'Aristocrazia e Stato in Sicilia nell'epoca de Filippo III', in M.A. Visceglia (ed.), *Signori, patrizi, cavalieri nell'età moderna* (Bari, 1992), pp. 76–93, in particular pp. 78–9.

16 For Naples see G. Muta, '"I Segni d'honore": Rappresentatzioni delle

dinamiche nobiliari a Napoli in età moderna', in Visceglia, *Signori*, pp. 171–92; cf. R. Villari, *The Revolt of Naples* (Cambridge, 1993), pp. 150–2, and G. Labrot, *Baroni in città. Residenze e comportamenti dell' aristocrazia napoletana, 1530–1740* (Naples, 1979).

17 A. Spagnoletti, *Principi italiani e Spagna nell' età barocca* (Milan, 1996), pp. 129–45, 154–9.

18 For the process of 'refeudalisation' see P. Hersche, *Italien im Barockzeitalter (1600–1750)* (Cologne, 1999), pp. 103–15 and C.F. Black, *Early Modern Italy: A Social History* (London, 2001), pp. 129–48. For the continuing commercial activities of the Gondi and Corsi in Florence, the Doria and Pallavincini in Genoa or the Bragadin and Dolfin in Venice see ibid. pp. 141–3. For Florence cf. J. Boutier, 'Una nobiltà urbana in età moderna. Aspetti della morfologia sociale della nobiltà fiorentina', in M.A. Visceglia (ed.), *Dimensioni e Problemi della Ricerca Storica* (1993), no. 2: *Identità nobiliari in età moderna*, pp. 141–59. For developments in Italy in general see also the survey by F. Angiolini, 'Les Noblesses italiennes à l'époque moderne: approches et interprétations', *RHMC* 45 (1998), pp. 66–88.

19 Black, *Early Modern Italy*, p. 139.

20 J. Dewald, *The Formation of a Provincial Nobility. The Magistrates of the Parlement of Rouen, 1499–1980* (Princeton, NJ, 1980), pp. 112–17; cf. F.-J. Ruggiu, *Les élites et les villes moyennes en France et en Angleterre, XVIIe–XVIIIe siècles* (Paris/Montreal, 1997), pp. 143–74; Gallet, *Seigneurs*, pp. 198–200, and M. Marraud, *La Noblesse de Paris au XVIIIe Siècle* (Paris, 2000). Marraud estimates that 40 per cent of all nobles lived in towns in the eighteenth century as opposed to 4 per cent at the end of the Middle Ages (p. 11).

21 R.M. Smuts, 'The Court and its Neighbourhood: Royal Policy and Urban Growth in the Early Stuart West End', *Journal of British Studies* 30 (1991), pp. 117–49; J.M. Rosenheim, *The Emergence of a Ruling Order: English Landed Society 1650–1750* (London, 1998), pp. 215–38; cf. for Germany M. Weidner, *Landadel in Münster 1600–1760. Stadtverfassung, Standesbehauptung und Fürstenhof* (2 vols., Münster, 2000), I, pp. 430 ff, and the conclusion pp. 565–78.

22 R. Endres, 'Adel und Patriziat in Oberdeutschland', in W. Schulze (ed.) *Ständische Gesellschaft und soziale Mobilität* (Munich, 1988), pp. 221–38.

23 M. Diefenbacher, 'Stadt und Adel – Das Beispiel Nürnberg', *Zeitschrift für die Geschichte des Oberrheins* 141 (1993), pp. 51–69; for the reverse of the coin K. Graf, 'Feindbild und Vorbild. Bemerkungen zur städischen Wahrnehmung des Adels', ibid., pp. 121–43; cf. further C. Ulrichs, *Vom Lehnhof zur Reichsritterschaft. Strukturen des fränkischen Niederadels am Übergang vom späten Mittelalter zur frühen Neuzeit* (Stuttgart, 1997), pp. 61–88 and V. Press, 'Die Reichsritterschaft im Reich der Frühen Neuzeit', in *idem, Adel im Alten*

Reich (Tübingen, 1998), pp. 205–32; for Alsace see A. Graf Kageneck, 'Das Patriziat im Elsaß unter Berücksichtigung der Schweizer Verhältnisse', in H. Rössler (ed.), *Deutsches Patriziat, 1430–1740* (Limburg, 1968), pp. 377–94; cf. E. Pelzer, *Der Elsässische Adel. 1648–1790* (Munich, 1990).

24 H.F.K. Nierop, *The Nobility of Holland: From Knights to Regents, 1500–1650* (Cambridge, 1993).

25 J.I. Israel, *The Dutch Republic: Its Rise, Greatness and Fall, 1477–1806* (Oxford, 1995), pp. 341–4; J.L. Price, 'The Dutch Noblility in the Seventeenth and Eighteenth Centuries', in Scott, *Nobilities*, I, pp. 82–113, at pp. 107–13; O. Kooijmans, 'Patriciaat en aristocratisering in Holland tijdens de zeventiendes en achttiendes eeuw', in J. Aalbers and M. Prak (eds.), *De Bloem der Natie. Adel en patriciaat en de Nordelijke Nederlanden* (Amsterdam, 1987), pp. 93–103; J.L. Price, *Dutch Society 1588–1713* (Harlow, 2000), pp. 163–86.

26 Jan Aalbers, 'Geboorte en geld. Adel in Gelderland, Utrecht en Holland tijdens de eerste helft van the achttiende eeuw', in Aalbers/Prak, *De Bloem der natie*, pp. 56–78, in particular pp. 66–9.

27 J.-M. Constant, 'Absolutisme et modernité', in G. Chaussinand-Nogaret et al. (eds.), *Histoire des élites en France du XVIe au XXe siècle* (Paris, 1991), pp. 145–216, at p. 187.

28 R. Mousnier, *La vénalité des offices sous Henri IV et Louis XIII* (Paris, 2nd edn., 1971); G. Huppert, *Les Bourgois Gentilshommes: An Essay on the Definition of Elites in Renaissance France* (Chicago, 1977); M. Greengrass, *France in the Age of Henri IV* (2nd edn., London, 1995), pp. 183–94.

29 Constant, 'Modernité', p. 157; 35 per cent had risen to noble status simply by living like a nobleman ('vivre noblement') or because their immediate ancestors had done so. Only 8 per cent had been formally ennobled by royal letters patent. In the country outside the cities and their immediate vicinity the *noblesse de robe* was of course a numerically much less significant group, although many *robins* tended to buy estates near the city in which they held office (Gallet, *Seigneurs*, pp. 197–8).

30 Constant, 'Modernité', p. 148.

31 A. Jouanna, 'Des "gros et gras" aux "gens d'honneur"', in Chaussinand-Nogaret, *Histoire des élites*, pp. 17–144, at pp. 74–5.

32 F. Bluche, *Les Magistrats du Parlement de Paris au XVIIIe siècle* (2nd edn., Paris, 1986), pp. 235–7.

33 Constant, 'Modernité', pp. 150–1: R. Chartier, 'La noblesse et les États de 1614: une réaction aristocratique?', in *idem* and D. Richet, *Représentations et vouloirs politiques: autour des États Généraux de 1614* (Paris, 1982), pp. 125–45.

34 Dewald, *The Formation of a Provincial Nobility*, pp. 107–8 quoting contemporary sources from 1578 and 1589.

35 R.G. Asch, 'Bürgertum, 'Universität und Adel. Eine württembergische Kontroverse des Späthumanismus', in K.R. Garber (ed.), *Stadt und Literatur im deutschen Sprachraum der Frühen Neuzeit* (Tübingen, 1998), pp. 384–410; cf. below, pp. 55–6.

36 Thompson, 'Nobility', pp. 204–5, B. Bennassar, *Un siècle d'or espagnol* (Paris, 1982), pp. 46–60; R.L. Kagan, *Students and Society in Early Modern Spain* (Baltimore, 1974); J.M. Pelorson, *Les letrados juristes castillans sous Philippe III* (Le Puy en Velay, 1980). Even in Castile, however the eldest sons of great noblemen hesitated to study at university and take a degree; see below, p. 57.

37 Lukowski, *Folly*, pp. 24 and 82, cf. Bush, *Rich Noble*, pp. 113–14.

38 Bush, *Rich Noble*, p. 116.

39 M. Nassiet, *Noblesse et pauvreté. La petite noblesse en Bretagne, XVE–XVIIIe siècles* (Banalec, 1993), p. 375.

40 J. Dewald, *Pont-St-Pierre 1398–1789: Lordship, Community and Capitalism in Early Modern France* (Berkeley, CA, 1987), pp. 98–100.

41 J.-M. Constant, *La Vie quotidienne de la noblesse française aux XVIe–XVIIe siècles* (Paris, 1985), pp. 71–4 and 219–23; R. Baury, 'Sentiment et reconaissance identitaires de la noblesse pauvre en France à l'époque moderne (XVIe–XVIIIe siècles)', in *L'identité nobiliaire. Dix siècles de métamorphoses (IXE–XIXe siècles)*, ed. Université du Maine (Le Mans, 1997), pp. 78–99.

42 Baury, 'Sentiment', p. 91; A. Corvisier, *Louvois* (Paris, 1998), pp. 337–43; cf. for the eighteenth century *idem* (ed.), *Histoire militaire de la France* (4 vols., Paris 1992), II, pp. 68–75, and generally D. Julia, art. 'Écoles militaires', in L. Bély (ed.), *Dictionnaire de l'Ancien Régime* (Paris, 1996), pp. 461–4.

43 L. Bourquin, 'Partage noble et droit d'ainesse dans les coutumes du royaume de France à l'époque moderne', in *L'identité nobiliaire*, pp. 136–65. For customs of inheritance cf. J. Russell Major, *From Renaissance Monarchy to Absolute Monarchy: French Kings, Nobles and Estates* (Baltimore, 1994), pp. 86–90.

44 A. Jouanna, *Le Devoir de révolte. La noblesse française et la gestation de l'État moderne, 1559–1661* (Paris, 1989), pp. 245–51.

45 S.A. Eurich, *The Economics of Power: The Private Finances of the House of Foix-Navarre-Albret during the Religious Wars* (Kirksville, MS, 1994), pp. 78–89; cf. M.P. Holt, 'Patterns of Clientèle and Economic Opportunity at Court during the Wars of Religion: The Household of François Duke of Anjou', *French Historical Studies* 13 (1984), pp. 305–22.

46 Dewald, *Pont-St-Pierre*, pp. 112–17. For Bohemia see V. Bůžek and P. Mat'a, 'Wandlungen des Adels in Böhmen und Mähren im Zeitalter des "Absolutismus" (1620–1740)', in R.G. Asch (ed.), *Der Adel im Ancien Régime* (Cologne, 2001), pp. 287–322, at p. 308, cf. G. Klingenstein, *Der Aufstieg des Hauses Kaunitz* (Göttingen, 1975), p. 134. For the

survival of the great households and clientage networks maintained by the *princes du sang* in France see Marraud, *Noblesse*, pp. 240–58.

47 Dewald, *Pont-St-Pierre*, pp. 109–12.

48 See L. Stone, *The Crisis of the Aristocracy, 1558–1641* (Oxford, 1965); D. Bitton, *The French Nobility in Crisis, 1560–1640* (Stanford, CA, 1969); C. Jago, 'The "Crisis of the Aristocracy" in Seventeenth-Century Castile', *PP* 84 (1979), pp. 60–90; T. Winkelbauer, 'Krise der Aristokratie? Zum Strukturwandel des Adels in den böhmischen und niederösterreichischen Ländern im 16. und 17. Jahrhundert', *MIÖG* 100 (1992), pp. 328–53; for a good critical survey of older research see Jouanna, *Devoir*, pp. 91–102.

49 For Spain, see Thompson, 'Nobility', pp. 210–15.

50 Clay, *Expansion*, I, pp. 152–8, and G. Batho, 'Landlords in England, 1500–1640, B: Noblemen, Gentlemen and Yeomen', in C. Clay (ed.) *Rural Society: Landowners, peasants and labourers, 1500–1750* (Cambridge, 1990), pp. 41–70, at pp. 45–50 and 55–65; as well as H.J. Habbakuk, 'The Rise and Fall of English Landed Families. III: Did the Gentry Rise?', *TRHS*, 5th ser. 31 (1981), pp. 195–217 and J.H. Hexter, 'Storm over the Gentry', in *idem*, *Reappraisals in History* (Chicago, 1979), pp. 149–62, all with references to less recent publications.

51 K.M. Brown, *Noble Society in Scotland: Wealth, Family and Culture From Reformation to Revolution* (Edinburgh, 2000), pp. 92–109, in particular pp. 97 and 108. For spending as a means to increase credit-worthyness see Eurich, *The Economics of Power*, p. 165.

52 The fifth Earl of Huntingdon, recently studied by Thomas Cogswell, is clearly an example of this phenomenon: T. Cogswell, *Home Divisions: Aristocracy, the State and Provinical Conflict* (Manchester, 1998); cf. for another similar case D.L. Smith, 'The Political Career of Edward Sackville, 4th Earl of Dorset 1590–1653' (unpubl. PhD thesis, University of Cambridge, 1989), pp. 260–86. See also Brown, *Noble Society*, p. 105.

53 Jouanna, *Devoir*, pp. 98–102, and, for the economic situation, pp. 90–8; cf. for the causes of economic problems (reduction of royal pensions, massive expenses incurred in royal service or local feuding) Greengrass, *France*, pp. 222–3; see further Russell Major, *Renaissance Monarchy*, pp. 75–86, who does not see much evidence for a lasting economic crisis affecting noble income. For the role of noble affinities see M. Greengrass, 'Noble Affinities in Early Modern France: The Case of Henri I de Montmorency, Constable of France', *European History Quarterly* 16 (1986), pp. 275–311; cf. further S. Kettering, *Patrons, Brokers and Clients in Seventeenth-Century France* (Oxford, 1986).

54 Thompson, 'Nobility', pp. 192–4; cf. Casey, *Spain*, pp. 149, 157–9. For the economic problems of the Spanish nobility see also García Hernán, *Nobleza*, pp. 34–5.

55 B. Yun Casalilla, *Sobre la transición al capitalismo en Castilla.*

Economía y sociedad en Tierra de Campos, 1500–1830 (Salamanca, 1987), pp. 230–44.

56 For France see Bourquin, 'Partage noble'.

57 J.P. Cooper, 'Patterns of Inheritance and Settlement by Great Landowners from the fifteenth to the eighteenth centuries', in J. Goody, J. Thirsk and E.P. Thompson (eds.), *Family and Inheritance. Rural Society in Western Europe 1200–1800* (Cambridge, 1976), pp. 192–327, at pp. 234–52, cf. B. Clavero Arévalo, *Mayorazgo y propiedad feudal en Castilla, 1369–1836* (Madrid, 1974) and C. Jago, 'The "Crisis of the Aristocracy"', pp. 74–8. For France where the entail remained rare see Russell Major, *Renaissance Monarchy*, pp. 89–90. Here noble property was protected by the *retrait lignager*, which gave the family the right to reclaim alienated property by reimbursing the original purchaser.

58 The *mayorazgo* system inherently favoured direct female descendants over more distant male relatives, Cooper, 'Patterns' p. 241–2; cf. Casey, *Spain*, pp. 145–8.

59 Cooper, 'Patterns', p. 251; H. Reif, *Westfälischer Adel 1770–1860* (Göttingen, 1979), pp. 81–2, Jouanna, '"gros et gras"', pp. 78–9; cf. A. Farge, 'The Honor and Secrecy of Families' in R. Chartier (ed.), *A History of Private Life*, vol. III: *Passions of the Renaissance* (Cambridge, MA, 1989), pp. 571–607.

60 H. Hofmeister, 'Pro conservanda familiae et agnationis dignitate. Der Liechtensteinische Familien-Fidekommiß als Rechtsgrundlage der Familien- und Vermögenseinheit', in E. Oberhammer (ed.), *Der ganzen Welt ein Lob und Spiegel. Das Fürstenhaus Liechtenstein in der frühen Neuzeit* (Vienna and Munich, 1990), pp. 46–63; cf. J. Van Horn Melton, 'The Nobility in the Bohemian and Austrian Lands, 1620–1780', in Scott, *Nobilities*, II, pp. 110–43, at p. 127.

61 Many of the families belonging to the peerage in the late sixteenth century had received their rank and laid the political and economic foundations of their position during the Reformation, with its major upheaval in landownership. In fact, of the 62 peers living in 1560 only 25 held a title which went back beyond 1509 (Batho, 'Landlords', p. 46). Cf. Stone, *Crisis*, p. 758, and for the modest growth of the peerage in later periods J.V. Beckett, *The Aristocracy in England, 1660–1914* (Oxford, 1986), pp. 26–31.

62 Beckett, *Aristocracy*, pp. 296–7; for the development of the strict settlement see H.J. Habbakuk, *Marriage, Debt and the Estates System: English Landownership, 1650–1950* (Oxford, 1994), pp. 58–67; Clay, *Expansion*, I, pp. 160–2; B. English and J. Saville, *Strict Settlements* (Hull, 1983); for Spain Cooper, 'Patterns', pp. 243–5.

63 R. Schlögl, 'Absolutismus im 17. Jahrhundert – Bayerischer Adel zwischen Disziplinierung und Integration. Das Beispiel der Entschuldungspolitik nach dem Dreißigjährigen Krieg', *ZHF* 15 (1988),

pp. 151–86; for Spain cf. C. Jago, 'The Influence of Debt on the Relations between Crown and Aristocracy in Seventeenth-Century Castile', *Economic History Review* 26 (1973), pp. 216–36.

64 Winkelbauer, 'Krise'.

65 Ibid., pp. 341–3; W. Schulze, 'Das Ständewesen in den Erblanden der Habsburger Monarchie bis 1740: vom dualistischen Ständestaat zum organisch-föderativen Absolutismus', in W. Baumgart (ed.), *Ständetum und Staatsbildung in Brandenburg-Preussen* (Berlin, 1983), pp. 263–79.

66 G. Heilingsetzer, 'Das Jahre 1620 als Zäsur? Der oberösterreichische Adel im Vergleich mit dem Adel der böhmischen Länder', *Opera Historica* 7 (1999), pp. 115–37; *idem*, 'The Austrian Nobility, 1600–1650: Between Court and Estates', in R.J.W. Evans and T.V. Thomas (eds.), *Crown, Church and Estates; Central European Politics in the Sixteenth and Seventeenth Centuries* (Basingstoke, 1991), pp. 245–60; E. Maur, 'Der böhmische und mährische Adel vom 16. bis zum 18. Jahrhundert', in H. Feigl and W. Rosner (eds.), *Adel im Wandel* (Vienna, 1991), pp. 17–37. Cf. also K.J. MacHardy, *War, Religion and Court Patronage in Habsburg Austria: The Social and Cultural Dimensions of Political Interaction, 1521–1622* (Basingstoke, 2003), pp. 134–50.

67 E. Hassenpflug-Elzholz, *Böhmen und die böhmischen Stände in der Zeit des beginnenden Zentralismus. Eine Strukturanalyse der böhmischen Adelsnation um die Mitte des 18. Jahrhunderts* (Munich, 1982), pp. 306–10; cf. van Horn Melton, 'Nobility'.

68 Bůžek and Mat'a, 'Wandlungen', pp. 307–9.

69 R. Evans, *The Making of the Habsburg Monarchy* (Oxford, 1979), p. 179.

70 Van Horn Melton, 'Nobility', p. 127.

71 Hassenpflug-Elzholz, *Böhmen*, pp. 335 and 346.

72 Winkelbauer, 'Krise', p. 344; *idem, Fürst und Fürstendiener. Gundaker von Liechtenstein, ein österreichischer Aristokrat des konfessionellen Zeitalters* (Vienna/Munich 1999), pp. 24–46; Bůžek and Mat'a, 'Wandlungen', pp. 303–7.

73 Winkelbauer, *Fürst*, p. 367.

74 Hassenpflug-Elzholz, *Böhmen*, pp. 366–71; about 60 per cent of all princely Bohemian families were represented at court or elsewhere in the service of the Habsburgs by at least one member of their family.

75 See V. Bůžek (ed.), *Zivot na dvorech barokní Slechty (1600–1750)* [The Life at the Courts of the Baroque Nobility] (Opera Historica 5, Ceske Budejovice, 1996), in particular the contributions by V. Bůžek, P. Král and M. Korychová; cf. Winkelbauer, *Fürst*, pp. 291–313.

76 Winkelbauer, *Fürst*, pp. 365–7.

77 Bůžek and Mat'a, 'Wandlungen', pp. 302–4.

78 Evans, *Making*, p. 211–13.

79 Ibid., pp. 200 (quotation), 204–15.

80 H.J. Bömelburg, 'Die Magnaten: Avantgarde der Ständeverfassung oder olgarchische Clique', in J. Bahlcke (ed.), *Ständefreiheit und Staatsgestaltung in Ostmitteleuropa* (Leipzig, 1996), pp. 119–33, at p. 131.

81 F. Heal and C. Holmes, *The Gentry in England and Wales 1500–1700* (Basingstoke, 1994), pp. 10–14.

82 Ibid., p. 14; cf. A. Everitt, *The Community of Kent and the Great Rebellion, 1640–60* (Leicester, 1966), p. 41, and J. Morrill, 'The Northern Gentry and the Great Rebellion', in *idem, The Nature of the English Revolution* (London, 1993), pp. 191–213, at p. 196.

83 A. Fletcher, *Sussex 1600–1660: A County Community in Peace and War* (London, 1975), pp. 138–9; cf. *idem, Reform in the Provinces. The Government of Stuart England* (New Haven, CT, 1986). For later developments see also N. Landau, *The Justices of the Peace 1679–1760* (Berkeley, CA, 1984).

84 Heal and Holmes, *Gentry,* p. 167; A. Fletcher, 'Honour, Reputation and Local Officeholding in Elizabethan and Stuart England', in *idem* and J. Stevenson (eds.), *Order and Disorder in Early Modern England* (Cambridge, 1987), pp. 92–115; J.M. Rosenheim, *The Emergence of a Ruling Order: English Landed Society 1650–1750* (London, 1998), p. 113.

85 Rosenheim, *Emergence,* pp. 194–5, *idem,* 'Landownership, the Aristocracy and the Country Gentry, in L.K.J. Glassey (ed.), *The Reign of Charles II and James VII and II* (Basingstoke, 1997), pp. 152–70, at pp. 155–63; Heal and Holmes, *Gentry,* p. 187; E.P. Thompson, *Whigs and Hunters: The Origins of the Black Act* (New York, 1975).

86 Heal and Holmes, *Gentry,* pp. 289–93; cf. R.B. Manning, *Hunters and Poachers: A Social and Cultural History of Unlawful Hunting in England, 1485–1640* (Oxford, 1993), and D. Beaver, '"Bragging and Daring Words": Honour, Property and the Symbolism of the Hunt in Stowe, 1590–1642', in M.J. Braddick and J. Walter (eds.), *Negotiating Power in Early Modern Society: Order, Hierarchy and Subordination in Britain and Ireland* (Cambridge, 2001), pp. 149–65. Cf. for the history of the hunt in France, P. Salvadori, *La chasse sous l'Ancien Régime* (Paris, 1996).

87 K. Wrightson, *English Society, 1580–1680* (London, 1982), p. 28.

88 J.T. Cliffe, *The Yorkshire Gentry: From the Reformation to the Civil War* (London 1969), p. 84.

89 W.R. Prest, *The Rise of the Barristers: A Social History of the English Bar, 1590–1640* (Oxford, 1986), pp. 87–95; cf. *idem, The Inns of Court under Elizabeth I and the Early Stuarts 1590–1640* (London, 1972), and Heal and Holmes, *Gentry,* pp. 270–5. For later development see J. Rule, *Albion's People: English Society 1714–1815* (London, 1992), pp. 62–3.

90 For litigation see C.W. Brooks, *Pettyfoggers and Vipers of the*

Commonwealth: The 'Lower Branch' of the Legal Profession in Early Modern England (Cambridge 1986).

91 J.E. Neale, *The Elizabethan House of Commons* (London, 1949), pp. 140–61 is the classical account; cf. M.A. Kishlansky, *Parliamentary Selection: Social and Political Choice in Early Modern England* (Cambridge, 1986).

92 Heal and Holmes, *Gentry*, p. 221. For the impact of the Civil War on the counties see J. Morrill, *The Revolt of the Provinces* (2nd edn. Harlow, 1999), as well as a number of important county studies such as Everitt, *Kent*, or A. Hughes, *Politics, Society and Civil War in Warwickshire 1620–1660* (Cambridge 1987). For the cultural conflict underlying the war see D. Underdown, *Revel, Riot and Rebellion: Popular Politics and Culture in England, 1603–1660* (Oxford, 1985).

93 Heal and Holmes, *Gentry*, pp. 233–40, cf. below, p. 147.

94 F.-J. Ruggiu, 'Origines et identité des familles de la gentry de l'East Kent au milieu du XVIIIe siécle', in *L'identité nobiliaire*, pp. 62–73; cf. for the eighteenth century also P. Corfield, 'The Rivals: Landed and other Gentlemen', in N. Harte and R. Quinault (eds.), *Land and Society in Britain, 1700–1914* (Manchester, 1996), pp. 1–33.

Education, religion and civility

1 Nikodemus Frischlin, 'Oratio de vita rustica', in *idem, Orationes insigniores aliquot* (Strasburg, 1598), pp. 253–333, at pp. 305–13.

2 R.G. Asch, 'Bürgertum, Universität und Adel. Eine württembergische Kontroverse des Späthumanismus', in K. Garber (ed.), *Stadt und Literatur im deutschen Sprachraum der Frühen Neuzeit* (Tübingen, 1998), pp. 384–410.

3 K.M. Brown, *Noble Society in Scotland: Wealth, Family and Culture from Reformation to Revolution* (Edinburgh, 2000), p. 197; cf. H.C.E. Midelfort, 'Adeliges Landleben und die Legitimationskrise des deutschen Adels im 16. Jahrhundert', in G. Schmidt (ed.), *Stände und Gesellschaft im Alten Reich* (Wiesbaden, 1989), pp. 245–64.

4 See above, pp. 37–8 (noblesse de robe***); cf. K. Garber, 'Zur Statuskonkurrenz von Adel und gelehrtem Bürgertum im theoretischen Schrifttum des 17. Jhdts', in E. Blühm et al. (eds.), *Staat und Gesellschaft in der Literatur des 17. Jahrhunderts* (*Daphnis* 11, Amsterdam, 1982), pp. 115–43.

5 Fynes Moryson, *An Itinerary* (London, 1617, repr. Amsterdam 1971), part III, pp. 221–2; cf. G. Fouquet, '"Begehr nit doctor zu werden, und habs Gott seys gedanckht, nit im Sünn". Bemerkungen zu Erziehungsprogrammen ritterschaftlicher Adliger in Südwestdeutschland, 14. bis 17. Jahrhundert', in H.-P. Brecht and H. Schadt (eds.), *Wirtschaft – Gesellschaft – Städte* (Ubstadt-Weiher, 1998),

pp. 95–127. Cf. for similar incidents in early seventeenth-century France, J. Dewald, *Aristocratic Experience and the Origins of Early Modern Culture: France 1570–1715* (Berkeley, CA, 1993), p. 81.

6 M. Bogucka, *The Lost World of the Sarmatians: Custom as Regulator of Polish Social Life in the Early Modern Times* (Warsaw, 1996), p. 27.

7 J. Russell Major, From *Renaissance Monarchy to Absolute Monarchy: French Kings, Nobles and Estates* (Baltimore, 1994), pp. 101–2.

8 F. Heal and C. Holmes, *The Gentry in England and Wales 1500–1700* (Basingstoke, 1994), p. 264; L. Stone, *The Crisis of the Aristocracy, 1558–1641* (Oxford, 1965), pp. 687–92; cf. J.H. Gleason, *The Justices of the Peace in England, 1558–1640* (Oxford, 1969), pp. 88–95, who points out that in the 1630s almost 90 per cent of all JPs had attended either a university or one of the Inns of Court, whereas in the 1560s only a minority had received any academic education. However, for many, the social experience of attending a university may have been far more important than the academic training as such, as argued by A. Fletcher, *Reform in the Provinces. The Government of Stuart England* (New Haven, CT, 1986), p. 37.

9 R. Endres, *Adel in der Frühen Neuzeit* (Munich, 1993), p. 96; cf. R.A. Müller, *Universität und Adel. Eine soziokulturelle Studie zur Geschichte der bayerischen Landesuniversität Ingolstadt 1472–1648* (Berlin, 1974), and *idem*, 'Aristokratisierung des Studiums? Bemerkungen zur Adelsfrequenz an süddeutschen Universitäten im 17. Jahrhundert', *Geschichte und Gesellschaft* 10 (1984), pp. 31–46. For Austria see K. MacHardy, 'Cultural Capital, Family Strategies and Noble Identity in Early Modern Habsburg Austria 1579–1620', *PP* 163 (1999), pp. 36–75, at pp. 49–50. Cf. further M.R. di Simone, 'Admission', in W. Rüegg (ed.), *A History of the University in Europe*, vol. II: *Universities in Early Modern Europe (1500–1800)*, ed. H. de Ridder-Symons (Cambridge, 1996), pp. 285–325, at pp. 314–24.

10 MacHardy, 'Capital', p. 52, stresses that members of the newer nobility did take degrees, but often before being raised to noble status. For England Stone (*Crisis*, p. 688) also notes that peers' sons were reluctant to take degrees. Moreover, the sons and in particular the heirs of peers seem to have avoided the Inns of Court, the centre of legal education (ibid., pp. 690–2).

11 M. Hernández, *A la sombra de la corona. Poder local y oligarquía urbana (Madrid, 1606–1808)* (Madrid, 1995), pp. 184–5; cf. J. Hernández Franco, *Cultura y limpieza de sangre en la España moderna* (Murcia, 1996), pp. 152–6; R.L. Kagan, *Students and Society in Early Modern Spain* (Baltimore, 1974), and *idem*, 'Olivares y la educación de la nobleza española' in J. Elliott and A. García Sanz (eds.), *La España de conde duque de Olivares* (Valladolid, 1990), pp. 225–48.

12 See for France Dewald, *Experience*, pp. 86–90. For the attack on the more pedantic side of learned humanism see S. Stanton, *The Aristocrat*

as Art: A Study of the 'Honnête homme' and the Dandy in Seventeenth-Century French Literature (New York, 1980), pp. 21–5, and O. Roth, *Die Gesellschaft der 'honnêtes gens'. Zur Sozialethischen Grundlegung des 'honnêteté' Ideals bei La Rochefoucauld* (Heidelberg, 1981), pp. 142–5. Cf. generally for France J.F. Supple, *Arms versus Letters. The Military and Literary Ideals in the 'Essais' of Montaigne* (Oxford, 1984).

13 For the history of the *Kavaliersreise* or grand tour see *inter alia*, J. Black, *The British and the Grand Tour* (London, 1985); A. Stannek, *Telemachs Brüder. Die höfische Bildungsreise des 17. Jahrhunderts* (Frankfurt/M., 2001); H. de Ridder-Symons, 'Mobility', in *Universities in Early Modern Europe (1500–1800)*, ed. H. de Ridder-Symons (Cambridge, 1996), pp. 416–48, at pp. 431–6; and E. Chaney, *The Evolution of the Grand Tour* (London 1998); see also Stone, *Crisis*, pp. 692–702.

14 Von der Schulenburg reports in his short autobiography that while on tour in Europe in 1601–3, he not only took part in the siege of Oostend as an *aventurier* (adventurer, a volunteer who took part in a military campaign without an official commission as a sort of privileged camp follower), but was also offered a command by the Admiral of the Neapolitan galleys. He declined and also rejected an offer to serve as an *aventurier* in the fight against the Turks in Hungary. Alexander von der Schulenberg, *Lebenslauf*, ed. F. Schwerin (Halle, 1858), pp. 146–8; these passages refer to the life of Alexander's father (born 1578).

15 Dewald, *Experience*, p. 102.

16 For the history of the fencing academies see S. Anglo, *The Martial Arts of Renaissance Europe* (New Haven, CT and London, 2000), pp. 7–18, and, for France P. Brioist, H. Drévillon, P. Serna, *Croiser le fer. Violence et culture de l'épée dans la France moderne (XVIe–XVIIIe siècle)* (Seyssel, 2002), pp. 71–128.

17 E. Chaney, 'Quo Vadis? Travel as Education and the Impact of Italy in the Sixteenth Century', in *idem*, *Evolution*, pp. 58–101. For Protestant visitors to Italy see also V. Helk, 'Dänische Romreisen von der Reformation bis zum Absolutismus (1536–1660)', *Analecta Romana Instituti Danici* 6 (1971), pp. 126–9; *idem*, *Dansk Norske studierejser fra reformationen til enevaelden 1536–1660* (Odense, 1987), and P.M. Krieg, 'Hans Hoch/Giovanni Alto. Ein Schweizerischer Fremdenführer im Rom des 17. Jahrhunderts', *Römische Quartalsschrift* 48 (1953), pp. 225–36.

18 J. Black, *The British Abroad: The Grand Tour in the Eighteenth Century* (New York, 1992); B. Redford, *Venice and the Grand Tour* (New Haven, CT, 1996) and D. Arnold, 'The Illusion of Grandeur? Antiquity, Grand Tourism and the Country House', in *idem* (ed.), *The Georgian Country House* (Stroud, 1998), pp. 100–17.

19 Stannek, *Telemachs Brüder*, pp. 80–4; J. Boutier, 'L'institution politique

du gentilhomme. Le "Grand Tour" des jeunes nobles florentins en Europe, XVIe–XVIIe siècles' in *Istituzioni e società in Toscana nell'età moderna (Pubblicazionie degli Archivi di Stato, Saggi* 31, Rome, 1994), pp. 257–90; de Ridder-Symoens, 'Mobility', pp. 434–5.

20 Stannek, *Telemachs Brüder*, pp. 64–84; cf. K. Keller, 'Der sächsische Adel auf Reisen. Die Kavalierstour als Institution adliger Standesbildung im 17. und 18. Jahrhundert' in *idem* and J. Matzerath (eds.), *Geschichte des sächsischen Adels* (Cologne, 1997), pp. 257–74.

21 N. Conrads, *Ritterakademien der Frühen Neuzeit. Bildung als Standesprivileg im 16. und 17. Jahrhundert* (Göttingen, 1982), pp. 70–4.

22 J.W. Stoye, *English Travellers Abroad, 1640–1667: Their Influence in English Society and Politics* (London, 1952), pp. 63–9.

23 G. Heiß, 'Standeserziehung und Schulunterricht. Zur Bildung des niederösterreichischen Adels in der frühen Neuzeit', in *Adel im Wandel. Politik – Kultur – Konfession, 1500–1700*, ed. Niederösterreichisches Landesmuseum Wien (Vienna, 1990), pp. 391–407, at pp. 398–404; Conrads, *Ritterakademien*, pp. 238–72, in particular p. 267.

24 Conrads, *Ritterakademien*, pp. 271–2.

25 MacHardy, 'Capital', pp. 50–1. In central and eastern Europe Latin long retained its importance as a *lingua franca* not just for scholars but for noblemen as well. Thus, in the 1630s Gundaker von Liechtenstein stressed in the instruction for the education of his son that he should learn to speak Latin and other modern languages fluently while travelling abroad; see T. Winkelbauer, *Fürst und Fürstendiener. Gundaker von Liechtenstein, ein österreichischer Aristokrat des konfessionellen Zeitalters* (Vienna and Munich, 1999), p. 474. In fact, and this was unusual, Gundaker insisted that his daughters should learn to write and speak good Latin as well (p. 475).

26 Stannek, *Telemachs Brüder*, pp. 230–43.

27 Conrads, *Ritterakademien*, pp. 27–96, M. Motley, *Becoming a French Aristocrat: The Education of the Court Nobility, 1580–1715* (Princeton, New Jersey, 1990), pp. 123–68.

28 Motley, *Aristocrat*, pp. 126–38.

29 Conrads, *Ritterakademien*, in particular pp. 154–220; cf. K. Bleeck, *Adelserziehung auf deutschen Ritterakademien. Die Lüneburger Adelsschulen 1655–1850* (2 vols., Frankfurt/M., 1977), I, pp. 120–48; cf. G. Klingenstein, *Der Aufstieg des Hauses Kaunitz* (Göttingen, 1975), p. 139.

30 Klingenstein, *Aufstieg*, pp. 136–9; for similar problems a century and a half earlier in Tübingen see Asch, 'Bürgertum', pp. 408–9.

31 M. Feingold, 'The Humanities', in *The History of the University of Oxford*, vol. IV: *The Seventeenth Century*, ed. N. Tyacke (Oxford, 1997), pp. 211–356, pp. 238–55, in particular p. 239, where Feingold quotes Casaubon's statement (1668), 'one word consisting of but two

syllables, hath undone (or much damaged) good learning: it is ... the word "pedant"'.

32 H. Decker-Hauff and W. Setzler (eds.), *Die Universität Tübingen von 1477–1977 in Bildern und Dokumenten* (Tübingen, 1977), p. 115; Bleeck, *Ritterakademien*, I, pp. 88–130.

33 G. Walter, 'Adel und Antike. Zur politischen Bedeutung gelehrter Kultur für die Führungselite der Frühen Neuzeit', *HZ* 266 (1998), pp. 359–85; cf. Arnold, 'Illusion of Grandeur'. For one of the foremost collectors of antiquities north of the Alps, the Earl of Arundel, see D. Howarth, *Lord Arundel and his Circle* (New Haven, CT, 1985).

34 Beauvais-Nangis who had attended the prestigious *College de Navarre* in Paris as a young man in the late sixteenth century and had learnt Latin very thoroughly ceased to read serious academic books at court with the exception of works on history, which he thought every noble-man should know. See *Mémoires du Marquis de Beauvais-Nangis*, ed. M. Mommerqué and A.H. Taillander (Paris, 1862), p. 62.

35 Dewald, *Experience*, pp. 83–5; cf. for the education of noblemen G. Rowlands, *The Dynastic State and the Army under Louis XIV: Royal Service and Private Interest, 1661–1701* (Cambridge, 2002), pp. 178–85.

36 Frischlin, 'Oratio', p. 304.

37 Nikolaus Selnecker, *Der ganzte Psalter Davids ausgelegt* (Leipzig, 1571), f. 126v: 'was nach den Herren den Adel belanget, ist es fast dahin kommen das alle Christen wissen, das der mehrer Theil ... verechter Gotts wort sind ... ihr recht heist gewalt ... ihr zier heist frantzosen, stinckende athem, reudige hende, und füs, keuchen und schnauben ... da ist nun kein wunder, das sie von dem gemeinen mann fast an allen orten verachtet werden und schier niemands mehr etwas rechts von ihnen halten kan.'

38 A. Jouanna, *Ordre social, mythe et hiérarchies dans la France du XVIe siècle* (Paris, 1977), pp. 187–97; A.H. Williamson, 'A Patriot Nobility? Calvinism, Kin-Ties and Civic Humanism', *Scottish Historical Review* 72 (1993), pp. 1–21, at p. 1, quoting Andrew Melville's autobiography.

39 Dewald, *Experience*, p. 133; cf. A. Adam (ed.), *Les libertins au XVIIe siècle* (Paris, 1964); R. Pintard, *Le libertinage érudit dans la première moitié du XVIIe siècle* (2 vols., Paris, 1943).

40 G. Ashe, *The Hell-Fire Clubs: A History of Anti-Morality* (rev. edn., Stroud, 2000); A. Bryson, *From Courtesy to Civility: Changing Codes of Conduct in Early Modern England* (Oxford, 1998), pp. 243–75.

41 J. Youings, 'The Church', in C. Clay (ed.), *Rural Society: Landowners, Peasants and Labourers, 1500–1750* (Cambridge, 1990), pp. 71–121, at pp. 103–20.

42 For the problem of ecclesiastical property and the role it played in the debate on the reformation between nobilities and territorial rulers see V. Press, 'Adel, Reich und Reformation' in *idem, Das Alte Reich.*

Ausgewählte Aufsätze (Berlin, 1997), pp. 329–78, at pp. 348–51, and F. Göse, 'Adlige Führungsgruppen in nordostdeutschen Territorialstaaten des 16. Jahrhunderts', in P.-M. Hahn and H. Lorenz (eds.), *Formen der Visualisierung von Herrschaft: Studien zu Adel, Fürst und Schloßbau vom 16. zum 18. Jahrhundert* (Potsdam, 1998), pp. 139–210, at pp. 185–8.

43 B. Nischan, *Prince, People and Confession: The Second Reformation in Brandenburg* (Philadelphia, 1994); L. Schorn-Schütte, *Evangelische Geistlichkeit in der Frühneuzeit. Deren Anteil an der Entfaltung frühmoderner Staatlichkeit und Gesellschaft* (Gütersloh, 1996), pp. 416–48; M. Honecker, *Cura religionis magistratus Christiani. Studien zum Kirchenrecht im Luthertum des 17. Jahrhunderts, inbesondere bei Johann Gerhard* (Munich, 1968).

44 N. Canny, *The Upstart Earl: A Study of the Social and Mental World of Richard Boyle, first Earl of Cork, 1566–1643* (Cambridge, 1982).

45 J.D. McCafferty, 'John Bramhall and the Reconstruction of the Church of Ireland 1633–1641' (PhD thesis, Cambridge University, 1996); H. Kearney, *Strafford in Ireland: A Study in Absolutism* (Manchester 1959, 2nd edn. Cambridge, 1989), pp. 104–29.

46 M. Lee, *The Road to Revolution: Scotland under Charles I, 1625–37* (Urbana, IL, 1985), pp. 53–64; Brown, *Noble Society*, pp. 238–44; A. Foster, 'The Clerical Estate Revitalised', in K. Fincham (ed.), *The Early Stuart Church, 1603–42* (Basingstoke, 1993), pp. 139–60, at pp. 150–2; C. Hill, *Economic Problems of the Church from Archbishop Whitgift to the Long Parliament* (Oxford, 1956).

47 P. Hersche, *Die deutschen Domkapitel im 17. und 18. Jahrundert* (3 vols, Bern, 1984) (cf. above, pp. 20–21); S. Kremer, *Herkunft und Werdegang geistlicher Führungsschichten in den Reichsbistümern zwischen Westfälischem Frieden und Säkularisation* (Freiburg, 1992) and C. Duhamelle, *L'Héritage Collectif: La noblesse d'èglise rhénane, 17e et 18e siècles* (Paris, 1998). For France see M. Péronnet, *Les Evêques de l'ancienne France* (2 vols., Lille, 1978); N. Ravitch, *Sword and Mitre: Government and Episcopacy in France and England in the Age of Aristocracy* (The Hague, 1966). For Italy, however, where many sees, in particular in the south, were too poor to attract noblemen from wealthy families as candidates, see M. Papenheim, *Karrieren in der Kirche. Bischöfe in Nord- und Süditalien, 1676–1903* (Tübingen, 2001).

48 For France see J.A. Bergin, 'The Counter-Reformation Church and its Bishops', *PP* 165 (1999), pp. 30–73; cf. for other countries R. Po-Chia Hsia, *The World of Catholic Renewal, 1540–1770* (Cambridge, 1998), pp. 106–21.

49 J.A. Bergin, *The Making of the French Episcopate, 1598–1661* (New Haven, CT, 1996), p. 488; cf. *idem, Cardinal Richelieu: Power and the Pursuit of Wealth* (New Haven, CT, 1985).

50 R.M. Kingdon, 'Calvinism and Resistance Theory, 1550–1580', in J.H.

Burns (ed.), *The Cambridge History of Political Thought, 1450–1700* (Cambridge, 1991), pp. 193–218; cf. R. v. Friedeburg (ed.), *Widerstandsrecht in der frühen Neuzeit. Erträge und Perspektiven der Forschung im deutsch-britischen Vergleich* (Berlin, 2001).

51 R.R. Harding, *Anatomy of a Power Elite: The Provincial Governors of Early Modern France* (New Haven, CT, 1978), pp. 84–6, for France.

52 On the revival of chivalry in England see R. McCoy, *The Rites of Knighthood. The Literature and Politics of Elizabethan Chivalry* (Berkeley, CA, 1989); on the redefinition of aristocratic honour see M. James, 'English Politics and the Concept of Honour, 1485–1642' in *idem, Society, Politics and Culture. Studies in Early Modern England* (Cambridge, 1986), pp. 308–415, in particular pp. 332 ff.

53 For Austria see B. Bastl, *Tugend, Liebe, Ehre. Die adelige Frau in der Frühen Neuzeit* (Vienna, Cologne and Weimar, 2000), pp. 531–61, cf. *idem*, 'Tugend, Ehre, Eigensinn, Religiöse Selbstzeugnisse adeliger öster-reichischer Protestantinnen in der Frühen Neuzeit', in J. Dantine, K. Thien and M. Weinzierl (eds.), *Protestantische Mentalitäten* (Vienna, 1999), pp. 43–68.

54 A good example of the strong religious conviction which could inspire noblewomen is provided by Jeanne d'Albret, the mother of Henry IV. Born in 1528 she converted to Calvinism in 1560 and remained a stead-fast defender of the faith until her death in 1572; see N.L. Roelker, *Queen of Navarre: Jeanne d'Albret* (Cambridge, MA, 1968); cf. for the role of women also M. Cassan, *Le Temps des Guerres de Religion. Le cas du Limousin (vers 1530–vers 1630)* (Paris, 1996), pp. 100–1.

55 For France, see J. Garrisson, *Protestants du Midi, 1559–1598* (Toulouse, 1980); for Austria, see G. Reingrabner, *Adel und Reformation* (Vienna, 1976), and W. Ziegler, 'Nieder- und Oberösterreich', in A. Schindling and W. Ziegler (eds.), *Die Territorien des Reiches im Zeitalter der Reformation und Konfessionalisierung,* I: *Der Südosten* (Münster, 1989), pp. 119–33. See also K.J. MacHardy, *War Religion and Court Patronage in Habsburg Austria* (Basingstoke, 2002), pp. 47–56.

56 J. Cornette, 'Les nobles et la foi, du siècle des réformes au siècle de l'état absolu' in *Société, culture vie religieuse aux XVIe et XVIIe siècles (Association des Historiens Modernistes, Bulletin 20, Paris, 1995),* pp. 139–96, at pp. 163–7; cf. J.B. Wood, *The Nobility of the Election of Bayeux, 1463–1666* (Princeton, NJ, 1980), pp. 167–8, but see also Cassan, *Limousin,* pp. 94–5, for a different perspective.

57 *Die Selbstbiographie des Burggrafen Fabian zu Dohna (1550–1621),* ed. C. Krollmann (Leipzig, 1905), pp. 26–7, cf. V. Press, *Calvinismus und Territorialstaat. Regierung und Zentralbehörden in der Kurpfalz (1559–1619)* (Stuttgart, 1970), pp. 312–13.

58 J. Wormald, *Court, Kirk and Community, Scotland 1470–1625* (London, 1981), p. 137; for the Scottish Reformation, cf. I.B. Cowan,

The Scottish Reformation (London, 1982), and further Brown, *Noble Society*, pp. 228–50.

59 R. Mitchison, *Lordship to Patronage: Scotland 1603–1745* (London, 1983), pp. 137–8.

60 T. Winkelbauer, 'Sozialdisziplinierung und Konfessionalisierung durch Grundherren in den österreichischen und böhmischen Ländern im 16. und 17. Jahrhundert', *ZHF* 19 (1992), pp. 317–39.

61 J. Wormald, *Lords and Men: Bonds of Manrent 1442–1625* (London, 1981), p. 163.

62 J. Bergin, 'The Guises and their Benefices 1588–1641', *EHR* 99 (1984), pp. 34–58; cf. S. Carroll, *Noble Power during the French Wars of Religion* (Cambridge, 1998), pp. 252–4. Carroll comes to the conclusion that 'the importance of the church to the fortunes of the Guise can not be overstated' (p. 254).

63 Cf. R. Taveneaux, 'L'Esprit de croisade en Lorraine aux XVIe et XVIIe siècles' in *L'Europe, l'Alsace et la France. Études Reunies en l'honneur du doyen George Livet* (Colmar, 1986), pp. 256–63.

64 See A. Jouanna et al., *Histoire et dictionnaire des Guerres de Religion* (Paris, 1998), pp. 1095–7; Philippe-Emmanuel de Lorraine, Duc de Mercoeur, died in Nuremberg on his way back from the fight against the Turks.

65 H. Germa-Romann, *Du 'Bel Mourir' au 'Bien Mourir'. Le sentiment de la mort chez les gentilshommes français (1515–1643)* (Geneva, 2001), p. 293.

66 Winkelbauer, *Fürst*, p. 136–8; Cornette, 'Les nobles', pp. 173, 180; D. Parrott, 'A *prince souverain* and the French Crown: Charles de Nevers 1580–1638', in R. Oresko, G. Gibbs and H.M. Scott (eds.), *Royal and Republican Sovereignty in Early Modern Europe* (Cambridge, 1997), pp. 149–87; for Nevers' father Louis see M. Wolfe, 'Piety and Political Allegiance: The Duc de Nevers and the Protestant Henri IV, 1589–93', *French History* 2 (1989), pp. 1–21.

67 Jouanna, *Histoire et Dictionnaire*, pp. 1003–5; cf. Cornette, 'Les nobles', p. 173.

68 D. Albrecht, *Maximilian I. von Bayern 1573–1651* (Munich, 1998), p. 289; for a similar mentality among Bohemian and Austrian magnates see Winkelbauer, *Fürst*, pp. 500–5.

69 On Jansenism see R. Briggs, *Communities of Belief: Cultural and Social Tensions in Early Modern France* (Oxford, 1989), pp. 339–63.

70 On the importance of François de Sales for aristocratic piety see Winkelbauer, *Fürst*, pp. 494–500; cf. V. Mellinghof-Bourgerie, *François de Sale, un homme des lettres spirituel, 1567–1622* (Geneva, 1999).

71 At least until the middle decades of the seventeenth century Jesuit confessors seem to have been less strict in their condemnation of the duel among noblemen than theologians inspired by more rigorous principles. See F. Billacois, *Le Duel dans la société française des XVIe–XVIIe*

siècles: essai de psychologie historique (Paris, 1986), pp. 164–82; cf. Blaise Pascal, *Lettres écrites à un provincial*, ed. A. Adam (Paris, 1967), lettre 7, pp. 96–108, and lettre 14, p. 192. Pascal like many Jansenists took a dim view of Jesuit casuistry.

72 On the phenomenon of conversion among noblemen see Winkelbauer, *Fürst*, pp. 66–158; cf. Dieter Stievermann, 'Politik und Konfession im 18. Jahrhundert', *ZHF* 18 (1991), pp. 177–99.

73 W. Sommer, *Gottesfurcht und Fürstenherrschaft. Studien zum Obrigkeitsverständnis Johann Arndts und lutherischer Hofprediger zur Zeit der altprotestantischen Orthodoxie* (Göttingen, 1988), pp. 287–91 on the attitude of German court preachers to the English Revolution.

74 J. Bérenger, *Turenne* (Paris, 1987), pp. 444–70.

75 See above, n. 72; cf. G. Haug-Moritz, 'Kaisertum und Parität. Reichspolitik und Konfessionen nach dem Westfälischen Frieden', in *ZHF* 19 (1992), pp. 445–82.

76 M. Fulbrook, *Piety and Politics: Religion and the Rise of Absolutism in England, Württemberg and Prussia* (Cambridge, 1983), pp. 166–9; C. Hinrichs, *Preußentum und Pietismus* (Göttingen, 1971); cf. for Zinzendorf: D. Meyer, 'Zinzendorf und Herrnhut', in M. Brecht et al. (eds.), *Geschichte des Pietismus*, vol. II: *Der Pietismus im achtzehnten Jahrhundert* (Göttingen, 1995), pp. 5–106. See also R.L. Gawthorp, *Pietism and the Making of Eighteenth-Century Prussia* (Cambridge, 1993).

77 V. Press, 'Reichsgrafenstand und Reich. Zur Sozial- und Verfassungsgeschichte des deutschen Hochadels in der Frühen Neuzeit' in *idem*, *Adel im Alten Reich* (Tübingen, 1998), pp. 113–38, at p. 131 with reference to the counts of Reuß, Waldeck, Wied, Solms, Ysenburg as 'the pious counts'.

78 J. Dewald, *The European Nobility, 1400–1800* (Cambridge, 1996), p. 182.

79 For Germany see H.R. Schmidt, *Konfessionalisierung im 16. Jahrhundert* (Munich, 1992), pp. 94–105; cf. for Europe in general H. Schilling (ed.), *Institutionen, Instrumente und Akteure sozialer Kontrolle und Disziplinierung im frühneuzeitlichen Europa* (Frankfurt, 1999).

80 Dewald, *Experience*, pp. 137–9.

81 D. Parker, *Class and State in Ancien Régime France: The Road to Modernity?* (London, 1996), p. 148, cf. pp. 191–3.

82 Cf. below, chapter 4 for the salons see C. Lougee, *Le paradis des femmes: Women, Salons and Social Stratification in Seventeenth-Century France* (Princeton, New Jersey, 1976).

83 J.M. Constant, 'Les barons français pendant les guerres de religion' in *Quatrième Centenaire des la bataille de Courtras (Colloque de Courtras, 1987*, Pau, 1988), pp. 48–62, at pp. 54–60; and Wood, *Bayeux*, pp. 81–90.

84 V. Groebner, 'Das Gesicht wahren. Abgeschnittene Nasen, abgeschnittene Ehre in der spätmittelalterlichen Stadt' in K. Schreiner and G. Schwerhoff (eds.), *Verletzte Ehre, Ehrkonflikte in Gesellschaften des Mittelalters und der frühen Neuzeit* (Cologne, 1995), pp. 361–80; J. Eibach, 'Städtische Gewaltkriminalität im Ancien Régime. Frankfurt am Main im Europäischen Kontext', *ZHF* 25 (1998), pp. 359–82, and J.R. Ruff, *Violence in Early Modern Europe, 1500–1800* (Cambridge, 2001), in particular pp. 75–83.

85 For the history of the feud see O. Brunner, *'Land' and Lordship: Structures of Governance in Medieval Austria* (Philadelphia, 1992), chapter 1 [German title, *Land und Herrschaft* (5th edn., Vienna, 1965)]; H. Zmora, *State and Nobility in Early Modern Germany: The Knightly Feud in Franconia, 1440–1567* (Cambridge, 1997), in particular pp. 1–15. Zmora points out that many feuding noblemen were territorial officeholders in the fifteenth century and often waged war by proxy for their own princes who connived in their acts of violence. See further G. Algazi, *Herrengewalt und Gewalt der Herren im späten Mittelalter* (Frankfurt/M. and New York, 1996), and H. Carl, *Der Schwäbische Bund, 1488–1534* (Leinfelden-Echterdingen, 2000), pp. 423–6.

86 For the following see V. Press, 'Wilhelm von Grumbach und die deutsche Adelskrise der 1560er Jahre' in *idem, Adel im Alten Reich* (Tübingen, 1998), pp. 383–420.

87 F. Ortloff, *Geschichte der Grumbachischen Händel* (4 vols., Jena, 1868–70), IV, p. 536.

88 Zmora, *State and Nobility*, pp. 122–46.

89 K.M. Brown, *Bloodfeud in Scotland, 1573–1625: Violence, Justice and Politics in Early Modern Scotland* (Edinburgh, 1986), p. 32.

90 J. Goodare and M. Lynch, 'The Scottish State and its Borderlands, 1567–1625', in *idem* (eds.), *The Reign of James VI* (East Linton, 2000), pp. 186–207; cf. Wormald, *Lords and Men*.

91 E. Muir, *Mad Blood Stirring: Vendetta and Factions in Friuli during the Renaissance* (Baltimore, 1993), in particular pp. 247 ff.

92 Billacois, *Le Duel*; cf. Stone, *Crisis*, pp. 242–50; but cf. also P. Brioist, H. Drévillon and P. Serna, *Croiser le fer*, which revises Billacois' interpretation considerably.

93 See D. Quint, 'Duelling and Civility in Sixteenth-Century Italy, *I Tatti Studies* 7 (1997), pp. 231–75, in particular p. 265: 'the codification of the duel thus partook of, even as it contested it, the growing legalism of modern society'.

94 S. Shapin, *A Social History of Truth: Civility and Science in Seventeenth-Century England* (Chicago, 1994), pp. 107–14; cf. for the early seventeenth-century discussion on the duel and its implications in England, M. Peltonen, 'Francis Bacon, The Earl of Northampton and the Jacobean anti-Duelling Campaign', *HJ* 44 (2001), pp. 1–28. see also M. Peltonen, *The Duel in Early Modern England. Civility, Politeness and Honour* (Cambridge, 2003).

95 Honour and truth were intimately connected in the ritual of the duel. Lying was not necessarily frowned upon if those whom one lied to were of inferior status, and therefore, it was assumed, had no right to the truth. But if one gentleman lied to another this was either a moral deficiency or an open affront, or as J. Pitt-Rivers has put it: 'The right to the truth and the right to withhold it both attach to honour, and to contest these rights is to place honour in jeopardy' (J. Pitt-Rivers, *The Fate of Shechem or the Politics of Sex* (Cambridge, 1977), p. 12).

96 M. Bellabarba, 'Honour, Discipline and the State: Nobility and Justice in Italy, Fifteenth to Seventeenth Centuries', in Schilling, *Institutionen, Instrumente und Akteure sozialer Kontrolle*, pp. 225–51, and D. Weinstein, 'Fighting or Flyting? Verbal Duelling in mid-sixteenth-century Italy', in T. Dean and K.J.P. Lowe (eds.), *Crime, Society and the Law in Renaissance Italy* (Cambridge, 1994), pp. 204–20.

97 Billacois, *Le duel*, pp. 115–16.

98 Stone, *Crisis*, p. 245.

99 Gervase Holles, *Memorials of the Holles Family, 1493–1656*, ed. A.C. Wood (*Camden Society, Third Series*, LV, London, 1937), pp. 90–1.

100 Harding, *Governors*, pp. 78–80.

101 William Segar, *Honor Military and Civill* (London, 1602), p. 122; Marc Vulson de la Colombiére, *Le vray théâtre d'honneur* (Paris, 1669), pp. 152–7.

102 P. Brioist, H. Drévillon and P. Serna, *Croiser le fer*, pp. 277–304, 323–4, 365–7. Cf. E. Le Roy Ladurie and J.-F. Fitou, *Saint-Simon ou le système de la cour* (Paris, 1977), pp. 81–2, and M. Cuénin, *Le duel sous l'Ancien Régime* (Paris, 1982).

103 R.J. Knecht, *Richelieu* (London, 1991), pp. 51–2. François Billacois comes to the conclusion that the Compagnie de Saint Sacrement, which tried to curb the duel in France, was proclaiming not so much the ideals of Christian charity as of the well-ordered police state, and that its members were in fact 'les prophètes du culte de Léviathan.' See Billacois, *Le duel*, pp. 294–5, for official policy cf. pp. 146–61 and 247–318.

104 Billacois, *Le duel*, pp. 284–94; cf. R.A. Schneider, 'Swordplay and Statemaking. Aspects of the Campaign against the Duel in Early Modern France' in C. Bright and S. Harding (eds.), *Statemaking and Social Movements* (Ann Arbor, 1984), pp. 265–96, at pp. 284–6.

105 Cf. A. Tallon, *La Société du Saint-Sacrement 1629–1667, spiritualité et société* (Paris, 1990).

106 Germa-Romann, *Du 'Bel Mourir' au 'Bien Mourir'*, pp. 271–306.

107 Schneider, 'Swordplay', p. 283; cf. G. Rowlands, 'The Ethos of Blood and Changing Values? *Robe*, *Epée* and the French Army, 1661–1715', *Seventeenth-Century French Studies* 19 (1997), pp. 95–108.

108 J. McManners, *Church and Society in Eighteenth-Century France*, vol. I, *The Clerical Establishment and its Ramifications* (Oxford, 1998), p. 224; cf. for the continuing popularity of duels among officers,

G. Rowlands, *The Dynastic State and the Army under Louis XIV: Royal Service and Private Interest, 1661–1701* (Cambridge, 2002), pp. 236–8.

109 C. Chauchadis, *La loi du duel. Le code du point d'honneur dans l'Espagne des XVIe–XVIIe siècles* (Toulouse, 1997), in particular, pp. 36–40 and 393–401, 439–73.

110 O. Mörke, *'Stadtholder' oder 'Staetholder'? Die Funktion des Hauses Oranien und seines Hofes in der politischen Kultur der Republik der Vereinigten Niederlande im 17. Jahrhundert* (Münster, 1997), pp. 206–10.

111 J. Childs, *The Army, James II and the Glorious Revolution* (Manchester, 1980), pp. 43–5; *idem, The British Army of William III* (Manchester, 1987), pp. 44–6.

112 V.G. Kiernan, *The Duel in European History* (Oxford, 1989), pp. 129–30; cf. for the late seventeenth and early eighteenth centuries V.L. Stater, *Duke Hamilton is dead! A Story of Aristocratic Life and Death in Stuart Britain* (New York, 1999).

113 Bryson, *Courtesy*, pp. 249–50.

114 N. Schindler, 'Ein inszenierter Jugendkrawall. Hegemoniespiele zwischen Adels- und Volkskultur im 16. Jahrhundert' in *idem, Widerspenstige Leute. Studien zur Volkskultur in der frühen Neuzeit* (Frankfurt/M., 1992), pp. 245–57, analysing an incident in which a gang of young noblemen – if only in jest – terrorised the small town of Meßkirch, residence of the Counts of Zimmern. For Spain see Hernández, *A la sombra*, p. 221, and H. Kamen, *Spain in the Later Seventeenth Century, 1665–1700* (London, 1980), pp. 171–2.

115 A. Lebigre, *Les Grands Jours d'Auvergne* (Paris, 1976). Apparently Louis XIV hesitated to take equally strong measures against noble violence in other provinces as he feared that this would encourage peasant resistance against the *seigneurs*. See R. Mettam, *Power and Faction in Louis XIV's France* (Oxford, 1988), pp. 204–7.

116 J.A. Sharpe, *Crime in Early Modern England, 1550–1750* (2nd edn., Edinburgh, 1999), p. 140.

117 Villari, *Revolt*, p. 141 with regard to the 1640s. For Spain see Casey, *Spain*, pp. 173–5, with particular reference to the Kingdom of Aragon, and Kamen, *Spain*, pp. 207–12; cf. Ruff, *Violence*, pp. 46–8. For Italy and an earlier period see I. Polverino Fosi, *La società violenta. Il banditismo dello stato pontificio nella seconda metà del Cinquecento* (Rome, 1985).

118 For the hunt see P. Salvadori, *La Chasse sous l'Ancien Régime* (Paris, 1996), and Heal and Holmes, *Gentry*, pp. 289–92.

119 Bryson, *Courtesy*, p. 113.

120 For this aspect see Bryson, *Courtesy*, pp. 241 ff.

121 S. Fairchilds, *Domestic Enemies, Servants and their Masters in Old Regime France* (Baltimore, 1984); S. Kettering, 'The Household Service

of Early Modern French Noblewomen', *French Historical Studies* 20 (1997), pp. 55–85; M. Girouard, *Life in the English Country House* (Yale, 1978), pp. 138–43.

122　O. Brunner, *Adeliges Landleben und Europäischer Geist* (Salzburg, 1959), pp. 332–3; C. Christie, *The British Country House in the Eighteenth Century* (Manchester, 2000), pp. 129–78, in particular pp. 162–6; cf. L. Stone and J.C. Fawtier Stone, *An Open Elite? England 1540–1880* (abr. edn., Oxford, 1986), pp. 237–40. For France see M. Girouard, *Life in the French Country House* (London, 2000); for Bohemia V. Bůžek and P. Mat'a, 'Wandlungen des Adels in Böhmen und Mähren im Zeitalter des "Absolutismus" (1620–1740)', in R.G. Asch (ed.), *Der Adel im Ancien Régime* (Cologne, 2001), pp. 287–322, at pp. 309–20.

123　See above, chapter 2, pp. 35–6.

124　P. Borsay, *The English Urban Renaissance: Culture and Society in the Provincial Town, 1660–1770* (Oxford, 1989), p. 307. For France cf. J.-L. Flandrin, 'Distinction through Taste' in R. Chartier (ed.), *A History of Private Life*, vol. III: *Passions of the Renaissance* (Cambridge, Mass., 1989), pp. 265–307, at pp. 300–5, and for Spain J.S. Amelang, *Honored Citizens of Barcelona: Patrician Culture and Class Relations, 1490–1714* (Princeton, New Jersey, 1986), p. 184.

The court: prison or showcase of noble life?

1　J. Adamson, 'Introduction: The Making of the Ancien-Régime Court 1500–1700' in *idem* (ed.) *The Princely Courts of Europe: Ritual, Politics and Culture under the Ancien Régime 1500–1750* (London, 1999), pp. 7–41, at p. 21. Cf. R.G. Asch, 'Introduction: Court and Household from the Fifteenth to the Seventeenth Century' in R.G. Asch and A.M. Birke (eds.), *Politics, Patronage and the Nobility: The Court at the Beginning of the Modern Age (c.1450–1650)*, (Oxford, 1991), pp. 1–39.

2　For the cultural impact of the Italian courts see M. Hollingsworth, *Patronage in Sixteenth Century Italy* (London, 1996), as well as the contributions by H.D. Fernández, Robert Oresko and Marcello Fantoni in Adamson, *Courts*. See further F. Fantoni, *La Corte Del Granduca* (Rome, 1994), L. Waage-Petersen, M. Pade and D. Quarta (eds.), *La Corte di Ferrara – The Court of Ferrara* (Copenhagen, 1990) and P. Merlin, *Tra guerre et tornei. La corte sabauda nell' età de Carlo Emmanuele I* (Turin, 1991).

3　For Castiglione's biography see E. Loos, *Baldassare Castigliones Libro de Cortegiano* (Frankfurt M., 1955), pp. 40–69; for the impact of his work see P. Burke, *The Fortunes of the Courtier: The European Reception of Castiglione's Cortegiano* (Cambridge, 1995); cf. C.

Ossola, *Dal Cortegiano al uomo di mondo* (Turin, 1987) and R.W. Hanning and D. Rosand (eds.), *Castiglione, The Ideal and the Real in Renaissance Culture* (New Haven, CT, 1983).

4 See Burke, *Courtier*, p. 36.

5 M. Hinz, *Rhetorische Strategien des Hofmannes. Studien zu den italienischen Hofmannstraktaten des 16. und 17. Jahrhunderts* (Stuttgart, 1992), pp. 91–2. Hinz's study is truly outstanding.

6 Baldassare Castiglione, *The Book of the Courtier*, transl. by Sir Thomas Hoby, ed. W.H.D. Rouse (London, 1928), pp. 31–4.

7 Ibid., pp. 35, 71.

8 Ibid, p . 46 (book I, § 26) renders this as 'to use in every thing a certaine disgracing to cover arte withall and seeme whatsoever he doth and saith, to doe it without paine, and as it were not minding it.' Cf. p. 48. See also E. Saccone, '*Grazia, sprezzatura* and *affettazione* in Castiglione's *Book of the Courtier*', in Hanning and Rosand, *Castiglione*, pp. 45–68.

9 Hinz, *Strategien*, pp. 122, 128.

10 Castiglione, *Cortegiano*, p. 31: 'I wil have this our courtier therefore to bee a gentleman borne and of a good house' cf. C. Donati, *L'idea di nobiltà in Italia, secoli XIV–XVIII* (Rome and Bari, 1995), pp. 38–44.

11 Hinz, *Strategien*, pp. 127–8.

12 Castiglione, *Cortegiano*, p. 106 (book II, § 28).

13 Ibid., p. 16, book I, § 1.

14 Ibid., pp. 16 and 298–9 (I, § 1 and IV, §§ 46–7).

15 Hinz, *Strategien*, pp. 379–82.

16 Lorenzo Ducci, *Arte aulica* (Ferrara, 1601), p. 53.

17 Ducci, *Arte*, p. 92.

18 Stephano Guazzo, *De Conversatione civili. Dissertationes politicae* (Lugduni Batavorum, 1650), IV, iii, pp. 221–2 and 238–9. Cf. Donati, *L'idea*, pp. 152–64.

19 See Ducci, *Arte*, pp. 397 ff, 452.

20 S. Neumeister and D. Briesmeister (eds.), *El mundo de Gracián. Actas del Coloquio Internacional Berlin 1988* (Berlin, 1991); P. Werle, "*El Héroe*". *Zur Ethik des Baltasar Gracián* (Tübingen, 1992), and M. Hinz, *Die menschlichen und göttlichen Mittel. Sieben Kommentare zu Baltasar Gracián* (Bonn, 2002).

21 Burke, *Courtier*, p. 119.

22 D. Frigo, *Il Padre de Famiglia, Governo della casa e governo civile nella tradizione dell' "Economica" tra cinque et seicent* (Rome 1985), p. 198, cf. pp. 193–200.

23 Even Faret could still write in the 1630s that 'stupidité brutale' was commonly seen as the true hallmark of an aristocrat and that French noblemen remained convinced that nobody could be at the same time a soldier and a 'savant'. See Nicolas Faret, *L'Honeste Homme, ou l'art de plaire à la cour* (Paris, 1637), pp. 37–8; cf. above, chapter 3, pp. 76–7.

24 M. Chatenet, 'Henri III et l'ordre de la cour. Evolution de l'étiquette à travers les règlements gèneraux de 1578 et 1585', in R. Sauzet (ed.), *Henri III et son temps* (Paris, 1992), pp. 133–9; J. Boucher, *Societé et mentalités autour des Henri III* (4 vols., Lille, 1981), I, pp. 198–200, and N. Le Roux, *La faveur du Roi. Mignons et courtisans au temps des derniers Valois (vers 1547–vers 1589)* (Seyssel, 2000), pp. 176–91.

25 See O. Ranum, 'Courtesy, Absolutism and the Rise of the French State', *JMH* 52 (1980), pp. 426–51.

26 J. Dewald, *Aristocratic Experience and the Origins of Early Modern Culture: France 1570–1715* (Berkeley, CA, 1993), p. 138; cf. Louis de Rouvroy, Duc de Saint-Simon, *Mémoires*, ed. Y. Coirault (8 vols., Paris, 1983–88), I, pp. 245–6.

27 In the later sixteenth century *honnêteté* had become associated with Christian notions of morality and decent manners. However the most influential version of *honnêteté* was developed for life at court. See A. Höfer and R. Reichardt, 'Honnêteté, Honnêtes gens', in R. Reichardt and E. Schmidt (eds.), *Handbuch politisch-sozialer Grundbegriffe in Frankreich 1680–1820*, vol. VII (Munich, 1986), pp. 7–73, at pp. 10–11.

28 P.M. Smith, *The Anti-Courtier Trend in Sixteenth Century French Literature* (Geneva, 1966), pp. 192–218.

29 Höfer and Reichart, 'Honnêteté', pp. 12–13; some contemporaries immediately criticised Faret's tendence to identify the *honnête homme* with the courtier and argued that his tract should have been called 'l'honneste courtisan'. H. Scheffers, *Höfische Konvention und die Aufklärung. Wandlungen des honnête-homme Ideals im 17. und 18. Jahrhundert* (Bonn, 1980), pp. 55–6.

30 See Faret, *L' Honeste Homme*, pp. 72–3, 182 ff. and 204.

31 Burke, *Courtier*, pp. 123–4.

32 Faret, *L' Honeste Homme*, pp. 6 and 10.

33 Ibid., pp. 14, 21, 37–54. The courtier had to have at least some arithmetic and geometry because these sciences were important for warfare, but more importantly, he had to read the historians and tracts on politics. History, Faret remarked, was the science of kings.

34 Ibid., pp. 186–7.

35 Höfer and Reichart, 'Honnêteté', p. 23; cf. O. Roth, *Die Gesellschaft der Honnêtes Gens. Zur sozialethischen Grundlegung des honnêté-Ideals bei La Rochefoucauld*, (Heidelberg, 1981), pp. 226–50.

36 M. Magendie, *La Politesse mondaine et les théories de l'honnêteté en France de 1600 à 1660* (Paris, 1925), pp. 730 ff.; cf. A. Coupire, *De Corneille à la Bruyere. Images de la cour* (2 vols., Lille, 1984).

37 For the latter see H. Kiesel, *'Bei Hof, bei Höll', Untersuchungen zur literarischen Hofkritik von Sebastian Brant bis Friedrich Schiller* (Tübingen, 1979).

38 [Joh. Christoph Wagenseil] *Directorium Aulicum de ratione Status, in*

aulis imperatorum, regum, principum (Hagae Comitis, 1687), p. 10: 'cum omnes externi habehantur pro nobilibus, et sine invidia responderi possint interroganti: quisnam sit peregrinus? je suis un Gentilhomme étranger. Nobiles enim in Gallia Anglia, Italia, et Hispania omnes reputantur, qui non manibus victum quaerunt.'

39 Johann Basilius Küchelbecker, *Allerneueste Nachricht vom Römisch-Kayserlichen Hofe* (Hanover, 1730), pp. 378–80.

40 A. Jouanna, art. 'Noblesse, noblesses' in *Dictionnaire de l'ancien Régime*, ed. L. Bély (Paris, 1996), at p. 892; according to the rules valid since 1732 which enshrined earlier customs, families who wanted to achieve the *honneurs de la cour* had to prove that they had been noble for at least 300 years. Cf. F. Bluche, *Les Honneurs de la Cour* (2 vols., Paris, 1957). Acccording to Bluche (*Les Magistrats du Parlement de Paris au XVIIIe siècle*, 2nd edn., Paris, 1986, p. 244) only about 10 per cent of the entire French nobility enjoyed the *honneurs de la cour*. The percentage of robe families entitled to claim this privilege was not really all that much lower (6.6 per cent), as the king could freely bestow this honour on families otherwise not entitled to it. Cf. Further, M. Marraud, *La noblesse de Paris au XVIIIe siècle* (Paris, 2000), pp. 399–400 for the exclusion of many provincial noblemen from the honours of the court.

41 For the courtly hierarchy in Versailles and its logic see J. Revel, 'La Cour', in P. Nora (ed.), *Les Lieux de Mémoire*, part III, *Les France*, vol. 2, *Traditions* (Paris, 1992), pp. 129–93, at pp. 143–59 and E. Le Roy Ladurie (avec la collaboration des Jean-François Fitou), *Saint-Simon ou le systéme de la Cour* (Paris, 1997), pp. 43–100.

42 For the role of ceremonial in early modern society and at court in particular see E. Muir, *Ritual in Early Modern Europe* (Cambridge, 1997), pp. 246–62; R.E. Giesey, 'La societé de cour' in *idem, Cérémonial et puissance souveraine. France, XVe–XVIIe siècles* (Paris, 1987), pp. 67–86; and the contributions by Giesey and J.H. Elliott to S. Wilentz (ed.), *Rites of Power: Symbolism, Ritual and Politics Since the Middle Ages* (Philadelphia, 1985); cf. further most recently B. Stollberg-Rilinger (ed.), *Vormoderne politische Verfahren* (Berlin, 2001) and J.J. Berns and T. Rahn (eds.), *Zeremoniell als höfische Ästhetik in Spätmittelalter und Früher Neuzeit* (Tübingen, 1995).

43 Hinz, *Strategien*, pp. 375 and 377. On the logic of patronage and gift-giving cf. L.L. Peck, *Court Patronage and Corruption in Early Stuart England* (Boston, 1990). For the mechanics of the French court see Revel, 'La Cour'.

44 The Duc de Saint-Simon's writings are a classical expression of such warnings. See, for example, his bitter account of the alleged humiliation of the French aristocracy by Mazarin and his successors as royal ministers in his memoirs (Saint-Simon, *Mémoires*, V, pp. 294–8).

45 For the changing position of servants see S. Fairchilds, *Domestic Enemies, Servants and their masters in Old Regime France* (Baltimore,

1984) and J.P. Gutton, *Domestiques et serviteurs dans la France de l'ancien régime* (Paris, 1981); S. Maza, *Servants and Masters in 18th Century France: The Uses of Loyalty* (Princeton, 1983).

46 As Matteo Peregrini pointed out in the early seventeenth century. See Matteo Peregrini (alias Pellegrini), *Difesa del savio in corte*, (In Macerata, 1634), pp. 241–4. For the implications of friendship for political culture see now also Peter N. Miller, 'Friendship and Conversation in Seventeenth-Century Venice', *JMH* 73 (2001), pp. 1–31.

47 Cf. R.G. Asch, *Der Hof Karls I von England: Politik, Provinz und Patronage, 1625–1640* (Cologne, 1993), pp. 288–321.

48 I.A.A. Thompson, 'The Institutional Background to the Rise of the Minister-Favourite', in J.H. Elliott and L.W.B. Brockliss (eds.), *The World of the Favourite* (New Haven and London, 1999), pp. 13–25, at p. 20.

49 F. Tomás y Valiente, *Los validos en la monarquía española del siglo XVII* (2nd. edn., Madrid, 1990); A. Alvarez-Osorio Alvariño, 'El favor real: liberalidad del príncipe y jerarquía de la república (1665–1700)', in C. Continisio and C. Mozzarelli (eds.), *Repubblica e virtú: Pensiero politico e Monarchia Cattolica fra XVI e XVII secolo* (Rome, 1995), pp. 393–453.

50 A. Feros, *Kingship and Favouritism in the Spain of Philip III, 1598–1621* (Cambridge, 2000); cf. F. Benigno, *L'ombra del re. Ministri e lotta politica nell Spagna del Seicento* (Venice, 1992).

51 Thompson, 'Background', p. 21.

52 G. Signorotti and M.A. Visceglia (eds.), *Court and Politics in Papal Rome, 1400–1800* (Cambridge, 2002); M. Völkel, *Römische Kardinalshaushalte des 17. Jahrhunderts* (Tübingen, 1993); V. Reinhardt, *Kardinal Scipione Borghese (1605–1633). Vermögen, Finanzen und sozialer Aufstieg eines Papstnepoten* (Tübingen, 1984); R. Ago, *Carriere e clientele nella Roma barocca* (Rome and Bari, 1990).

53 A. Feros, 'Images of Evil, Images of Kings: The Contrasting Faces of the Royal Favourite and the Prime Minister in Early Modern European Political Literature, *c.*1580–1650', in Elliott and Brockliss, *Favourite* , pp. 205–22.

54 Peck, *Court Patronage*, pp. 49–56, 190–6; cf. R. Lockyer, *Buckingham. The Life and Political Career of George Villiers, First Duke of Buckingham 1592–1628* (London, 1981).

55 Smith, *Anti-Courtier Trend*, pp. 193–202.

56 Le Roux, *La faveur*, p. 485 argues that Anne de Joyeuse appeared as the 'paragon of the cultivated and pacified (pacifiée) nobility which the King tried to create'.

57 Le Roux, *La faveur*, pp. 210–314, 463–505.

58 J. Bergin, *Cardinal Richelieu: Power and the Pursuit of Wealth* (New Haven, CT and London, 1985); D. Dessert, 'Pouvoir et fortune au XVIIe siècle: la fortune des Mazarin', *RHMC* 23 (1976), pp. 161–81.

59 R.G. Asch, 'Corruption and Punishment: the Rise and Fall of Matthäus Enzlin (1556–1613), Lawyer and Favourite', in Elliott and Brockliss, *Favourite*, pp. 96–111.

60 For Versailles see Revel, 'La Cour'; O. Chaline, 'The Valois and Bourbon Courts, c. 1515–1750', in Adamson, *Courts*, pp. 67–95; and J. Duindam, 'The Bourbon and the Austrian Habsburg Courts: Numbers, Ordinances, Ceremonies and Nobles', in R.G. Asch (ed.), *Der europäische Adel im Ancien Régime: Von der Krise der ständischen Monarchien bis zur Revolution (1600–1789)* (Cologne, 2001), pp. 181–206; as well as N. Elias, 'Die höfische Gesellschaft' (Darmstadt, 1969), engl. translation *The Court Society* (Oxford, 1983); G. Sabatier, *Versailles ou la figure du roi* (Paris, 1999) and P. Burke, *The Fabrication of Louis XIV* (New Haven, CT and London, 1992).

61 Elias, *Höfische Gesellschaft*, chapter VII. For a critical assessment of Elias's work, see most recently, J. Duindam, 'Norbert Elias und der frühneuzeitliche Hof – Versuch einer Kritik und Weiterführung', *Historische Anthropologie* 6 (1998), pp. 371–87 and G. Schwerhoff, 'Zivilisationsprozeß und Geschichtswissenschaft. Norbert Elias Forschungsparadigma in historischer Sicht', *HZ* 266 (1998), pp. 561–605. See also the new edition by Claudia Opitz, N. Elias, *Höfische Gesellschaft* (Frankfurt/M., 2002).

62 Saint-Simon, *Mémoires*, V, pp. 484–5, 527–30 and 479, where Saint-Simon writes: 'Encore lui fallait-il expliquer quelles étaient ces maisons, que leur nom ne lui aprenait pas' ('Thus one had to explain to the King what the position of these [great aristocratic] families was, as their name alone did not provide him with sufficient information').

63 For an analysis of the Spanish court which emphasises its theatrical function see J. Brown and J.H. Elliott, *A Palace for A King. The Buen Retiro and the Court of Philipp IV* (New Haven and London, 1980); cf. J.H. Elliott, 'Power and Propaganda in the Spain of Philip I', in Wilentz, *Rites*, pp. 145–76. See also C. Hofmann, *Das spanische Hofzeremoniell von 1500–1700* (Frankfurt/M. 1985).

64 P.R. Campbell, *Power and Politics in Old Regime France, 1720–1745* (London, 1996), p. 309.

65 See below, pp. 136–9.

66 J.M. Smith, *The Culture of Merit: Nobility, Royal Service and Making of Absolute Monarchy in France, 1600–1789* (Ann Arbor, 1996), in particular pp. 130 ff; cf. *idem*, '"Our Sovereign's Gaze": Kings, Nobles and State-Formation in Seventeenth-Century France', *French Historical Studies* 18 (1993), pp. 396–415.

67 Saint-Simon, *Mémoires*, V, pp. 484–6.

68 *Mémoires de Primi Visconti sur la cour de Louis XIV*, ed. J.-F. Solnon (Paris, 1988), p. 146.

69 G. Rowlands, 'Louis XIV, Aristocratic Power and the Elite Units of the French Army', *French History* 13 (1999), pp. 303–31; cf. *idem, The*

Dynastic State and the Army under Louis XIV: Royal Service and Private Interest, 1661–1701 (Cambridge, 2002), pp. 341–7.

70 F. Bluche, *Louis XIV* (Paris, 1986), p. 519, speaks of the French court as 'antichambre de la mort'.

71 Important studies of individual German courts are A. Winterling, *Der Hof des Kurfürsten von Köln, 1688–1794. Eine Fallstudie zur Bedeutung "absolutistischer" Hofhaltung* (Bonn, 1986) and S.J. Klingensmith, *The Utility of Splendor: Ceremony, Social Life and Architecture at the Court of Bavaria, 1600–1800* (Chicago, 1993).

72 For the Dresden court see now K. Keller, 'Der Hof als Zentrum adliger Existenz? Der Dresdner Hof und der sächsische Adel im 17. und 18. Jahrhundert', in Asch, *Adel*, pp. 207–33, in particular pp. 222–3.

73 P. Bahl, *Der Hof des Großen Kurfürsten. Studien zur höheren Amtsträgerschaft Brandenburg-Preußens* (Cologne, 2001), pp. 164–86; E. Melton, 'The Prussian Junkers 1600–1786', in H.M. Scott (ed.), *The European Nobilities in the Seventeenth and Eighteenth Centuries* (2 vols., London, 1995), II, pp. 71–109, at pp. 85–9.

74 W. Neugebauer, 'Staatsverwaltung, Manufaktur und Garnison. Die polyfunktionale Residenzlandschaft von Berlin – Potsdam – Wusterhausen zur Zeit Friedrich Wilhelms I', *Forschungen zur Brandenburgischen und Preußischen Geschichte*, Nene Folge 7 (1997), pp. 233–57; C. Hinrichs, 'Der Regierungsantritt Friedrich Wilhelms I' in *idem, Preußen als historisches Problem* (Berlin, 1964), pp. 91–137, in particular pp. 100–7.

75 V. Bauer, Hofökonomie, *Der Diskurs über den Fürstenhof in Zeremonialwissenschaft, Hausväterliteratur und Kameralismus* (Vienna, 1997), pp. 46–7; cf. *idem, Die höfische Gesellschaft in Deutschland von der Mitte des 17. bis zum Ausgang des 18. Jahrhunderts* (Tübingen, 1993), pp. 90–4.

76 On the general structure of the imperial court, see A. Pecar, 'Die Ökonomie der Ehre. Ressourcen, Zeremoniell und Selbstdarstellungspraxis des höfischen Adels am Kaiserhof Karls VI. (1711–1749)', (unpubl. PhD thesis, University of Cologne, 2001) and the forthcoming study (a Konstanz university PhD thesis) of the imperial court in the seventeenth century by Mark Hengerer. In the meantime see his article 'Zur symbolischen Dimension eines sozialen Phänomens: Adelsgräber in der Residenz (Wien im 17. Jahrhundert)', in A. Weigl (ed.), *Wien im Dreißigjährigen Krieg* (Vienna, 2001), pp. 250–352. I am grateful to both authors for sending me copies of their manuscripts and publications. See also Duindam, 'Numbers' and *idem, Vienna and Versailles: The Courts of Europe's Dynastic Rivals* (Cambridge, 2003).

77 H. Lietzmann, *Herzog Heinrich Julius zu Braunschweig und Lüneburg (1564–1613: Persönlichkeit und Wirken für Kaiser und Reich* (Brunswick, 1993).

78 Cf. above, pp. 15, 41.

79 For these aspects see V. Press, 'The Habsburg Court as a Centre of Imperial Government', *JMH* 85 (1986), pp. 23–45 and *idem*, 'The Imperial Court of the Habsburgs: From Maximilian I to Ferdinand III' in Asch, *Princes*, pp. 289–312.

80 J. Bérenger, *Finance et absolutisme autrichien dans le second moitié du XVIIe siècle* (Paris, 1975).

81 Pecar, 'Ehre', pp. 122–7.

82 Cf. above, chapter 2, pp. 47–8.

83 *Aus der Zeit Maria Theresias. Tagebuch des Fürsten Johan Josef Khevenhüller-Metsch, Kaiserlichen Obersthofmeister 1742–1776*, ed. R. Graf Khevenhüller-Metsch and H. Schlitter (8 vols., Vienna and Leipzig, 1907–25, 1972), II, pp. 43–4. For the court hierarchy see Pecar, 'Ehre', pp. 264–70.

84 H. Lorenz, 'The Imperial Hofburg, The Theory and Practice of Architectural Representation in Baroque Vienna' in W. Ingrao (ed.), *State and Society in Early Modern Austria* (West Lafayette, IN, 1994), pp. 93–109; cf. for the early eighteenth century F. Matsche, *Die Kunst im Dienste der Staatsidee Kaiser Karls VI* (2 vols., Berlin, 1981) and Pecar, 'Ehre', pp. 293–305.

85 W. Pircher, *Verwüstung und Verschwendung. Adeliges Bauen nach der Zweiten Türkenbelagerung* (Vienna, 1984); J.P. Spielman, *The City and the Crown: Vienna and the Imperial Court, 1600–1740* (West Lafayette, IN, 1993), pp. 157–70; cf. T. Winkelbauer, *Fürst und Fürstendiener. Gundaker von Liechtenstein, ein österreichischer Aristokrat des konfessionellen Zeitalters* (Vienna and Munich, 1999), pp. 410–14; Pecar, 'Ehre', pp. 311–20, with reference to Fouquet. For Fouquet cf. D. Dessert, *Fouquet* (Paris, 1987).

86 M. Goloubeva, *The Glorification of Emperor Leopold I in Image, Spectacle and Text* (Mainz, 2000), pp. 79–81 and 191–212; cf. A. Coreth, *Pietas Austriaca* (Munich, 1959).

87 See now Goloubeva, *Glorification,* pp. 67–81.

88 For Vienna see B. Bastl and G. Heiss, 'Hofdamen und Höflinge zur Zeit Kaiser Leopolds I. Zur Geschichte eines vergessenen Berufsstandes', in V. Bůžek (ed.), *Zivot no dvorech barokní slechty (1600–1750)* (Opera Historica 5, Ceske Budejovice, 1996), pp. 187–265.

89 S. Adams, 'Favourites and Factions at the Elizabethan Court', in Asch, *Princes,* pp. 265–87; cf. *idem, The Earl of Leicester and Elizabethan Court Politics* (Manchester, 2001). For the culture of the court see R. Strong, *The Cult of Elizabeth* (London, 1977) and H. Hackett, *Virgin Mother, Maiden Queen: Elizabeth and the Cult of the Virgin Mary* (Basingstoke, 1995).

90 Alvarez-Osorio Alvariño, 'El favor real', pp. 433–6; cf. the forthcoming study by the same author, *La corte de Madrid y el gobierno de la monarquía católica 1665–1733.*

Resistance and rebellion

1   A. Gindely, *Geschichte des Dreißigjährigen Krieges* (3 parts, Leipzig, 1882), I, p. 99; cf. G. Lorenz (ed.), *Quellen zur Vorgeschichte und zu den Anfängen des Dreißigjährigen Krieges* (Darmstadt, 1991), p. 327.

2   For a general survey see P. Zagorin, *Rebels and Rulers 1500–1600* (2 vols., Cambridge, 1982), in particular vol. II, *Provincial Rebellion: Revolutionary Civil Wars, 1560–1660*; cf. also Y.-M. Bercé, *Revolt and Revolution in Early Modern Europe. An Essay on the History of Political Violence* (Manchester, 1987), in particular pp. 46–54 and P. Blickle (ed.), *Resistance, Representation and Community* (Oxford, 1997), especially part II: J. Nicolas, J. Valdéon Baruque and Sergij Vilfan, 'The Monarchic State and Resistance in Spain, France and the Old Provinces of the Habsburgs, 1400–1800', pp. 65–114. For England see A. Wall, *Power and Protest in England, 1525–1640* (London, 2000), pp. 163–80.

3   This is one of the principal arguments of A. Jouanna, *Le devoir de révolte. La noblesse française et la gestation de l'État moderne, 1559–1661* (Paris, 1989), in particular pp. 102–19.

4   G. Parker, *The Dutch Revolt* (London, 1977), pp. 49–52; cf. R.H. Bremmer, *Reformatie en Rebellie. Willem van Oranje, de calvinisten en het recht van opstand. Tien onstuimige jaren 1572–1581* (Franeker, 1984) and K.W. Swart, *Willem van Oranje en de Nederlandes Opstand, 1572–1584* (The Hague, 1994).

5   M. Roberts, *The Early Vasas, A History of Sweden, 1523–1611* (Cambridge, 1986), pp. 327–93.

6   A. Fletcher, *Tudor Rebellions* (3rd edn., London, 1983), pp. 82–96; Wall, *Power and Protest*, pp. 174–7. Wall points out that the earls recruited their army less by appealing to the loyalty of their tenants than by other methods. For example, they might use their authority as royal officeholders at the local level, or pretend that they only wanted to liberate the Queen from the influence of evil counsellors, a fairly widespread device to legitimise rebellions (cf. Bercé, *Revolt*, pp. 29–33). For the attitude of the local population, see also A. Wood, *Riot, Rebellion and Popular Politics in Early Modern England* (Basingstoke, 2002), pp. 72–8. For the earlier history of the Tudor North see S. Ellis, *Tudor Frontiers and Noble Power: The Making of the British State* (Oxford, 1995), pp. 146–72, 233–50.

7   D. Stevenson, *The Scottish Revolution: 1637–1655: The Triumph of the Covenanters* (Edinburgh, 1973); A.I. Macinnes, *Charles I and the Making of the Covenanting Movement, 1625–1641* (Edinburgh, 1991).

8   C. Russell, *The Causes of the English Civil War* (Oxford, 1990), pp. 73–82, 105–7; J. Morrill, 'The Religious Context of the English Civil War' in *idem, The Nature of the English Revolution* (London, 1993), pp. 45–69. For the interpretation of the English Civil War as a

noble revolt cf. J.S.A. Adamson, 'The Baronial Context of the English Civil War', *TRHS*, 5th Ser., 40 (1990), pp. 93–120.

9 M. Stoyle, *Loyalty and Locality. Popular Allegiance in Devon during the English Civil War* (Exeter, 1994), pp. 141–8; cf. R. Ashton, *The English Civil War: Conservatism and Revolution 1603–1649* (London, 1978), and for the wider social and cultural context of local allegiance D. Underdown, *Revel, Riot and Rebellion* (Oxford, 1987).

10 L.G. Schwoerer (ed.), *The Revolution of 1688–89. Changing Perspectives* (Cambridge, 1992); J. Israel (ed.), *The Anglo-Dutch Moment, Essays on the Glorious Revolution and its World Impact* (London, 1991).

11 See in particular D. Crouzet, *Les Guerriers de Dieu. La violence au temps des troubles de religion* (2 vols., Seyssel, 1990). For recent surveys of the Wars of Religions see R.J. Knecht, *The French Civil Wars* (Harlow, 2000) and M.P. Holt, *The French Wars of Religion, 1562–1629* (Cambridge, 1995).

12 J.-M. Constant, *La Ligue* (Paris, 1996), pp. 325–9, cf. *idem*, 'Les barons français pendant les guerres de religion', in *Quatriéme Centenaire des la bataille de Courtras* (*Colloque de Coutras organisé par le GRAHC, 1987*, Pau, 1988), pp. 48–62, at pp. 54–60; for the number of noblemen in active military service cf. also J.B. Wood, *The Nobility of the Election of Bayeux, 1463–1666* (Princeton, NJ, 1980), pp. 81–90, who argues that at the beginning of the seventeenth century about 40–45 per cent of all noblemen had seen some military service, but only 15–20 per cent really had experience as professional soldiers serving in a series of campaigns, not just in one or two.

13 Wood, *Bayeux*, pp. 167–8; but cf. the somewhat different assessment of the situation in Limousin by M. Cassan, *Le temps des Guerres de Religion. Le cas du Limousin (vers 1530–vers 1630)* (Paris, 1996), pp. 94–5. For Anjou see L. Bourquin, *Les nobles, la ville et le roi. L'autorité nobiliaire en Anjou pendant les Guerres de Religion* (Paris, 2001).

14 A. Jouanna, *La France du XVIième siècle* (Paris, 1996), pp. 235–6; H. Morel, 'La fin du duel judiciaire en France et la naissance du point d'honneur', *Revue d'histoire de droit Français et étranger* 42 (1964), pp. 574–639, for the last judicial trial by combat (1547) staged in the King's presence in the sixteenth century. It ended in defeat for the nobleman the King had favoured, La Châtaigneraye, and thus indirectly for the King himself.

15 S. Carroll, *Noble Power during the French Wars of Religion: the Guise Affinity and the Catholic Cause in Normandy* (Cambridge, 1998), p. 146.

16 R.R. Harding, *Anatomy of a Power Elite: The Provincial Governors of Early Modern France* (New Haven, CT, 1978), pp. 84–5, cf. p. 86: 'In a variety of ways therefore the governors looked to religious partisanship to provide the discipline and moral commitment within their regimes

that royal service and its values could no longer provide. Party loyalty became a new focus for aristocratic values, one that often displaced royal service while pretending only to supplement it.'

17 Harding, *Governors*, p. 215. For a noble dynasty 'in search of a cause' hoping thus to find loyalty and support among lesser nobles, cf. Carroll, *Noble Power*, p. 181.

18 Jouanna, *La France*, pp. 497–8, quoting Antonie Batailler, *Mémoires sur les guerres civiles à Castres*, ed. C. Pradel (Albi, 1894), pp. 42–3.

19 A. Jouanna, 'Le théme polémique du complot contre la noblesse lors des prises d'armes nobiliaires sous les derniers Valois', in Y.-M. Bercé and E. Fasano Guarini (eds.), *Complots et Conjurations dans l'Europe moderne* (Rome, 1996), pp. 475–90.

20 Jouanna, *Devoir*, pp. 154–79, 342–48.

21 Knecht, *Civil Wars*, pp. 236–7; P. Chevallier, *Henri III, Roi shakespearien* (Paris, 1985), pp. 696–704; cf. E.J. Baumgartner, *Radical Reactionaries: The Political Thought of the French Catholic League* (Geneva, 1976) and Constant, *La Ligue*.

22 J.-M. Constant, *Les Guises* (Paris, 1984) and *idem*, *La Ligue*, pp. 112–16.

23 R. Descimon, *Qui étaient les Seize? Mythes et réalités de la ligue Parisienne (1585–1594)* (Paris, 1983); A. Jouanna, J. Boucher, D. Biloghi and G. Le Thiec, *Histoire et dictionnaire des Guerres de Religion* (Paris, 1998), pp. 355–78.

24 François Cromé, *Dialogue dentre le maheustre et le manant*, ed. P.M. Ascoli (Geneva, 1977), pp. 72, 80, 66.

25 Jouanna, *Devoir*, p. 197, quoting Pierre de Saint-Julien de Balleure, *Meslanges historiques* (Lyon, 1588), p. 592. De Balleure was a nobleman from Burgundy who took great pride in Burgundy's autonomy and ancient privileges; cf. Jouanna, *Devoir*, pp. 195–6, for the similar thoughts of Jean de Saulx-Tavanes.

26 For Normandy see Caroll, *Noble Power*, pp. 241–2.

27 A. Jouanna, *Ordre social, mythe et hiérarchies dans la France du XVIe siècle.* (Paris, 1977), pp. 187–97.

28 Jouanna, *Devoir*, pp. 202–3; *idem* et al., *Histoire et dictionnaire*, pp. 400–4.

29 Ibid., pp. 398–9.

30 J. Bahlke, *Regionalismus und Staatintegration im Widerstreit. Die Länder der Böhmischen Krone im ersten Jahrhundert der Habsburgerherrschaft (1526–1619)* (Munich, 1994), pp. 430–45; cf. for the events of 1618–20 R.G. Asch, *The Thirty Years War* (Basingstoke, 1997), pp. 47–72 and for the wider context R.J.W. Evans and T.V. Thomas (eds.), *Crown, Church and Estates; Central European Politics in the Sixteenth and Seventeenth Centuries* (Basingstoke, 1991), and, most recently, K.J. MacHardy, *War Religion and Court Patronage in Habsburg Austria* (Basingstoke, 2002).

31 R.J.W. Evans, *The Making of the Habsburg Monarchy* (Oxford, 1979), pp. 201–13, cf. pp. 169–80.

32 R.G. Asch, *Der Hof Karls I. von England* (Cologne, 1993), pp. 105–19; cf. for factions at court in the late 1630s K. Sharpe, *The Personal Rule of Charles I* (Newhaven, CT, 1992), pp. 837–48 and for the outbreak of the Civil War C. Russell, *The Fall of the British Monarchies, 1637–1642* (Oxford, 1991).

33 R.J. Knecht, Richelieu (London, 1991), p. 54; cf. G. Dethan, *Gaston d'Orleans, conspirateur et prince charmant* (Paris, 1959) and J.-M. Constant, *Les Conjurateurs. Le premier libéralisme politique sous Richelieu* (Paris, 1987), pp. 147–65.

34 R. McCoy, *The Rites of Knighthood. The Literature and Politics of Elizabethan Chivalry* (Berkeley, CA, 1989).

35 P.E.J. Hammer, 'Patronage at Court, Faction and the Earl of Essex' in J. Guy (ed.), *The Reign of Elizabeth I: Court and Culture in the Last Decade* (Cambridge, 1995), pp. 65–86; cf. P. Williams, *The Later Tudors: England 1547–1603* (Oxford, 1995), pp. 366–76.

36 P.E.J. Hammer, *The Polarisation of Elizabethan Politics. The Political Career of Robert Devereux, 2nd Earl of Essex* (Cambridge, 1999), pp. 199–223, 235–41.

37 Hammer, *Polarisation*, pp. 297–300, 338–9; McCoy, *Rites*, pp. 88–94.

38 M. James, 'At a crossroads of the Political Culture: the Essex Revolt, 1601' in *idem, Society, Politics and Culture: Studies in Early Modern England* (Cambridge, 1986), pp. 416–66, at p. 455.

39 Ibid. p. 459.

40 V. Snow, *Essex the Rebel* (Lincoln, NE, 1971); cf. R.C. McCoy, 'Old English Honour in an Evil Time: Aristocratic Principle in the 1620s', in R. Malcolm Smuts (ed.), *The Stuart Court and Europe: Essays in Politics and Culture* (Cambridge, 1996), pp. 133–55.

41 See J.S.A. Adamson, 'Chivalry and Political Culture in Caroline England', in K. Sharpe and P. Lake (eds.), *Culture and Politics in Early Stuart England* (Basingstoke, 1994), pp. 161–98.

42 For the wider context see most recently J. Scott, *England's Troubles: Seventeenth-Century English Political Instability in European Context* (Cambridge, 2000); for aristocratic republicanism *idem, Algernon Sidney and the English Republic 1623–1677* (Cambridge, 1988) and its sequel, *Algernon Sidney and the Restoration Crisis 1677–1683* (Cambridge, 1991).

43 R.M. Smuts, *Court Culture and the Origins of a Royalist Tradition in Early Stuart England* (Philadelphia, 1987), in particular pp. 247–53; Thomas Howard, Earl of Arundel, Earl Marshal of England was the most prominent example of the new type of aristocrat: cultured, well educated and a great collector of art and antiquities; see D. Howarth, *Lord Arundel and his Circle* (New Haven, CT, 1985).

44 See above, pp. 74, 77.

45 F. Heal and C. Holmes, *The Gentry in England and Wales 1500–1700* (Basingstoke, 1994), p. 172, speak of the 'tangential link to the chivalric elements still associated with gentility' provided by positions of command in the militia, but clearly even before 1642 military virtue was less important in defining status for the English gentry than, for example, the French *noblesse d'epée.*

46 The most important works on the Fronde are E. Kossman, *La Fronde* (Leiden, 1954), A. Lloyd Moote, *The Revolt of the Judges: The Parlement of Paris and the Fronde (1643–52)* (Princeton, 1971), M. Pernot, *La Fronde* (Paris, 1994) and O. Ranum, *The Fronde: A French Revolution 1648–1652* (New York, 1993).

47 For the rebellions in early seventeenth-century France see Jouanna, *Devoir*, pp. 212–80; Constant, *Les conjurateurs.*

48 M. Greeengrass, *France in the Age of Henry IV* (2nd edn., London, 1995), pp. 226–32; Jouanna, *Devoir*, pp. 203–6.

49 Ibid., pp. 225–6.

50 Greengrass, *France*, p. 229; cf. K. Béguin, *Les Princes de Condé. Rebelles, courtisans et mécènes dans la France du grand siècle* (Paris, 1999).

51 Jouanna, *Dévoir*, pp. 237–40.

52 J. Berenger, *Turenne* (Paris, 1987), pp. 41–52, and 269–304; for the *princes étrangers* see also D. Parrott, 'A *prince souverain* and the French Crown: Charles de Nevers 1580–1638' in R. Oresko et al. (eds.), *Royal and Republican Sovereignty in Early Modern Europe* (Cambridge, 1997), pp. 149–87.

53 Béguin, *Princes de Condé*, pp. 38–55. For Condé see also J. Inglis-Jones, 'The Grand Condé in Exile: Power Politics in France, Spain and the Spanish Netherlands' (D. phil. diss., University of Oxford, 1994).

54 D. Dessert, 'Pouvoir et fortune au XVIIe siècle: la fortune de Mazarin', *RHMC* 23 (1976), pp. 161–81; P. Goubert, *Mazarin* (Paris, 1990).

55 Béguin, *Princes de Condé* , pp. 98–111, in particular pp. 108–10.

56 Lloyd Moote, *Revolt*, pp. 225–30.

57 Cf. R. Descimon and C. Jouhaud, 'La Fronde en mouvement: la développent de la crise politique entre 1648 et 1652', *Dix-septième Siècle* 145 (1984), pp. 305–22.

58 For the lesser nobility see J.-M. Constant, 'La troisième Fronde: Les gentilshommes et les libertés nobiliaires', *Dix-septième Siècle* 145 (1984), pp. 341–54.

59 Constant, *Conjurateurs*; cf. *idem*, 'Les Frondes' in J. Cornette (ed.), *La France de la Monarchie absolue, 1610–1715* (Paris, 1997), pp. 185–203.

60 Jouanna, *Dévoir*, pp. 273–8.

61 For this problem see most recently T. Cogswell, *Home Divisions: Aristocracy, the State and Provincial Conflict* (Manchester, 1998); cf J. Morrill, *The Revolt of the Provinces* (2nd edn., Harlow, 1999) and for

the appointment of Justices of the Peace see Wall, *Power and Protest,* pp. 47–61.

62 An important study of such tension in a particularly faction-ridden county is P. Salt, 'Sir Thomas Wentworth and the Parliamentary Representation of Yorkshire, 1614–1628', *Northern History* 16 (1980), pp. 130–68; cf. A. Wall, 'Patterns of Politics in England 1558–1625', *HJ* 31 (1988), pp. 947–63.

63 A. Hughes, *The Causes of the English Civil War* (Basingstoke, 1991), pp. 32–41.

64 J.B. Collins, *Fiscal Limits of Absolutism: Direct Taxation in Early Seventeenth-Century France* (Berkeley, CA, 1988), pp. 98–107, 194–5; M. Foisil, *La révolte des Nu-Pieds et les révoltes normandes de 1639* (Paris, 1970); cf. Y.-M. Bercé, *Croquants et Nu-Pieds Le soulèvements en France du XVIe au XIXe siècle* (Paris, 1974).

65 Collins, *Limits*, pp. 202–13.

66 K.M. Brown, 'The Scottish Aristocracy, Anglicization and the Court, 1603–1638', *HJ* 36 (1993), pp. 543–76.

67 For the crisis of the Spanish monarchy in 1640 see J.H. Elliott, R. Villari and A.M. Hespanha (eds.), *1640: La monarquía hispánica en crisis* (Barcelona, 1992) and M. Angels Pérez Samper, *Catalunya i Portugal en 1640. Dos pobles en una cruilla* (Barcelona, 1992); for Hungary see R.J.W. Evans, *The Making of the Habsburg Monarchy, 1530–1700* (Oxford, 1979), pp. 265–6 and C.W. Ingrao, *The Habsburg Monarchy, 1618–1815* (2nd edn., Cambridge, 2000), pp. 115–17.

68 For Scotland (although here the nobility was less united in the 1640s than it had at first appeared) D. Stevenson, *Revolution and Counter-Revolution in Scotland 1644–1651* (Edinburgh, 1977); see also the contributions by K.M. Brown and R.J.W. Evans on Scotland and Hungary respectively to R.G. Asch (ed.), Der *Adel im Ancien Régime* (Cologne, 2001).

69 J.H. Elliott, *The Revolt of the Catalans* (Cambridge, 1963); and *idem*, 'A Provincial Aristocracy: The Catalan Ruling Class in the Sixteenth and Seventeenth Centuries' in *idem, Spain and its World, 1500–1700* (New Haven, CT, 1989), pp. 71–91.

70 Bercé, *Revolt*, pp. 29–33.

71 A. Clarke, *The Old English in Ireland*, 1625–1642 (London, 1966), J. Ohlmeyer (ed.), *Ireland from Independence to Occupation, 1641–1660* (Cambridge, 1995) and N. Canny, *Making Ireland British, 1580–1650* (Oxford, 2001), pp. 461–550.

72 For the debate on the crisis of the seventeenth century see G. Parker and L.M. Smith (eds.), *The General Crisis of the Seventeenth Century* (London, 1978); H.G. Koenigsberger, 'The Crisis of the Seventeenth Century: A Farewell?' in *idem, Politicians and Virtuosi* (London, 1986), pp. 149–68 and more recently S.C. Ogilvie, 'Germany and the Seventeenth-Century Crisis', *HJ* 35 (1992), pp. 417–41; cf. also

H. Zmora, *Monarchy, Aristocracy and the State in Europe, 1300–1800* (London, 2001), pp. 73–5 for a cautious attempt to revive the idea of a general crisis.

73 For the political effects of warfare on the structure of the state see R.G. Asch, 'Warfare in the Age of the Thirty Years War 1598–1648' in J. Black (ed.), *European Warfare, 1453–1815* (Basingstoke, 1999), pp. 45–68.

74 For the confessional problems affecting the British multiple monarchy see J. Morrill, 'The War(s) of the Three Kingdoms' in G. Burgess (ed.), *The New British History: Founding a Modern State 1603–1715* (London, 1999), pp. 65–91. For the position of the Scottish aristocracy within the Stuart composite monarchy see also K.M. Brown, 'The Scottish Aristocracy, Anglicization and the Court, 1603–1638', *HJ* 36 (1993), pp. 543–76; and for the later seventeenth century, *idem*, 'The Origins of a British Aristocracy: Integration and its Limitation before the Treaty of Union', in S.G. Ellis and S. Barber (eds.), *Conquest and Coalescence: Fashioning a British State, 1485–1725* (London, 1995), pp. 222–49.

75 For later seventeenth-century Scotland see B. Lenman, 'The Scottish Nobility and the Revolution of 1688–90' in R. Beddard (ed.), *The Revolution of 1688*, (London, 1991), pp. 137–62; for resistance theories in Scotland see M. Steele, 'The Politick Christian: The Theological Background of the National Covenant' in J. Morrill (ed.), *The Scottish National Covenant in its British Context* (Cambridge, 1990), pp. 31–67; R. v. Friedeburg, *Widerstandsrecht und Konfessionskonflikt. Notwehr und gemeiner Mann im deutsch-britischen Vergleich 1530 bis 1669* (Berlin, 1999), pp. 130–47 and J. Coffey, *Politics, Religion and the British Revolutions: The Mind of Samuel Rutherford* (Cambridge, 1997); for Poland see E. Opalinski, 'Die Freiheit des Adels. Ideal und Wirklichkeit in Polen-Litauen im 17. Jahrhundert' in Asch, *Adel im Ancien Régime*, pp. 77–104. For developments in Poland – with special reference to the nobility's military role – cf. R.I. Frost, *The Northern Wars, 1558–1721* (Harlow, 2000), pp. 44–73 and 254–62.

76 For Wentworth's ambivalent attitude towards royal authority see R. Cust, 'Wentworth's "Change of Sides"' in J.F. Merritt (ed.), *The Political World of Thomas Wentworth, Earl of Strafford, 1621–1641* (Cambridge, 1996), pp. 63–80 and R.G. Asch, art. 'Wentworth, Thomas, first Earl of Strafford' in *New Dictionary of National Biography* (forthcoming).

77 For England see C. Russell, 'Parliamentary History in Perspective, 1604–1629' in *idem*, *Unrevolutionary England 1603–1642* (London, 1990), pp. 31–58 and *idem*, 'Monarchies, Wars and Estates in England, France and Spain, *c.*1580–*c.*1640', ibid., pp. 121–36; for the Continent R. G. Asch, 'Estates and Princes in Germany after 1648: The results of the Thirty Years' War', *GH* 6 (1988), pp. 113–32; V. Press, 'Vom

"Ständestaat" zum Absolutismus: 50 Thesen zur Entwicklung des Ständewesen in Deutschland' in P. Baumgart (ed.), *Ständetum und Staatsbildung in Brandenburg-Preussen* (Berlin, 1983), pp. 319–26; and the surveys by M.R. Graves, *The Parliaments of Early Modern Europe* (London, 2001), pp. 114–51 and Blickle, *Resistance, Representation and Community*.

Noble power and state formation: towards a new symbiosis?

1   For the debate on absolutism see R.G. Asch and H. Duchhardt (eds.), *Der Absolutismus – ein Mythos? Strukturwandel monarchischer Herrschaft in West- und Mitteleuropa (ca.1550–1700)* (Cologne, 1996); N. Henshall, *The Myth of Absolutism* (London, 1992), as well as J. Miller (ed.), *Absolutism in Seventeenth-Century Europe* (Basingstoke, 1990).

2   Cf. the various contributions to W. Reinhard (ed.), *Power Elites and State Building* (Oxford, 1996), in particular A. Maczak, 'The Nobility–State Relationship', pp. 189–234; cf. further W. Reinhard, *Geschichte der Staatsgewalt* (Munich, 1999), pp. 211–34.

3   R.G. Asch, 'Kriegsfinanzierung, Staatsbildung und ständische Ordnung in Westeuropa im 17. und 18. Jahrhundert', *HZ* 268 (1999), pp. 636–71; cf. T. Ertman, *Birth of the Leviathan: Building States and Regimes in Medieval and Early Modern Europe* (Cambridge, 1997) and Reinhard, *Staatsgewalt*, pp. 343–69.

4   On military developments in general see G. Parker, *The Military Revolution* (Cambridge, 1988), F. Tallett, *War and Society in Early-Modern Europe, 1495–1715* (London, 1992), pp. 168–216, C.J. Rogers (ed.), *The Military Revolution Debate* (Boulder, CO, 1995) and C. Storrs and H.M. Scott, 'The Military Revolution and the European Nobility, *c.*1600–1800', *War in History* 3 (1996), pp. 1–41; see also J.R. Ruff, *Violence in Early Modern European History, 1500–1800* (Cambridge, 2001), pp. 44–72.

5   In France the Crown's efforts to mobilise the feudal host, the *ban et arrière-ban,* in case of war had very unsatisfactory results in the sixteenth century. The whole of France could rarely raise more than 2,000 or at most 3,000 men for the royal army and, according to some sources, most were either newly ennobled commoners or noblemen's retainers. See P. Contamine, 'La premiére modernité: des Guerres d'Italie aux Guerres de Religion: un nouvel art militaire' in A. Corvisier (ed.), *Histoire militaire de la France*, vol. I: *Des origines à 1715* (Paris, 1992), pp. 233–56, at pp. 249–50.

6   P. Williams, *The Tudor Regime* (Oxford, 1979), pp. 128–9; on military organisation in England cf. M.J. Braddick, *State Formation in Early Modern England, c.1550–1700* (Cambridge, 2000), pp. 180–202.

7 The fundamental work on this problem remains F. Redlich, *The German Military Enterpriser and his Workforce: A Study in European Economic and Social History* (2 vols., Wiesbaden, 1964–5).

8 G. Hanlon, *The Twilight of a Military Tradition: Italian Aristocrats and European Conflicts, 1560–1800* (London, 1998), pp. 241–56; cf. for the Thirty Years War, R.G. Asch, *The Thirty Years War* (Basingstoke, 1997), pp. 155–66 and M.S. Anderson, *War and Society in Europe of the Old Regime, 1618–1789* (Stroud, 1988), pp. 33–76.

9 Hanlon, *Twilight*, p. 254; for the military career of Italian noblemen in the seventeenth century cf. A. Spagnoletti, *Prìncipi italiani e Spagna nell' età barocca* (Milan, 1996), pp. 183–214; for Savoy, W. Barberis, *Le armi del principe. La tradizione militare sabauda* (Turin, 1988).

10 G. Mann, *Wallenstein* (London, 1976), H. Diwald, *Wallenstein* (Munich, 1969) and A. Ernstberger, *Hans de Witte, Finanzmann Wallensteins* (Wiesbaden, 1954).

11 Redlich, *Enterpriser*, I, pp. 234–5; cf. G. Droysen, *Bernhard von Weimar* (Leipzig, 1885); D. Parrott, *Richelieu's Army: War, Government and Society in France, 1624–1642* (Cambridge, 2001), pp. 293–9.

12 O. Büsch, *Militärsystem und Sozialleben im alten Preußen, 1713–1807* (2nd edn., Frankfurt/M., 1981), pp. 113–34.

13 P. Pierson, *Commander of the Armada: The Seventh Duke of Medina Sidonia* (New Haven, CT, 1989).

14 I.A.A. Thompson, *War and Government in Habsburg Spain 1560–1620* (London, 1976), pp. 103–59, in particular p. 155; but cf. J. Casey, *Early Modern Spain: A Social History* (London, 1999), pp. 160–2 for the decline of the aristocracy's military power in other places.

15 I.A.A. Thompson, 'The Impact of War and Peace on Government and Society in Seventeenth-Century Spain' in R.G. Asch and M. Wrede (eds.), *Frieden und Krieg in der Frühen Neuzeit: Die europäische Staatenordnung und die außereuropäische Welt* (Munich, 2001), pp. 161–79, at p. 170.

16 I.A.A. Thompson, '"Money, Money, and yet more Money!" Finance, the Fiscal-State and the Military Revolution: Spain 1500–1600' in Rogers, *Revolution Debate*, pp. 273–98.

17 D. Potter, *War and Government in the French Provinces: Picardy, 1470–1560* (Cambridge, 1993); J.B. Wood, *The King's Army: Warfare, Soldiers and Society During the Wars of Religion in France, 1562–1576* (Cambridge, 1996).

18 G. Rowlands, 'The Monopolisation of Military Power in France, 1515 to 1715' in Asch and Wrede, *Frieden und Krieg*, pp. 139–60, in particular pp. 146–9; A. Blanchard, 'Vers la ceinture de fer, milieu du XVIe – début du XVIIIe siécle' in Corvisier, *Histoire Militaire*, I, pp. 449–84, at pp. 458–9.

19 Rowland, 'Monopolisation', pp. 148–9.

20 D. Parrott, 'Strategy and Tactics in the Thirty Years' War: The Military Revolution' in Rogers, *Revolution Debate*, pp. 227–53, at pp. 241–3; *idem*, 'French Military Organization in the 1630s: the Failure of Richelieu's Ministry', *Seventeenth-Century French Studies* 9 (1987), pp. 151–67; *idem, Richelieu's Army*, pp. 313–65, in particular pp. 317 and 364. Cf. also J.A. Lynn, *Giant of the Grand Siècle. The French Army 1610–1715* (Cambridge, 1997), pp. 221–38. Lynn speaks of a 'semi-entrepreneurial' system combining 'the worst of two worlds', at least for the officers (p. 223). Cf. G. Rowlands, *The Dynastic State and the Army under Louis XIV: Royal Service and Private Interest, 1661–1701* (Cambridge, 2002), which argues that Louis XIV went a long way towards resolving these problems.

21 A. Corvisier, *Louvois* (Paris, 1983), pp. 80–1, cf. p. 103; see further *idem, La France de Louis XIV* (Paris, 1979), pp. 178–81.

22 Lynn, *Giant*, pp. 221–81, in particular p. 239, and B. R. Kroener, '*Législateur de ses* armées: Verstaatlichungs- und Feudalisie- rungstendenzen in der militärischen Gesellschaft der Frühen Neuzeit am Beispiel der französischen Armee im Zeitalter Ludwigs XIV' in Asch and Duchhardt, *Absolutismus*, pp. 311–28; cf. Rowlands, *The Dynastic State*, pp. 167–71.

23 Lynn, *Giant*, p. 261 and A. Corvisier, 'Renouveau militaire et misères de la guerre, 1635–1659' in *idem, Histoire Militaire*, I, pp. 353–82, at pp. 373–4. In a different context A. Corvisier came to the conclusion that about 50 per cent, if not more of all nobles of military age served in the King's army (Corvisier, *La France*, p. 62).

24 Rowlands, *Dynastic State*, pp. 154–8.

25 Ibid., p. 359.

26 G. Rowlands, 'Louis XIV, Aristocratic Power and the Elite Units of the French Army', *French History* 13 (1999), pp. 303–31 and *idem, Dynastic State*, pp. 341–7, and pp. 154–6 for the social composition of the officer corps in general.

27 Ibid., pp. 324–6; Kroener, 'Législateur', p. 319; cf. J. Chagniot, 'Mobilité sociale et armée (vers 1660–1760)', *Dix-septiéme Siècle* 122 (1979), pp. 37–49, at p. 39 and *idem, Guerre et société à l'époque mod- erne* (Paris, 2001), p. 106 and, for the eighteenth century, M. Marraud, *La Noblesse de Paris au XVIIIe siécle* (Paris, 2000), pp. 225–40.

28 Lynn, *Giant*, pp. 56–8.

29 G. Rowlands, 'The Ethos of Blood and Changing Values? *Robe, Epée* and the French Armies, 1661–1715', *Seventeenth-Century French Studies* 19 (1997), pp. 95–108.

30 J. Brewer, *The Sinews of Power: War, Money and the English State, 1688–1783* (London, 1989), pp. 29–34. For the seventeenth century cf. J. Scott Wheeler, *The Making of a World Power: War and the Military Revolution in Seventeenth-Century England* (Stroud, 1999), pp. 66–93 and J. Childs, *The Army, James II and the Glorious Revolution*

(Manchester, 1980), as well as *idem, The British Army of William III, 1689–1702* (Manchester, 1987).

31 Büsch, *Militärsystem*, pp. 77–143, but see now also the cautionary remarks by F. Göse, 'Zwischen Garnison und Rittergut. Aspekte der Verknüpfung von Adelsforschung und Militärgeschichte am Beispiel Brandenburg-Preußens' in R. Pröve (ed.), *Klio in Uniform?* (Cologne, 1997), pp. 109–42, as well as D. Showalter, 'Prussia's Army: Continuity and Change, 1713–1830', in P.G.G. Dwyer (ed.), *The Rise of Prussia, 1700–1830* (Harlow, 2000), pp. 220–36, and the survey by P.H. Wilson, 'Social Militarization in Eighteenth-Century Germany', *GH* 18 (2000), pp. 1–39.

32 P.-M. Hahn, 'Aristokratisierung und Professionalisierung. Der Aufstieg der Obristen zu einer militärischen und höfischen Elite in Brandenburg-Preußen von 1650 bis 1725', *Forschungen zur Brandenburgischen und Preußischen Geschichte*, New Series 1 (1991), pp. 161–208.

33 F. Göse, 'Zum Verhältnis von landadliger Sozialisation zu adliger Militärkarriere. Das Beispiel Preußen und Österreich im ausgehenden 17. und 18. Jahrhundert', *MIÖG* 109 (2000), pp. 118–53.

34 M. Hochedlinger, 'Mars Ennobled: The Ascent of the Military and the Creation of a Military Nobility in Mid-Eighteenth-Century Austria', *GH* 17 (1999), pp. 141–76, in particular pp. 171–73; Göse, 'Verhältnis', pp. 126–7.

35 Y.-M. Bercé, *La Naissance dramatique de l'absolutisme, 1598–1661* (*Nouvelle Histoire de la France Moderne*, vol. 3, Paris, 1992), pp. 134–9; R.J. Knecht, *Richelieu* (London, 1991), pp. 49–63, in particular pp. 56–7.

36 J. Bergin, *Cardinal Richelieu: Power and the Pursuit of Wealth* (New Haven, CT and London, 1985).

37 D. Parrott, 'Richelieu, the *Grands* and the French Army' in J. Bergin and L. Brockliss (eds.), *Richelieu and his Age* (Oxford, 1992), pp. 135–73, at pp. 155–65.

38 R.R. Harding, *Anatomy of a Power Elite: The Provincial Governors of Early Modern France* (New Haven, CT, 1978), pp. 216–7, argues, 'It [the increasing reliance on intendants] was a response to the weakness of governors not to their strength'.

39 J.B. Collins, *The State in Early Modern France* (Cambridge, 1995), pp. 79–85; cf. D. Bohanan, *Crown and Nobility in Early Modern France* (Basingstoke, 2001), pp. 58–69 and F. Bluche, *Louis XIV* (New York, 1990).

40 R. Mettam, *Power and Faction in Louis XIV's France* (Oxford, 1988), p. 203.

41 L. Bourquin, *Noblesse seconde et pouvoir en Champagne aux XVIe et XVIIe siècles* (Paris, 1994), pp. 194–205; cf. J. Goldstone, *Revolution and Rebellion in the Early Modern World* (Berkeley, CA, 1991), pp. 193–6 and E. Le Roy Ladurie, 'De la crise ultime à la vraie

croissance 1660–1789' in G. Duby and A. Wallon (eds.) *Histoire de la France rurale*, vol. II: *L'Age classique des paysans, de 1340 à 1789* (2nd edn. Paris, 1992), pp. 345–596, at p. 381.

42 On royal finances see R. Bonney, 'The State and its Revenues in Ancien Régime France', *Historical Research* 65 (1992), pp. 150–76 and P.T. Hoffman, 'Early Modern France, 1450–1700' in P.T. Hoffman and K. Norberg (eds.), *Fiscal Crises, Liberty and Representative Government* (Stanford, CA, 1994), pp. 226–52.

43 Collins, *State*, pp. 85–87, and 106–13; Collins points out that finances had already begun to recover after 1653, during the period when the *surintendant* Fouquet (disgraced in 1661) had controlled financial policy.

44 J.M. Smith, *The Culture of Merit: Nobility, Royal Service and the Making of Absolute Monarchy in France 1600–1789* (Ann Arbor, 1996), pp. 137 ff; cf. Mettam, *Power*, pp. 202–10.

45 Rowlands, 'Elite Units'.

46 See – for the eighteenth century – Marraud, *Noblesse*, pp. 264–9, but cf. the different interpretation, for Louis XIV's reign, by Rowlands, 'Ethos', pp. 102–5.

47 D. Parker, 'Sovereignty, Absolutism and the Function of Law in Seventeenth-Century France', *PP* 122 (1989), pp. 36–47; cf. R. Bonney, 'Bodin and the French Monarchy' in *idem, The Limits of Absolutism in ancien régime France* (Aldershot, 1995), ch. II.

48 Collins, *State*, pp. 138–9, 147; for the relationship between royal authority and noble power see also J.B. Collins, *Classes, Estates and Order in Early Modern Brittany* (Cambridge, 1994), p. 14: 'The king did not want to destroy these elites or to eliminate their power; he could not want such a thing, because his power rested on their power. He wanted their power to emanate from him, rather than from some independent source.'

49 For these financial mechanisms see W. Beik, *Absolutism and Society in Seventeenth-Century France: State Power and Provincial Aristocracy in Languedoc* (Cambridge, 1985), pp. 245–78. Languedoc was admittedly a *pays d'états* where the local elite could exert power through the provincial estates. Nevertheless, Beik's main argument that certain sections of the elite – in so far as they did not drift away to Versailles or to faraway army garrisons – now defined their role as the state's agents much more than before, is convincing for other provinces as well.

50 D. Dessert, Argent, *Pouvoir et société au Grand Siècle* (Paris, 1984), p. 367; cf. pp. 341–68.

51 Collins, *State*, pp. 165–8; R. Bonney, 'Le secret de leurs familles: the Fiscal and Social Limits of Louis XIV's *dixième*', *French History* 7 (1993), pp. 383–416; for the eighteenth century see M. Kwass, *Privilege and the Politics of Taxation in Eighteenth-Century France: Liberté, Égalité, Fiscalité* (Cambridge, 2000).

52 Bourquin, *Noblesse seconde*, pp. 205–19.
53 This titled nobility was quite small. In most provinces around 1700 there were barely more than 20 or 30 counts and marquesses, constituting the core of the *noblesse seconde*. See Collins, *State*, p. 134.
54 This is strongly emphasised for the eighteenth century by Marraud, *Noblesse*, pp. 76–84, but cf. pp. 42–5 for the different mentalities of provincial and metropolitan nobilities.
55 J.-F. Dubost, 'Absolutisme et centralisation en Languedoc au XVIIe siècle' *RHMC* 37 (1990), pp. 369–97; R.A. Schneider, *Public Life in Toulouse, 1463–1789* (Ithaca and London, 1989), pp. 255–7; cf. Beik, *Absolutism*, pp. 316–28.
56 B. Nachison, 'Absentee Government and Provincial Governors in Early Modern France: The Princes of Condé and Burgundy, 1660–1720', *French Historical Studies* 21 (1998), pp. 265–97.
57 D. Parker, *Class and State in Ancien Régime France: The Road to Modernity?* (London, 1996), pp. 203–6, cf. – in a similar vein – Beik, *Absolutism*, pp. 333–8. Collins, *Classes*, also uses some Marxist vocabulary but adopts a somewhat different approach.
58 Collins, *Classes*, pp. 275–8.
59 E. Le Roy Ladurie (avec la collaboration de Jean-François Fitou), *Saint-Simon ou le systéme de la Cour* (Paris, 1997), pp. 9–16.
60 This paragraph and the following are based on P.-M. Hahn, *Struktur und Funktion des brandenburgischen Adels im 16. Jahrhundert* (Berlin, 1979).
61 Hahn, *Struktur*, pp. 180–3.
62 E. Melton, 'The Prussian Junkers, 1600–1786' in H.M. Scott (ed.), *The European Nobilities in the Seventeenth and Eighteenth Centuries* (2 vols., London, 1995), II, pp. 71–109, at p. 75.
63 Hahn, *Struktur*, p. 10 and p. 128.
64 For the development of *Gutsherrschaft* see W.W. Hagen, 'Seventeenth-Century Crisis in Brandenburg: The Thirty Years' War, The Destabilization of Serfdom, and the Rise of Absolutism', *American Historical Review* 94 (1989), pp. 302–35; E. Melton, 'Population Structure, the Market Economy and the Transformation of *Gutsherrschaft* in East Central Europe, 1650–1800: the Cases of Brandenburg and Bohemia', *GH* 16 (1999), pp. 297–327; cf. for earlier developments H. Harnisch, 'Grundherrschaft oder Gutsherrschaft. Zu den wirtschaftlichen Grundlagen des niederen Adels in Norddeutschland zwischen spätmittelalterlicher Agrarkrise und Dreißigjährigem Krieg' in R. Endres (ed.), *Adel in der Frühneuzeit. Ein regionaler Vergleich* (Cologne, 1991), pp. 73–98.
65 P.-M. Hahn, 'Aristokratisierung und Professionalisierung', in particular pp. 194, 197; cf. *idem*, 'Landesstaat und Ständetum im Kurfürstentum Brandenburg während des 16. und 17. Jahrhunderts' in P. Baumgart (ed.), *Ständetum und Staatsbildung in Brandenburg-Preußen* (Berlin,

1983), pp. 41–79, in particular p. 67. Cf. further P. Bahl, *Der Hof des Großen Kurfürsten. Studien zur höheren Amtsträgerschaft Brandenburg-Preußens* (Cologne, 2001), pp. 145–80 and D. McKay, *The Great Elector* (Harlow, 2001).

66 P.-M. Hahn, *Fürstliche Territorialhoheit und lokale Adelsgewalt. Die herrschaftliche Durchdringung des ländlichen Raumes zwischen Elbe und Allter (1300–1700)* (Berlin, 1989), pp. 319–82; cf. W. Neugebauer, 'Brandenburg im absolutistischen Staat. Das 17. und 18. Jahrhundert', in I. Materna and W. Ribbe (eds.), *Brandenburgische Geschichte* (Berlin, 1995), pp. 291–394, at pp. 326–30.

67 W. Neugebauer, *Die Hohenzollern*, vol. I, *Anfänge, Landesstaat und monarchische Autokratie bis 1740* (Stuttgart, 1996), pp. 155–67; *idem*, *Politischer Wandel im Osten. Ost-und Westpreussen von den alten Ständen zum Konstitutionalismus* (Stuttgart, 1992); for the Seven Years War see *idem*, 'Zwischen Preußen und Rußland. Rußland, Ostpreußen und die Stände im Siebenjährigen Krieg' in E. Hellmuth, A.I. Meenken and M. Trauth (eds.), *Zeitenwende. Preußen um 1800* (Stuttgart, 1999), pp. 43–76.

68 See, for example, F.L. Carsten, *A History of the Prussian Junkers* (Aldershot, 1989).

69 For a more balanced view see Melton, 'Junkers', and W. Neugebauer, 'Der Adel in Preußen im 18. Jahrhundert' in R.G. Asch (ed.), *Der europäische Adel im Ancien Régime: Von der Krise der ständischen Monarchien bis zur Revolution (1600–1789)* (Cologne, 2001), pp. 49–76. See now also F. Göse, 'Rittergut – Garnison – Residenz. Studien zur Sozialstruktur und politischen Wirksamkeit des brandenburgischen Adels, 1648–1763' (Dr. phil. habil. thesis, Potsdam University, 2002).

70 K.J.V. Jespersen, 'The Rise and Fall of the Danish Nobility' in Scott, *Nobilities*, II, pp. 41–70, at p. 56.

71 G. Lind, 'Den Dankse Adel og den Militære Revolution' in P. Ingesman and J.V. Jensen (eds.), *Riget, Magten og æren. Den Danske Adel 1350–1660* (Aarhus, 2001), pp. 576–603 (English summary).

72 R.I. Frost, *The Northern Wars 1558–1721* (Harlow, 2000), pp. 193–98, in particular p. 197. Cf. E. Ladewig Petersen, *The Crisis of the Danish Nobility, 1580–1660* (Odense, 1967) and Jespersen, 'Rise', pp. 49–64.

73 M. Busch, *Absolutismus und Heeresreform. Schwedens Militär am Ende des 17. Jahrhunderts* (Bochum, 2000), pp. 76–107.

74 A.F. Upton, 'The Swedish Nobility, 1600–1772' in Scott, *Nobilities*, II, pp. 11–40, at pp. 22–8, cf. *idem*, 'The Riksdag of 1680 and the Establishment of Royal Absolutism in Sweden', *EHR* 102 (1987), pp. 281–308.

75 A.F. Upton, *Charles IX and Swedish Absolutism* (Cambridge, 1998), pp. 68–9.

76 Ibid. In 1650 there were about 1,000 male adult noblemen, about 50 per cent of whom belonged to newly ennobled families. In 1700 there were

already 2,500 adult male noblemen in Sweden, of whom 2,000 came from 'new' families. See Busch, *Absolutismus*, pp. 95–6, and n. 512 ibid., cf. I. Elmroth, *För kung och fosterland. Studier i den svenska adelsn demografi och offentliga funktioner 1600–1900* (Lund, 1981).

77 Upton, 'Swedish Nobility', pp. 32–9.

78 See I. Atienza Hernández, *Aristocracia, poder y riqueza en la España moderna. La casa de Osuna, siglos xv–xix* (Madrid, 1987), pp. 227–33; cf. B. Yun Casalilla, *Sobre la transición al capitalismo en Castilla. Economía y sociedad en Tierra de Campos, 1500–1830* (Salamanca, 1987), pp. 319–20.

79 B. Yun Casalilla, 'The Castilian Aristocracy in the Seventeenth Century: Crisis, Refeudalisation or Political Offensive?' in I.A.A. Thompson and B. Yun Casalilla (eds.), *The Castilian Crisis of the Seventeenth Century: New Perspectives on the Economic and Social History of Seventeenth-Century Spain* (Cambridge, 1994), pp. 277–300, in particular p. 284.

80 I.A.A. Thompson, 'The Nobility in Spain' in Scott, *Nobilities*, I, pp. 174–236, at pp. 210–19, in particular p. 216.

81 Juan E. Gelabert, 'Urbanisation and deurbanisation in Castile, 1500–1800' in Thompson and Yun Casalilla, *Crisis*, pp. 182–205, at pp. 197–201, in particular p. 199.

82 Casey, *Spain*, p. 106, cf. p. 103.

83 I.A.A. Thompson, 'Castile' in Miller, *Absolutism*, pp. 69–98, at p. 93.

84 A. Calabria, *The Cost of Empire: The Finances of the Kingdom of Naples in the time of Spanish Rule* (Cambridge, 1991), p. 69.

85 L.A. Ribot García, 'La época del conde-Duque de Olivares y el Reino de Sicilia', in J. Elliott und A. García Sanz (eds.), *La España del Conde Duque de Olivares* (Valladolid, 1990), pp. 653–77; F. Benigno, 'Aristocrazia e stato in Sicilia nell'epoca de Filippo III' in M.A. Visceglia (ed.), *Signori, patrizi, cavalieri nell'età moderna* (Bari, 1992), pp. 76–93, in particular pp. 86–7; cf. for Milan, A. Alvarez Osorio Alvariño, 'Gobernadores, agentes y corporaciones: la corte de Madrid y el Estado de Milán (1669–1675)' in G. Signorotto (ed.), *L'Italia degli Austrias. Monarchia Cattolica e domini italiani nei secoli XVI e XVII* (Mantua, 1993), pp. 183–288; for Naples, Spagnoletti, *Principi*, pp. 129–54 and A. Musi, 'Integration and Resistance in Spanish Italy, 1500–1800' in P. Blickle (ed.), *Resistance, Representation and Community* (Oxford, 1997), pp. 305–20, in particular pp. 308–11. For Castile see Yun Casalilla, *Sobre la transición*, p. 330.

86 H. Zmora, *Monarchy, Aristocracy and the State in Europe, 1300–1800* (London, 2001), p. 97.

87 Ibid, pp. 92–4; cf. R. Brenner, *Merchants and Revolution: Commercial Change, Political Conflict and London's Overseas Traders, 1550–1653* (Cambridge, 1993), pp. 647–66.

88 L.K.J. Glassey, *Politics and the Appointment of Justices of the Peace 1675–1720* (Oxford, 1979), pp. 72–92; cf. for the Lord-Lieutenancy

V.L. Stater, *Noble Government: The Stuart Lord Lieutenancy and the Transformation of English Politics* (Athens, GA, 1994), pp. 165–7.

89 M.A. Kishlansky, *Parliamentary Selection: Social and Political Choice in Early Modern England* (Cambridge, 1986).

90 J.C.D. Clark, *English Society, 1660–1832* (2nd edn., Cambridge, 2000), pp. 48–52, 70–2; J. Scott, *Algernon Sidney and the English Republic 1623–1677* (Cambridge, 1988) and its sequel, *Algernon Sidney and the Restoration Crisis 1677–1683* (Cambridge, 1991); cf. A. Swatland, *The House of Lords in the Reign of Charles II* (Cambridge, 1996).

91 J. Cannon, *Aristocratic Century: The Peerage of Eighteenth-Century England* (Cambridge, 1984), in particular pp. 93–125.

92 B. Yun Casalilla, *Sobre la transición*, pp. 230–5.

93 Beik, *Absolutism*, p. 225.

94 S. Hindle, *The State and Social Change in Early Modern England, c.1550–1640* (Basingstoke, 2000), p. 89.

95 See the critical remarks by M. Dinges, 'Justiznutzung als soziale Kontrolle in der frühen Neuzeit' in A. Blauert and G. Schwerhoff (eds.), *Kriminalitätsgeschichte. Beiträge zur Sozial-und Kulturgeschichte der Moderne* (Konstanz, 2000), pp. 503–44. On the relationship between litigation and noble culture see also R.-P. Fuchs, *Um die Ehre. Westfälische Beleidigungsprozesse vor dem Reichskammergericht (1525–1805)* (Paderborn, 1999), pp. 194–209. Christoph Wieland (Bielefeld and Freiburg) is presently working on a major study of noble litigation in sixteenth-century Bavaria.

96 Hindle, *The State and Social Change*, pp. 89, 232.

97 Braddick, *State Formation*, p. 162, cf. pp. 163–5 and 77–85. Braddick does not focus primarily on the role of the gentry let alone the peerage. Rather, like Hindle, he concentrates on the middling sort from which local officeholders were recruited, for example. Nevertheless these arguments also apply to the role of the nobility, though probably more on the Continent than in England itself.

Conclusion

1 For France see M. Marraud, *La Noblesse de Paris au XVIIIe Siècle* (Paris, 2000), pp. 264–79.

2 J.S. Amelang, *Honored Citizens of Barcelona: Patrician Culture and Class Relations, 1490–1714* (Princeton, NJ, 1986), p. 151: 'It is a delicious irony that the self-definition of patricians should rely so crucially upon their social inferiors. The elite's strikingly holistic vision of social hierarchy left no alternative to fixing the contours of its own image by distancing itself from the sphere of the "lower" classes. Prospero obviously could not exist without the physical labors of Caliban.'

3 A. Jouanna, 'Des "Gros et Gras" aux "Gens d'Honneur"' in G. Chaussinand-Nogaret et al. (eds.), *Histoire des élites en France du XVIe au XXe siècle* (Paris, 1991), pp. 17–144, at pp. 96–100; cf. for England D. Underdown, *Revel, Riot and Rebellion* (Oxford, 1987), pp. 63–8.

4 For the increasing importance of literacy cf. R. Muchembled, *L'Invention de l'homme moderne* (Paris, 1988), pp. 350–4.

5 For England see F. Heal, *Hospitality in Early Modern England* (Oxford, 1990), pp. 23–90.

6 Cf. O. Brunner, *Adeliges Landleben und Europäischer Geist* (Salzburg, 1959), pp. 332–3.

7 P. Borsay, *The English Urban Renaissance: Culture and Society in the Provincial Town, 1660–1770* (Oxford, 1989), p. 285, with reference – in this case – to urban life. Cf. for Spain Amelang, *Honored Citizens*, pp. 198–201.

8 Cf. above, pp. 40–1, however, and Marraud, *Noblesse*, pp. 70–84, for the kinship ties between metropolitan and provincial nobilities.

9 For the strong coherence of the great clan-like aristocratic houses with their many different branches and cadet lines see Marraud, *Noblesse*, pp. 234–49. Cf. also J.B. Wood, *The Nobility of the Election of Bayeux, 1463–1666* (Princeton, New Jersey, 1980), pp. 48–53 for the survival of older families.

10 D. Arnold, 'The Illusion of Grandeur? Antiquity, Grand Tourism and the Country House' in *idem* (ed.), *The Georgian Country House* (Stroud, 1998), pp. 100–17, at p. 116.

11 P. Salvadori, *La Chasse sous l'Ancien Régime* (Paris, 1996), p. 189: 'Désormais se dessinent au contraire les conditions d'une divulgation des savoirs, savoir-faire et savoir-vivre par l'école, les sociétés savantes, les cercles conviviaux. En un temps où fleurissent les écoles militaires et les académies protégées par l'État, ce qui était *l'école sans école* de la noblesse est passé de mode'.

12 *Mémoires et Lettres de François-Joachim de Pierre Cardinal du Bernis*, ed. F. Masson (2 vols., Paris, 1878), I, p. 103: 'On entendait autrefois par le terme de "grand seigneur" un homme d'un naissance illustre qui possédait des grands biens, les grandes charges de la couronne, ou qui, maître dans ses terres, ne dédaignait pas d'y habiter, avait du crédit auprés du roi et ne se montrait à la cour que rarement. Ces anciens seigneurs avaient presqu'autant de créatures que de vassaux, et la noblesse ne rougissait pas de leur être attachée, la raison en est bien simple: les grands seigneurs avaient alors le crédit de faire la fortune des gentilshommes. Les temps sont bien changés: les possesseurs des grands fiefs n'habitent plus leurs terres, et les seigneurs d'aujourd'hui ont à la vérité des titres et des dignités, mais aucun crédit qui leur soit propre.' Cf. J. Gallet, *Seigneurs et paysans en France, 1600–1793* (Rennes, 1999), p. 199.

13 François-René de Chateaubriand, *Mémoires d'outre-tombe*, ed. J.-C. Berchet, (Paris, 2000), p. 39.

Index